The Grand Union Canal

(South)

Nick Corble

TEMPUS

First published 2005

Tempus Publishing Limited
The Mill, Brimscombe Port,
Stroud, Gloucestershire, GL5 2QG

British Library Cataloguing in Publication Data.
A catalogue record for this book is available from the British Library.

ISBN 0 7524 3539 6

Typesetting and design by Liz Rudderham
Origination by Tempus Publishing Limited
Printed and bound in Great Britain

CONTENTS

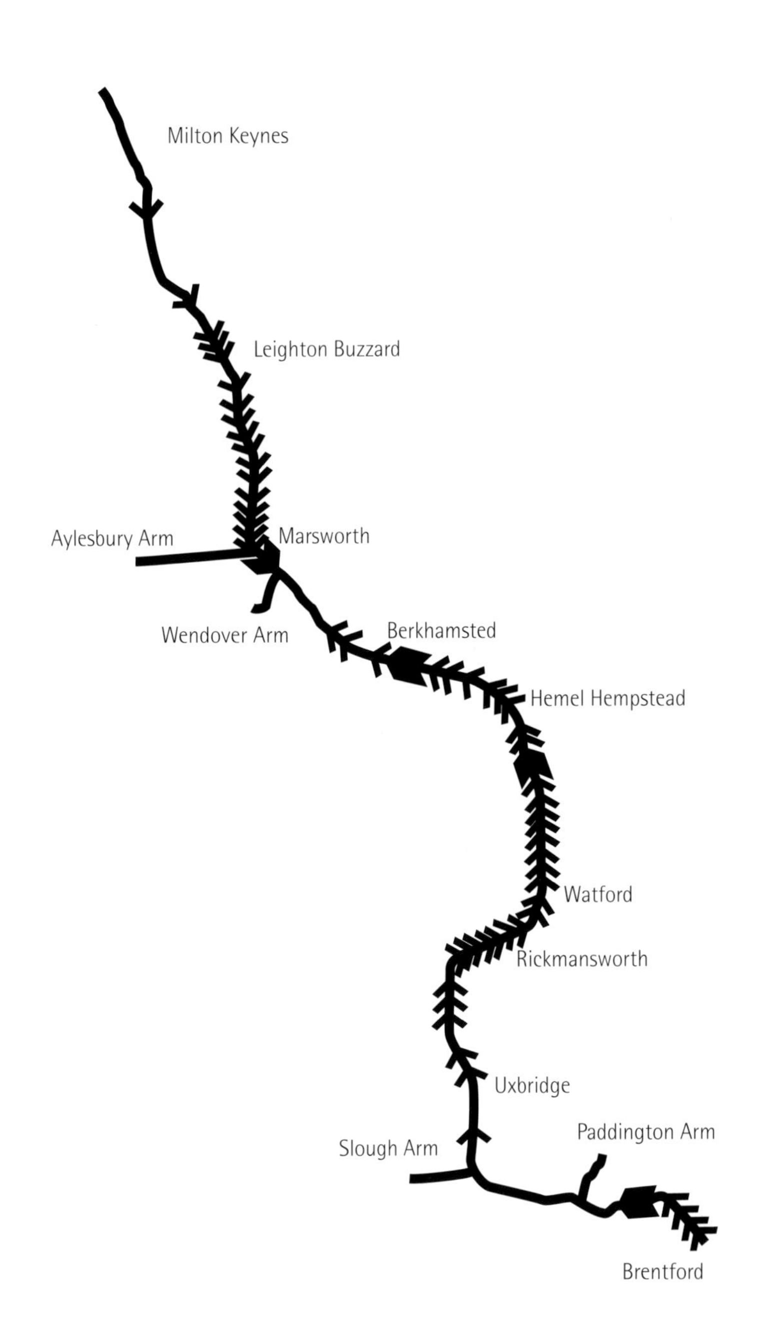
Milton Keynes
Leighton Buzzard
Aylesbury Arm
Marsworth
Wendover Arm
Berkhamsted
Hemel Hempstead
Watford
Rickmansworth
Uxbridge
Slough Arm
Paddington Arm
Brentford

INTRODUCTION

The renaissance of the canals towards the latter end of the last century was one of the country's greatest, but largely unsung, success stories. A major new leisure resource emerged that somehow managed to bring together our collective love of the countryside, our pride in our past and our growing need for an escape from the fast pace of modern living. There is no doubt about it; the canals, once in danger of being filled in and erased from history, are here to stay.

Perhaps the most distinguishing feature of our canal system is the boats that ply their way slowly but steadily through it. However, although boaters clearly represent the most visible group of canal users, they are by no means the only ones to appreciate their worth. It has been estimated that over 400 million visits are made to the canal system each year, only 2 million of which are by boaters.

The reality is that the canals have become more than simply a transport system; they have evolved into visitor corridors. Walkers, riders, anglers, cyclists or simply those among the half of the population who live within 5 miles of an inland waterway, now regularly pass through these corridors. Cyclists alone account for three times as many visits as boaters and the total number to utilise the canals is expected to double over the coming decade.

These new Guides have been written to reflect this burgeoning reality. They will appeal to boaters but will also reach out beyond them to these other groups – the backpacker planning a towpath walk, motorists looking to spend a long weekend staying in bed and breakfasts, riders looking to discover the joy of towpath routes... the list goes on.

The Guides have been prepared to inform, amuse and spark an interest in the areas surrounding the canals, with the visitor corridor being defined as spanning 2 miles either side of the towpath. Anecdotes and interesting facts are scattered throughout the Guides to provide colour and bring these areas to life for the reader, with only the most resilient likely to resist the temptation to repeat at least some of these to their companions.

For ease of use, each canal is broken down into sections, split into the following four groupings:

SHAPERS

Describing the route of the canal, the local history associated with it and details of the natural landscape and transport links, this section provides the basic background to each section.

BASICS

Where to shop, find a pub or locate a place to stay as well as places to eat. All these topics are covered here, taking the sting out of finding your way around and the essentials of getting by.

SEEING AND DOING

What to look out for and where it's worth making a diversion to see that oddity or curiosity you might not otherwise find, plus where to find that something a bit special culturally or where to go if you simply want to be entertained.

SAMPLING

Ways to dip into the local area and become part of the landscape, whether you are walking or cycling (a recommended route is provided for both in each section), riding, fishing or want to wander around a golf course.

Each section is accompanied by maps complete with symbols to show you where to find places highlighted in the text, and larger symbols indicating a concentration of pubs, hotels, etc. . Phone numbers and websites are given as appropriate and the 'Learn More and Links' section provides pointers on where to look if you want to follow up on items covered in the Guide – making it simple if you want to check a pub's opening hours, whether a leisure centre has a squash court or the times of a local bus.

We hope that these new Guides will encourage more people to enjoy our inland waterways and help to deepen their appreciation of the symbiotic relationship between the canals and the towns and villages that surround them.

Nick Corble
Series Editor

NOTE: *Cyclists need a permit from British Waterways – either apply direct or download one from their website www.britishwaterways.co.uk. Likewise, anglers should check who controls fishing rights on particular stretches and details are provided in this Guide.*

The Aylesbury Arm is marked by high rushes on both banks.

OVERVIEW

The Grand Union Canal, the 'M1' of the canal system, is perhaps one of the most famous waterways in the country, linking as it does the country's capital with its 'second city'.

The section described in this guide, its southern half, starts in Milton Keynes in the north and carves a passage through the Home Counties of Buckinghamshire, Bedfordshire, Hertfordshire and finally Middlesex before joining the Thames at Brentford in the heart of West London. Along the way it runs along a deep cutting through the Chilterns, an engineering triumph of its day, before relaxing a little by adopting the valleys of different rivers seeking the easiest route to the sea.

Today, this route is a favourite for the modern leisure boater, but it was originally built to serve a very different purpose. By the end of the eighteenth century the coalfields of the Midlands needed a means to get their black gold to markets in the south and the natural advantages of water transport for bulk freight were well understood. After considerable struggle a canal had been cut from Coventry to Oxford, and thence via the Thames to London, its first cargo of coal arriving in the university city in 1790.

Although effective, the Oxford route was less than efficient. Having spent a long time in gestation, it had been built using early canal thinking. The route valued the avoidance of locks over directness, and as such followed a tortuous meandering course, adding days to the journey time. What was more, Oxford still sat some way up the Thames, which was a less than easy waterway to negotiate, with boaters having to 'ride' weirs rather than use locks to manage the slope down to sea level.

There was scope for an alternative. An Act of Parliament in 1793 authorised the construction of a canal from Braunston in Northamptonshire, where there were other waterway links into Birmingham, down to Brentford. The canal engineer William Jessop was given the role of Chief Engineer and the new canal was given the name the Grand Junction. Work began straightaway.

The new company had an eye to the future and recognised the limitations of its main competitor. Their chosen route was direct, even if it meant quite literally blasting their way through any obstacles along the way, and their favoured dimension was broad. The Grand Junction was to be a wide, as opposed to a narrow, canal, with locks wide enough to take two narrowboats, or one broad-beamed river barge.

The canal was also intended to act as a main artery through the agricultural areas north-west of London. Like an crystal that is just forming, separate arms splintered off the main line to serve surrounding markets. Three of these remain today along the southern half of the canal, those at Aylesbury, Slough and Paddington, with a fourth at Wendover slowly being restored; but many others, such as one leading to Buckingham, have since disappeared. Although not covered in detail in this Guide, these still offer good towpaths and diversions for those with the time to explore them.

The Paddington Arm was undoubtedly the most significant of these. Even Brentford, it seemed, was too high up the Thames, and the year after the canal

A handful of swing bridges remain to inconvenience the boater on the Grand Union.

started, its backers recognised the potential of a separate arm heading west into Paddington, where a new road had been built connecting it with the heart of the city.

The new canal was not only grander in its thinking, but was also more efficient in its construction. Whereas it had taken the best part of thirty years to complete the Oxford Canal, the Grand Junction was completed as a through route in August 1805, a mere twelve years after the first turf had been cut, despite considerable engineering challenges. The Paddington Arm, just over 12 miles of canal cut through an increasingly built-up area, was completed by 1801.

Once opened, the new canal achieved all its backers' aspirations. Trade flowed through their new waterway and the basin at Paddington, currently the focus of a major redevelopment, was a modern wonder. At its head lay a 400-yard-long basin, 30 yards wide, surrounded by wharves. The noise and bustle 200 years ago would match those of the builders there today. Recovering livestock waited in pens for the final leg of their journey to Smithfield, hay and straw markets sat alongside warehouses and bargees mingled boisterously, taking a short break before setting off north once again.

> The canal company's first chairman was William Praed. Perhaps ironically, given the history that followed, his name is best remembered in the name of the street that runs outside Paddington Station.

It was to be a short moment in the sun, less than a generation. It was inevitable that once railway technology became established, one of the first major trunk routes the new breed of engineers would build would be one linking London and Birmingham. Work started on such a route in 1835, and it would have come as little consolation to the canal's founders that Robert Stephenson selected a route that more or less replicated their own.

The two transport routes were destined to co-exist, and today's towpath traveller will come across a number of examples of railway engineering along this section of the Grand Union, including some by Brunel. For a long while there was enough trade to keep both routes going, but the canals only survived by paring their costs back to a minimum. It is from around this time that bargee wages were slashed to such an extent that they were forced to make homes on their boats alongside their families.

The canal was further hampered by the fact that the canals which the Grand Junction linked with to provide the final route into Birmingham had initially resisted the widening of their waterways, creating a bottleneck and structural inefficiency that contributed to the waterway's decline.

Having just about withstood the impact of the railways, the canal found itself unable to resist the coming of the car. Like struggling businesses through time, the company had followed a strategy of expansion in a desperate search for growth, and had swallowed up the Leicester line in 1897. With the Great Depression of the late 1920s, the Grand Union as we know it today came into being when the Grand Junction joined forces with the Regent's Canal and the canals north and west of Braunston, whose pursuit of self-interest had been a thorn in its side for over a century.

Government assistance aimed at creating jobs saw the narrow locks closer to Birmingham widened, and in 1934 the Grand Union Canal Carrying Co., the GUCCC, whose initials became a regular feature along the canal on signs, bridges and boats, was formed.

> Negotiating for land along the Paddington Arm was a real problem for the canal company, with the Bishop of London presenting a particular obstacle.

The large fleet of boats built for the company came too late. The days of canal freight as a realistic alternative to the roads and railways were over. Nationalisation followed in 1949, and most of the boats carrying the company's insignia were scrapped, although some still ply the waters today, either restored to their original form or converted to leisure use.

This Guide picks up the Grand Union at Milton Keynes, a new city that has embraced the legacy of tradition offered by the canal with enthusiasm. It is a fitting place to start, just after the aqueduct over the Ouse that caused the canal's engineers so many headaches, and at the very tip of Buckinghamshire, where attention starts to be drawn more south than north.

The long lockless sweep around the edge of Milton Keynes is an extravagant one, but worth it. The new city is never far away, but far enough. The landscape is open and the towpath very well kept up – a tradition maintained almost without exception along this half of the canal.

> In its early years, the canal company ran a passenger packet service out of Paddington, using crews wearing smart blue uniforms with yellow capes and buttons. The service is remembered in the name of a pub in Cowley.

Bedfordshire and its chalk downs follow, with the lion carved into the hillside at Whipsnade a companion to the towpath traveller for a good half a day. Linslade and Leighton Buzzard, two towns that have become one, offer good places to stop as the rise towards the summit gathers momentum.

The reservoirs at Marsworth, where the arm to Aylesbury also begins with the only staircase lock on the canal, make a clear statement that the summit is reached, and shortly afterwards the deep cutting through to Tring follows, succeeded by Berkhamsted, a historical town with claims to have once been the nation's capital.

Having started at the new city of Milton Keynes our route takes us through a new town with an old heart, Hemel Hempstead, where the canal flows at a discrete distance from the centre through ancient common land. The names of Kings Langley and Abbots Langley sum up the history of the countryside that follows, the two divided by the modern icon that is the M25.

After Watford, the regional focus of West Hertfordshire, it is back for a final brief sojourn into Buckinghamshire before entering the now-defunct (but still very much alive in many peoples' consciousness), county of Middlesex. Destination: Brentford and the Thames, passing through three London boroughs and scraping past the outskirts of Heathrow.

The dead water of the canal meets the tidal flow of the Thames via two sets of double narrow locks in an area of London that is currently the subject of a massive regeneration. The vast majority of the southern section of the Grand Union can be classified as rural, and even along its final few miles through west London it is surprisingly green, passing as it does through the parks of Ostlerley and Syon.

The Grand Union Canal is perfect for the canal initiate and old hand alike. It is a waterway of contrasts, encompassing old and new towns and rural and urban landscapes. Its scale is impressive, its execution even more so. If the canal is new to you we hope this Guide will act as a deserved introduction; if you've been before we hope it deepens your appreciation of all the wonders it holds.

SECTION A

MILTON KEYNES

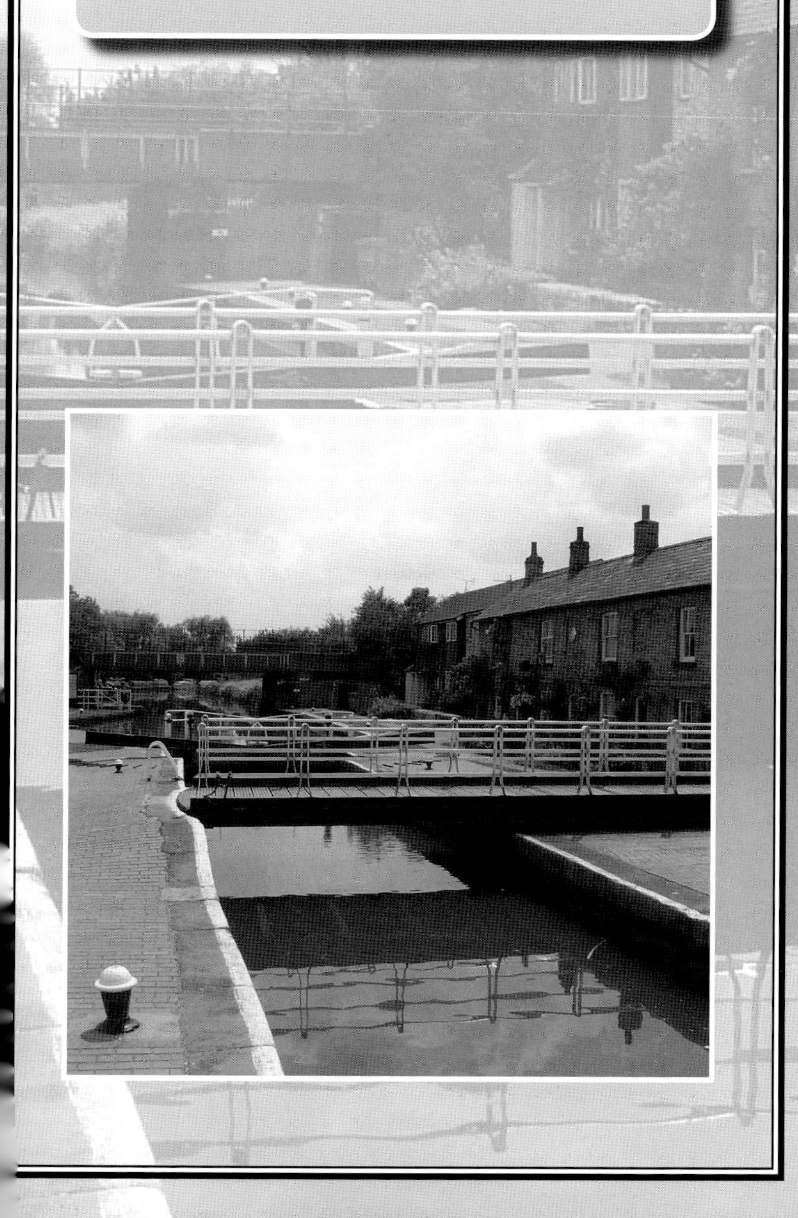

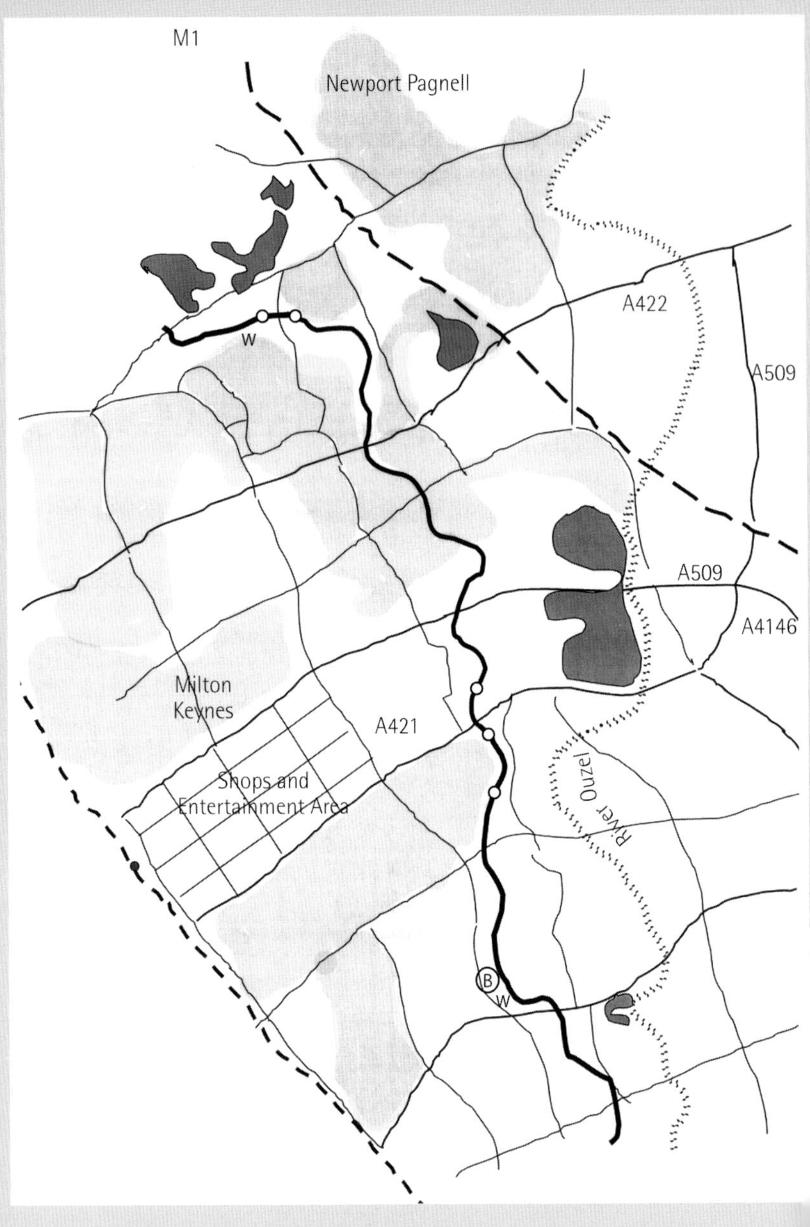
M1
Newport Pagnell
A422
A509
A509
A4146
Milton Keynes
A421
Shops and Entertainment Area
River Ouzel
W
W
B

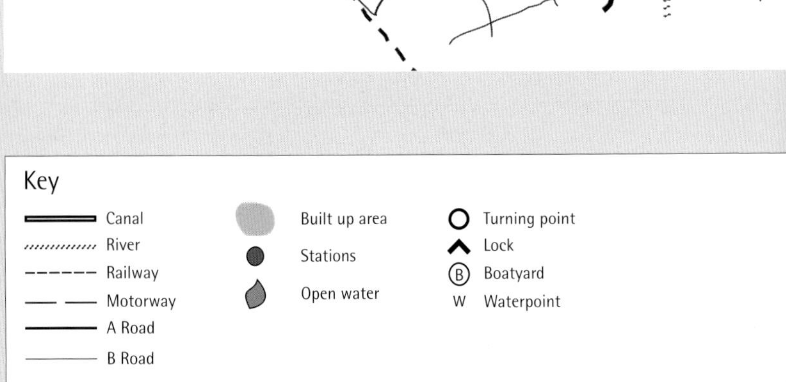
Key
Canal
River
Railway
Motorway
A Road
B Road
Built up area
Stations
Open water
Turning point
Lock
Boatyard
Waterpoint

SHAPERS

THE CANAL ON THIS STRETCH

KEY FACTS

LENGTH: 8.5 miles

BOATYARDS: 2
- Milton Keynes Marina
- Willowbridge Marina

WATERPOINTS:2
- Linford Wharf
- Milton Keynes Marina

TURNING POINTS: 7
- Linford Wharf
- Linford Wharf Bridge
- Newlands
- Little Woolstone
- Great Woolstone
- Fenny Stratford
- Water Eaton Mill

LOCKS: 1
- Fenny Stratford (1ft 1in)

There is a long flat sweep around the at times defiantly new and experimental town of Milton Keynes, with plenty of opportunities to strike into the centre of the city or to enjoy the open spaces and lakes the planners incorporated into the town's design. Wander off the towpath and there are chances to sample the area before the bulldozers moved in and learn more about its ancient antecedents.

The 'proud' in the Proud Perch's name could be put down to its apparent willingness to be associated with the canal which it sits on top of. Irregular decking offers the possibility of watching craft go by from this pub and this is as good a place as any to start the odyssey down to Brentford and the Thames along the southern stretch of the Grand Union.

This stretch of the canal is often lined with boats which have either just completed the long sweep round this newest of cities or are about to attempt it, and are taking advantage of the free availability of moorings. By Bridge 77 there is a small alleyway opposite the turning point in the canal by an information board. This leads down Gifford Pond, a remnant of the now redundant Newport Pagnell Canal.

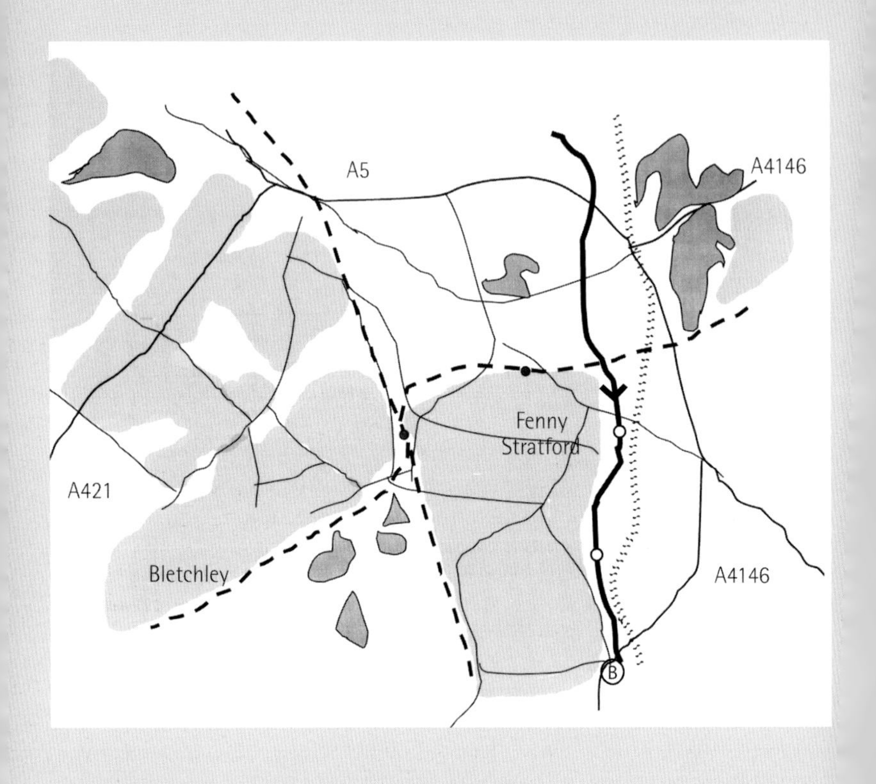
A5
A4146
Fenny
Stratford
A421
Bletchley
A4146
B

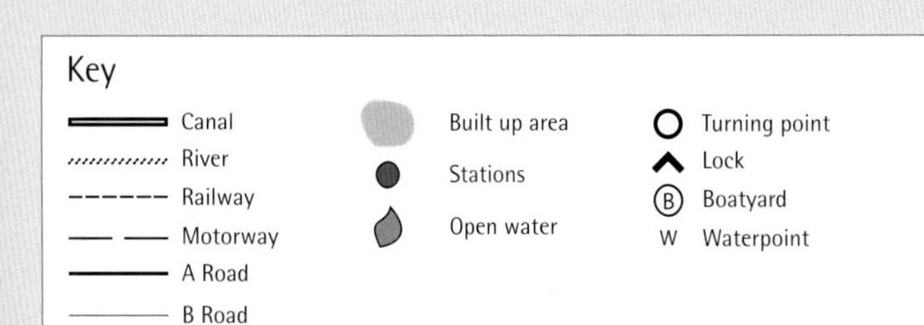
Key
Canal
River
Railway
Motorway
A Road
B Road
Built up area
Stations
Open water
Turning point
Lock
B Boatyard
W Waterpoint

> The Newport Pagnell Canal was a short (14 miles) narrow canal, which managed to pack eight locks into its short passage from Linford to Newport Pagnell. Opened in 1817, it lasted less than fifty years.

Ropes tied to mooring rings in the middle of the towpath can cause problems, so walkers need to watch out here. There is a sanitary station just before the Gifford Park Pub, which sits right on the side of a bend in the canal, and the park itself soon becomes visible to the right. The canal is on a slight embankment here with housing below and to the left and, by Milton Keynes' usually exemplary standards, the towpath is a bit rough and ready along this section.

> The brick kilns in Great Linford (accessible from Bridge 78A) once produced 10lb-bricks used to build homes in New Bradwell, Wolverton, Cosgrove and Castlethorpe at the turn of the nineteenth century, with the finished goods transported by canal to their final destination.

The route twists and turns a lot here and the towpath is soon joined once again by its tree-lined broadwalk or boulevard by Bridge 78B, just before the massed boats of the Lionheart Crusing Club. For a mile or so the boulevard is the walker's best bet, although it is still possible for the more hardy to take the towpath. The boulevard in fact diverts for a short while at Willen Park, crossing over a slated raised wooden walkway and through a children's playground. There is a school here with a running track and playing fields, which all look like they've seen better days.

After Bridge 81 the vista opens up to reveal Campbell Park, and at the park itself the towpath extends to both banks, with the park offering both living and static sculptures as well as a cricket pitch. There is ringed mooring on the park side, although mooring is rarely a problem along this stretch.

At the modern Bridge 81B there is a footpath to Willen Lake to the left, but sticking with the canal there is a winding hole just after Bridge 82, after which the towpath temporarily takes on a more traditional shape and feel, being uneven although firm. This said, the path is tracked throughout most of this stretch with a properly paved path to the left behind a hedge. There is a genuine feel of 'rurality' here, even if the large open spaces and seemingly countless children's parks, as well as the occasional glimpse of red-brick housing behind some trees, are all clearly man-made and contemporary

Further bridges follow, some of the traditional type, others determinedly modern, and after Bridge 86 the towpath becomes asphalt, although showing some signs of wear. The Peartree Marina soon follows, complete with its own pub and Chinese takeaway. After Bridge 88 the banks become more overgrown although the towpath remains easy-going. A long steady sweep to the right ends by Bridge 90C, which in turn is immediately followed by a more traditional brick version (Bridge 91). A more determined curve to the right then follows, taking in the 'sci-fi'-themed Trekkers Pub along the way, with two more swings to the left after a short straight before the canal resumes its previous course. This convoluted diversion is to avoid an area of low ground to the left.

Bridges 92 and 93 bookend a long straight and are both traditional in style, although 92A between them is a vast modern concrete affair carrying the A5. If you are starting to think you are nearing the end of Milton Keynes, you would be partly right. First though, there is a series of light industrial units and distribution centres to pass before the delights of Fenny Stratford. These are reached via a sharp bend at Bridge 94, after which there is a long run of fourteen-day moorings just before Fenny Lock, where there is also a water point.

This lock is worth noting for two reasons: first, the fact that there is a pub (The Old Red Lion) directly alongside it, and second because there is a swing bridge right across it. Although usually open, this can sometimes present a problem for boaters; while unusual now, this arrangement was once quite common. The lock has won awards for its upkeep and is significant for being close to the site where the proposed Bedford–Milton Keynes Waterway will join the Grand Union.

Long-term moorings follow the lock, and there is a winding hole just after the bridge, which provides handy access to Fenny Stratford, the last real town for some distance. A lift bridge carries the towpath over the entrance to a private marina, and the path remains solid throughout this section. The canal becomes wide and serene with good moorings.

A sense of leaving Milton Keynes behind begins to invade around this point as the canal twists and turns and the nearby housing looks as if it has seen a few decades. The tree-lined boulevard that has marked the passage of the canal through the city remains, hidden behind a hedge to the left, and at one point dipping down into a hollow. There is also the characteristic open parkland beyond the trees here as well as access to the Riverside Walk, all of which is visible through occasional gaps in the hedge, a view that also reveals some gentle hills rising to the east surrounded by farmland.

Cows (real ones, not concrete) graze in the meadows to the right, and, as the grass tapers away, the road that has been kept at bay finally comes alongside the canal, although this is not on the towpath side. There is a long straight section that leads to Bridge 99 and beyond, with the busy Willowbridge Marina sitting on the right just before the end. Bridge 99 itself carries the A4146, and there is a good view of the canal from the top of it.

It is here that the tree boulevard to the left of the towpath finally ends, and with it Milton Keynes' jurisdiction of the canal. If you look behind after passing through the bridge you will see a rather modest sign welcoming boaters going the other way to the city. For those travelling south it has been an interesting experience, but now it is time to move on.

PRINCIPAL TOWNS AND VILLAGES ALONG THIS STRETCH

BLETCHLEY:

Split into old and new parts, the former is characterised by terraced housing painted various colours, while the latter seems to suffer from being in the shadow of Milton Keynes, having taken on many of the features of a new town without commensurate investment. Attempts are currently being made to tackle this, with much accent being placed on use of the Bletchley Park 'brand' to entice hi-tech companies into the town.

FENNY STRATFORD:

Fenny Stratford has its roots in Roman times, being a crossing point over the River Ouzel for Watling Street, a position which later allowed it to become a staging post for the mail. These days it seems to struggle to maintain a separate identity, being squeezed between the encroachment of the burgeoning Milton Keynes and the larger and more significant town of Bletchley. The canal gives the place some sense of being, but otherwise its focus is its High Street.

MILTON KEYNES:

Milton Keynes remains a 'love it or loathe it' city. To this day, it is something of a curate's egg, and perhaps this is part of its attraction. Large open spaces combined with long tree-lined boulevards and a host of lakes allow the city to breathe, while an intricate network of cycle paths show at least good intent on the part of its planners. As you might expect not every experiment works, but at least experimentation is part of its ethos and for this it should be applauded. The planners also had sufficient foresight to realise the asset the canal offered, and although it does not pass through the more built-up areas, it is well guarded and used thoughtfully as circumstance demands.

Fenny Stratford once had its own market, but bubonic plague in 1665 led to its collapse and it was never revived.

NEWPORT PAGNELL:

Perhaps best known to outsiders as the home of Aston Martin or as a service station on the M1, Newport Pagnell is in fact a compact market town defined by the coming together of the Rivers Great Ouse and Ouzel. Most shops and services lie to the east, while the motorway just allows the houses to the west to avoid being absorbed into Milton Keynes.

HISTORY

It is tempting to assume that the history of this section began in 1967 when the Milton Keynes Development Corporation came into being – tempting, but wrong.

Contrary to many peoples' views, Milton Keynes did not gain its name as a homage to either the poet John Milton or the economist John Maynard Keynes, but from a small village that lay on the current site. Known variously as Milton or Middleton Keynes, the village got its name from the ancient family of

Newport Pagnell High Street.

Keynes who owned the local manor in the twelfth and thirteenth centuries. After that time the manor changed hands a few times, never growing significantly, so that by the end of the nineteenth century its total population was still only around 300, most of whom were employed in either agriculture or the local art of pillow-lace.

The area's history extends to prehistory, with the earliest evidence of occupation on the present site of Milton Keynes being dated to 2000BC, and further evidence of Neolithic and Bronze Age peoples choosing the Ouse Valley and its tributaries as settling points. Bronze Age burial sites have been found near Milton Keynes village and the remains of a large circular timber house dated to 1000BC have been found at Bancroft to the north of the city. From this point on, Iron Age settlements developed in various locations, and evidence of an Iron Age camp enclosed within a large bank and ditch can be seen at Bow Brickill.

Bancroft was clearly a favoured area as it was selected by the Romans as the spot for a villa, along with other nearby sites. Archaeologists have concluded that these served as the focus for some intensive farming, serving markets in Lactodorum (Towcester) and Magiovinium (Fenny Stratford), which sat in the busy Watling Street, today's A5 trunk road. Roman settlement was also significant around Olney to the north.

Evidence that settlement was lasting here is provided by the fact that a mausoleum has also been found as well as the remains of the area's first house, a solid structure with timer-framed walls and a thatched roof supported by ten large timber posts. Built around AD100, this precursor to tens of thousands of dwellings was destroyed by fire seventy years later. Like the 'three little piggies', the Romans learned from their mistakes and it was replaced by a house built of stone with a tiled roof.

Slowly, native Britons adopted Roman ways and the lines between the two sets of people became blurred. Farming continued until around AD400-500, when it is thought that plague wiped out the nearby towns and with them the markets for their produce, and the area fell into the slumber of the Dark Ages. Evidence of Saxon villages has been found at Milton Keynes village and Great Linford, as well as Bancroft, but they grew and fell back according to harsh economic realities.

Newport Pagnell lay as the northern limit of Saxon control, with the Danelaw dominant to the north. The Ouse and Ouzel, or Lovat, provided a natural boundary and defence, with the water contributing to the conclusion that it was a good place to settle.

By the time of the Norman invasion, Newport Pagnell had become a substantial settlement, acting as a market town for the surrounding area as well as being the location of Tickford Priory. Dissolved by Henry VIII, the priory passed into the hands of Cardinal Wolsey, and thence into private hands when he fell from grace. There is next to no remaining evidence of the Priory other than the money it was able to lavish on the local church, which even now seems large for the town.

This protection was in contrast to the fate of the villages to the south that these days comprise modern Milton Keynes, many of which existed as part of much larger land holdings. Bletchley did enjoy the benefits of ownership by a single family for 400 years, or ten generations, of the descendents of Lord Grey of Wilton, but this ended in 1603 when the lands were forfeited to the Crown.

The Duke of Buckingham was given the estate by James I and was able to recover it after it was again confiscated during the Commonwealth period. It was then given to an eminent physician by the name of Thomas Willis, and remained in this family for a further 100 years.

Campbell Park in Milton Keynes is home to a variety of sculptures.

Milton Keynes village meanwhile was vested in the Stafford family for around 250 years until it was bought by Baron Finch of Daventry in 1678, who went on to become Lord High Chancellor of England. The village then remained with the Finch family until more recent times. Fenny Stratford continued to enjoy the benefits of its strategic location on Watling Street, and became something of a stopping point, with plenty of inns with coaching stations appearing from the fifteenth century.

Newport Pagnell, for a long time the most significant settlement in the area, was occupied by the Roundheads during the Civil War, who promptly fortified it and eventually used it as a base for 2,000 soldiers who went on the fight at the decisive Battle of Naseby. If the end of the war came as something of a relief it was short-lived, as the plague of 1666 sliced through the population.

Previous economic prosperity began to wane in the face of challenges to the local industry of lace-making, and although Newport Pagnell retained its role as a market town it endured a period of relative decline, relieved only towards the end of the eighteenth century with the enclosures, and the decision to replace the town's two bridges with a single iron construction which incurred a toll. This bridge, Tickford Bridge, remains the oldest such bridge still in use.

The canal soon followed and a link to the Grand Junction Canal was made from Newport Pagnell, and although this link was short lived – its bed was used as the base for the railway that replaced it – the main arm of the canal proved to be more beneficial for Fenny Stratford in the south.

Wharves were built in Fenny and the population of this previously relatively small town doubled in the early 1800s. Furthermore, canal and railway were able to co-exist with the arrival of the latter in 1846. Together, these two transport routes revived the fortunes of the village, which had also been decimated by the plague which had led to the disastrous diversion of Watling Street to avoid it, and effectively ended its role as market town.

Bletchley's fortunes also improved with the arrival of the canal and railway, with the town attracting a major Victorian railway terminus. Fenny Stratford and Bletchley grew together, the line between them, as now, not always clear, and provided a clear centre of economic activity towards the south of this section to match that of Newport Pagnell in the north.

Although fortunes fluctuated, this was to remain the situation for a further century until the area began to attract the eye of planners looking for somewhere to house overspill population from London, in particular its East End. The site, ideally placed midway between Birmingham and London and just off the M1 motorway, was an ideal spot. Originally planned to take 40,000, this grew rapidly to 100,000, and is now moving towards the 200,000 mark.

It may be a new city, but Milton Keynes can boast a long history!

> During the excavation of Caldecotte Lake, archaeologists found the remains of an Ichithyosaur, dated to over 150 million years ago, as well as evidence of flint tool manufacture, dated to around 6000BC.

Within a few short decades the sleepy village of Milton Keynes expanded to overshadow those settlements with a longer and more noble history. Today the motorway helps Newport Pagnell retain its distinctive character, but it is hard to say the same of either Bletchley or Fenny Stratford, which cling to, rather than enjoy, a separate identity. With Milton Keynes an undoubted success story, and one whose history is still unfolding, it will be interesting to see what the future holds.

THE NATURAL LANDSCAPE

Man has had a tremendous impact on the local landscape in this section. Much of what was once a collection of villages surrounded by open pastures and cultivated fields is now thoroughly urbanised. That said, Mother Nature provided a near perfect canvas for man to cover, with gently undulating land, plenty of water and forgiving soil.

Man had recognised these advantages long before he decided to build a new town here, and first the railway and then the motorway carved their respective swathes through the scenery.

Oolites, successively lower, middle and then upper, define the countryside from the north of Buckinghamshire down to south of Stoke Hammond. These produce a gravelly soil, but a fertile one, and the area was intensely cultivated for centuries, with farms tending sheep and cattle to help to keep the land fecund, while wheat and oats grew well in the soil.

To the north, the River Great Ouse sweeps round the top of Newport Pagnell on its long journey east, while the Ouzel or Lovat, which rises as a chalk stream near the Dunstable Downs, heads north to join it. The latter's natural valley was exploited by engineers for both the railway and the canal, and as such is a constant companion to the traveller who heads through this section.

A distinguishing feature of the modern landscape is the number of lakes scattered around it. Many of these are man-made, although nature played its part by providing soggy marshland unsuitable for building. Some of these are known as 'balancing lakes', their position chosen deliberately to provide both reservoirs for the new town and places for recreation, as well as something to leaven the view.

Caldecotte and Willen Lakes both define an edge to Milton Keynes, while the Linford Lakes, a complex of fisheries and wildfowl centres, provide a good wedge between the northern part of modern housing and Newport Pagnell. The often-forgotten Furzton Lake, south of the centre, provides yet more water, while Bletchley is not without its own lakes, although these are more the result of disused extractive industries such as clay and sand.

ACCESS AND TRANSPORT

ROADS

The M1 Motorway cuts an arc across the top right-hand corner of this section and can be accessed at Junction 14 just east of Willen Lake, south-east of Newport Pagnell. Not surprisingly, Milton Keynes is well served with roads. Despite its original ambitions to become a cycle-city, most people take to their cars to get around. That said, the network of 'redways' or cycle paths that criss-cross the metropolis via subways, avoiding the need to cross busy roads, is excellent and is a pleasure to use.

The A5 passes near to the centre of the town and then sweeps down to the south-east, and provides a convenient marker for the town of Bletchely to maintain its separate identity. The A422, A509 and A421 all spur off this road and cut across the town to the north-east, while the A4146 provides a route south from the junction with the motorway to the A5.

Elsewhere there is a plethora of minor roads, notoriously clustered by the new town's planners into a grid system using the alphabet and numbering. Supposedly foolproof, this system can be frustratingly efficient in its ability to confuse, not least because not all roads are the same length and junctions do not always appear when you expect them to.

RAIL

Both Milton Keynes and Bletchley lie on the London line out of Euston, with the new town's modern but surprisingly modest station often the first stop out of the capital for trains heading up to Birmingham. There is also a station at Fenny Stratford, part of the Bletchley to Bedford line.

Train operators serving this area are:

- Silverlink Trains (01923 207258)
- South Central Trains (0870 8306000)
- Virgin (0870 789 1234)

Otherwise, National Train Enquiries can be reached on 08457 484950

BUSES

A number of bus operators and services ply routes covering this section and an excellent guide is produced by Milton Keynes Council, which is available from them either direct (01908 252302), or can be downloaded from their website (see Learn More and Links).

Alternatively, Traveline (www.traveline.org.uk) on 0870 6082608 can give details of specific services between 7 a.m. and 10 p.m.

There are a variety of special rates available for frequent travellers, day users and those linking with the rail service or those eligible for concessions, and it is worth checking with different operators if any of these are applicable to you.

The following list sets out the main bus services on this stretch, although it is advisable to check before using them as some buses only run on certain days and others may have been withdrawn since publication of this Guide:

Some key local routes with their operators are as follows:

- 1 – *Milton Keynes, Newport* Pagnell and Olney (MK Metro 01908 225100 and Z&S International 01296 415468)
- 4/4E – *Bletchley, Milton Keynes and Wolverton (MK Metro)*
- 7 – *Milton Keynes, the Hospital, Bletchley and Fenny Stratford (MK Metro)*
- 16 – *Fenny Stratford to Bletchley (MK Metro and Z&S International)*
- 19 – *Newport Pagnell to Bletchley (MK Metro)*
- 30/31 – *Bletchley to Newport Pagnell via Wolverton (MK Metro)*

Long-distance routes include:

- X2 – *From Northampton to Bedford via Olney*
- X4 – *Milton Keynes to Peterborough*
- X5 – *Oxford to Cambridge via Milton Keynes*
- X15 – *Milton Keynes to Aylesbury via Bletchley and Leighton Buzzard*
- X66 – *Milton Keynes to Luton Airport*

TAXIS

The following list gives a selection of the taxi operators in this section:

- Ace Cars, Bletchley (01908 366666)
- Apple Cars, Bletchley (01908 641010)
- Cabco, Milton Keynes (01908 261616)
- Circle Cars, Milton Keynes (01908 222444)
- Direct Cars, Bletchley (01908 646565)
- MK Taxis, Milton Keynes (01908 313030)
- Milton Keynes Cars, Milton Keynes (01908 567890)
- Raffles Private Hire, Bletchley (01908 632632)
- Wheelchair Taxi Service, Milton Keynes (07802 847503)

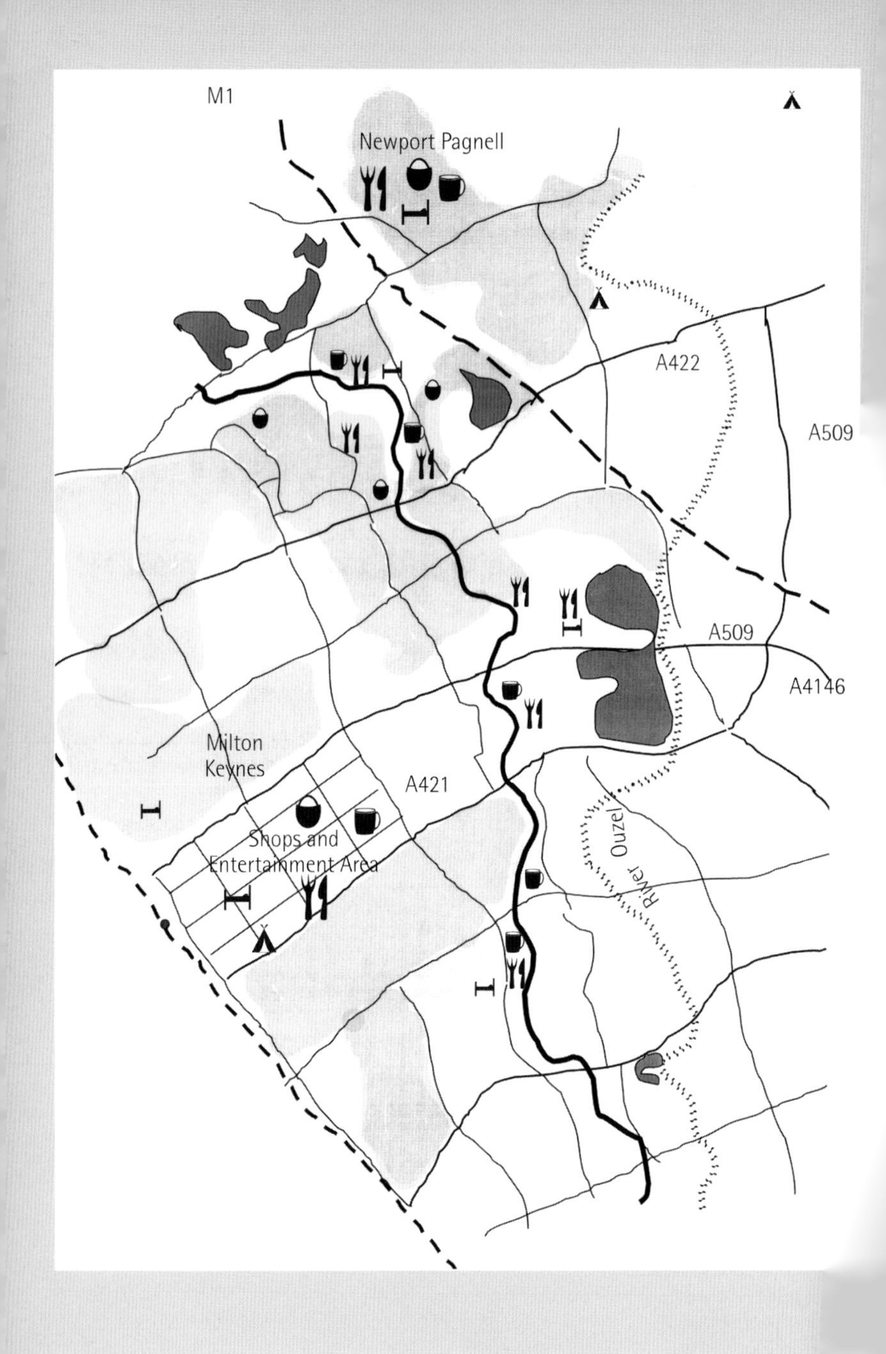
M1
Newport Pagnell
A422
A509
A509
A4146
Milton
Keynes
A421
Shops and
Entertainment Area
River Ouzel

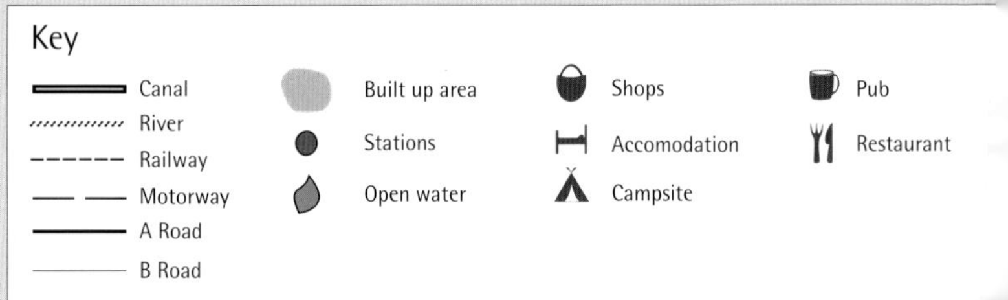
Key
Canal
River
Railway
Motorway
A Road
B Road
Built up area
Stations
Open water
Shops
Accomodation
Campsite
Pub
Restaurant

BASICS

INTRODUCTION

Newport Pagnell continues to exist as a separate entity from Milton Keynes, and still retains its own shopping centre and selection of places to stay. While the new city itself clearly dominates this section in terms of shopping, the casual visitor may still choose to look to the north or south of the section when searching for places to stay. It is here that more traditional inns and guest houses thrive, although Milton Keynes has, over the last few years, been active in developing more of a hotel sector.

Milton Keyes is also home to the nearest General Hospital (01908 611767), although non-emergency health concerns can be addressed by calling NHS Direct on 0845 4647.

SHOPPING

Newport Pagnell offers a full range of shops including chemists, most major banks and building societies, a post office, off-licence and both a Somerfield and a Co-Op supermarket, all within the compact main High Street.

At the lower end of this High Street there is also a store specialising in pianos and a couple of shops selling antiques and curios. The Tickford Arcade also houses a range of local shops, from card outlets to hairdressers. Moulsoe Buildings Farm in Newport Pagnell (01908 617016) sells pick-your-own strawberries and asparagus from its farm shop when they are in season.

Milton Keynes is, of course, notorious for its shopping centre, which was one of the first landmarks the city acquired. These days it is branded as 'thecentre: mk', and regards itself as in a European league when it comes to shopping malls. The centre itself radiates out from Midsummer Place, which was recently the subject of a £150 million upgrade with a Debenhams store at its core.

As a consequence, there is practically every large High Street name you can think of here, ranging from banks through to snack outlets, international clothes brands, bookshops and hairdressers. There are also plenty of supermarkets and even an oak tree, 150 years old, in the centre of the revamped development, and a stained glass window by the artist Ann Smyth, giving her interpretation of Milton Keynes' highway grid system.

The centre is not the only place you can shop: most of the outlying districts, many of which are accessible from the canal, have their own local shops, usually offering a newsagent or convenience store. In addition, there are a number of large out-of-town superstores dotted around the city.

Fenny Stratford has a Londis along with a good range of other shops and banks, as well as a post office and various fast-food and more formal restaurants. The large outlets do not seem to bother with Fenny, which means that the smaller local independents have had a chance to establish themselves, which can make it worthwhile to browse a little.

Bletchley has a large Tesco on its outskirts, as well as a free shoppers' car park opposite the Leisure Centre. The centre of Bletchley is partially pedestri-

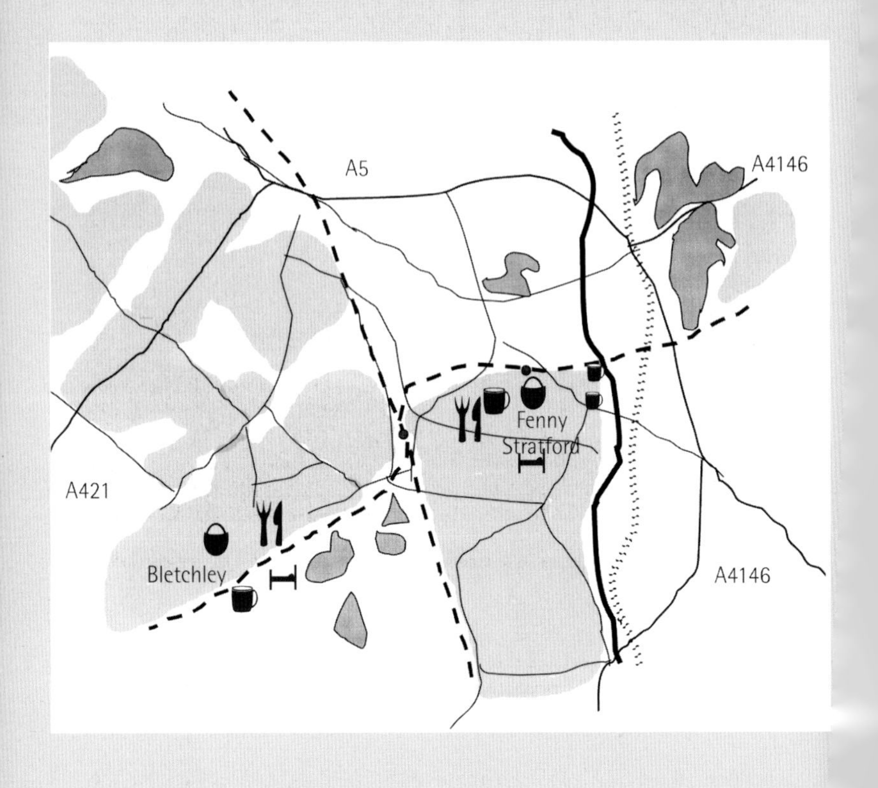
A5
A4146
Fenny
Stratford
A421
Bletchley
A4146

Key
Canal
River
Railway
Motorway
A Road
B Road
Built up area
Stations
Open water
Shops
Accomodation
Campsite
Pub
Restaurant

Bletchley and Fenny Stratford struggle to maintain a separate identify from the presence of nearby Milton Keynes.

anised and comprises a long High Street with a modern bandstand at one end and a contemporary rectangular black glass-fronted mall, the Brunel Centre, at the other. The latter has a few major High Street names such as WH Smith and Boots.

The shops along the High Street are not very inspiring, and the fact that this area has probably seen better days is confirmed by signs of ongoing investment in regeneration. Mingling among the charity shops and estate agents, however, it is possible to find pharmacies, all the major banks, a post office, a town-centre Somerfields supermarket and a larger Co-Op.

If you are looking for something a bit different, then Continental Foods (01908 376096) at the Brunel Centre end of town has a selection of Asian foods. Bletchley also has a parade of shops towards Fenny Stratford, including a Londis. G. Doyle in Denmark Street, (01908 372355) close to Bridge 96, sells farm-fresh fruit, vegetables and eggs.

EATING AND DRINKING

There are, of course, a number of pubs and restaurants in Milton Keynes and its surrounding area, but with the exception of Newport Pagnell and Bletchley, the following list confines itself to those within easy reach of the canal and can only offer a selection of the variety available, but hopefully will act as a useful starting point. Most of the pubs serve food, as do the hotels listed in the next section.

- The Bull Inn, Newport Pagnell (01908 650325)
- The Cannon, Newport Pagnell (01908 211495)
- The Kings Arms, Newport Pagnell (01908 610033)
- The Swan Revived, Newport Pagnell (01908 610565)
- The Gifford Park, Milton Keynes (01908 210025) – *Near Bridge 78, a Brewers Fayre pub*
- The Proud Perch, Great Linford, Milton Keynes (01908 398461)
- The Barge Inn, Little Woolstone, Milton Keynes (01908 208891) - *100 yards to the left of Bridge 83*
- The Peartree Bridge Inn, Milton Keynes (01908 691515) – *Adjacent to the marina and Bridge 88*
- Trekkers, Milton Keynes (01908 670015) – *Sci-fi themed pub after Bridge 91*
- The Bridge at Fenny, Fenny Stratford (0800 298 8015)
- The Bull and Butcher, Fenny Stratford (01908 372964)
- The Foundary Arms, Fenny Stratford (01908 377621)
- The Maltsters Arms, Fenny Stratford (01908 377621)
- The Old Red Lion, Fenny Lock (01908 372317) – *Next to Fenny Lock*

Cafés and fast-food outlets along the route and in surrounding areas include the following:

- The Coffee Pot, Newport Pagnell (01908 617931)
- The Golden Fry, Newport Pagnell (01908 616484) – *traditional fish and chips*
- The Picture House Café, Newport Pagnell (01908 216540)
- The Truffle, Newport Pagnell (01908 614132) – *sandwiches*
- Camphill Café, Willen Park, Milton Keynes (01908 235000) – *vegetarian meals and snacks, 50 yards east of Bridge 81.*
- Dail a Curry, Milton Keynes (01908 695225)
- Great Linford Takeaway, Milton Keynes (01908 231004)
- Sam's Chinese Takeaway, Peartree Marina (01908 695695)
- Colosseo Sandwich Bar, Fenny Stratford (01908 645588)
- Fryday's Fish Bar, Fenny Stratford (01908 373486)
- Napolis Fish Bar, Fenny Stratford (01908 372457)
- Café Mediterraneo Bar, Bletchley (01908 377099)
- Frydays Fish Bar, Bletchley (01908 373486)
- Smarts Fish and Chips, Bletchley (01908 370449)
- Mr. T's Café, Bletchley (01908 367049)
- Tony's Bakery, Bletchley (01908 648911) – *all-day breakfasts and hot snacks*

More formal dining establishments include the following:

- The East Ocean, Newport Pagnell (01908 616588) – *Peking and Cantonese restaurant*
- The Golden Tree, Newport Pagnell (01908 211110) - *African and Caribbean restaurant*
- The Magic Wok, Newport Pagnell (01908 610490) – *Chinese restaurant,*
- Robinsons Restaurant, Newport Pagnell (01908 611450) – *up-market bistro*
- The Syllett Dynasty, Newport Pagnell (01908 617771) – *Indian restaurant*
- Fatty Arbuckles, Midsummer Boulevard, Milton Keynes (01908 673656) – *American Diner*
- Jaipur, Grafton Gate East, Milton Keynes (01908 669796) – *Indian restaurant*

Fenny Lock is unusual for having a swing bridge right across its middle.

This wooden boat is moored just outside Fenny Stratford.

- Maharajas, Grafton Gate East, Milton Keynes (01908 200522) – *Indian restaurant*
- Marcellos Ristorante, Midsomer Boulvevard, Milton Keynes (01908 608787) – *Italian restaurant*
- Royal Lido, Midsummer Boulevard, Milton Keynes (01908 240128)
- No.15 Watling St, Fenny Stratford (01908 373018) – *Tapas bar*
- Aromas Chinese Restaurant, Fenny Stratford (01908 642274)
- Chutney's Tandoori, Fenny Stratford (01908 645886)
- Dinajpur, Fenny Stratford (01908 376234) – *Indian restaurant*
- Ganges Café, Indian Restaurant, Fenny Stratford (01908 376332)
- Viva Pizza, Fenny Stratford (01908 631316) – *Pizza restaurant*
- Voongs Restaurant (01908 370292) – *Chinese restaurant*
- The China Garden, Bletchley (01908 641007)
- Royal Emperor, Old Bletchley (01908 370733) – *Chinese restaurant*
- Veggie-World.com, Bletchley (01908 632288) – *Vegetarian Chinese restaurant*

SLEEPING

There is a reasonable selection of places to stay in this section. Some of the larger hotels chains have recently moved into the centre of Milton Keynes, while there is also a mix of bed and breakfasts and guest houses, as well as inns, scattered around. The following list features some you may wish to investigate if you intend staying in the area:

HOTELS

- Marriott Courtyard, London Road, Newport Pagnell (01908 613688) – *forty-seven rooms, six suites, superior style hotel*
- The Swan Revived, Newport Pagnell (01908 610565) – *former fifteenth-century coaching inn*
- The Church House Hotel, Gifford Park, Milton Keynes (01908 216030) – *eleven en suite rooms*
- Holiday Inn, Central Milton Keynes (08704 009057) – *166 rooms and two minutes from the city centre*
- Novotel, Central Milton Keynes (01908 322212) – *a new hotel with 125 rooms close to the city centre*
- Peartree Bridge Inn, Milton Keynes (01908 691515) – *canalside pub with ten twin rooms and five double rooms*
- Shenley Church Inn, Milton Keynes (01908 505467)
- Travel Inn Milton Keynes East (0870 1977185) – *by Willen Lake*
- Travelodge, Milton Keynes (0870 1911698) – *budget hotel on the edge of town*
- Campanile, Fenny Stratford (01908 649819) – *eighty rooms with all services*
- Swan Hotel, Fenny Stratford (01908 370100) – *nine rooms*
- The Shenley Hotel, Bletchley (01908 372485) – *eight rooms, including one family room*

BED AND BREAKFASTS/GUEST HOUSES

- Acorn Uplands B&B, Newport Pagnell (01234 391992)
- The Bull Inn, Newport Pagnell (01908 650325) – *two rooms*
- The Clitheroes B&B, Newport Pagnell (01908 611643) – *four rooms*
- High Street B&B, Newport Pagnell (01908 618989) – *town centre accommodation*
- Rosemary House B&B, Newport Pagnell (01908 612198) – *three rooms*
- A Rovers Return, Milton Keynes (01908 310465)
- Conifers, Woolstone, Milton Keynes (01908 674506) – *large bungalow within walking distance of the city centre*
- Fallty Towers, Milton Keynes (01908 315867)
- Kingfishers Guest House, Milton Keynes (01908 310231) – *four rooms*
- The Malt House B&B, Milton Keynes (01908 501619)
- Abbey's, Fenny Stratford (01908 643872)
- Shanballa, Fenny Stratford (01908 379150)
- The Hatch B&B, Bletchley (01908 630633)
- The Townhouse, Bletchley (01908 368713)

Tickford Bridge in Newport Pagnell.

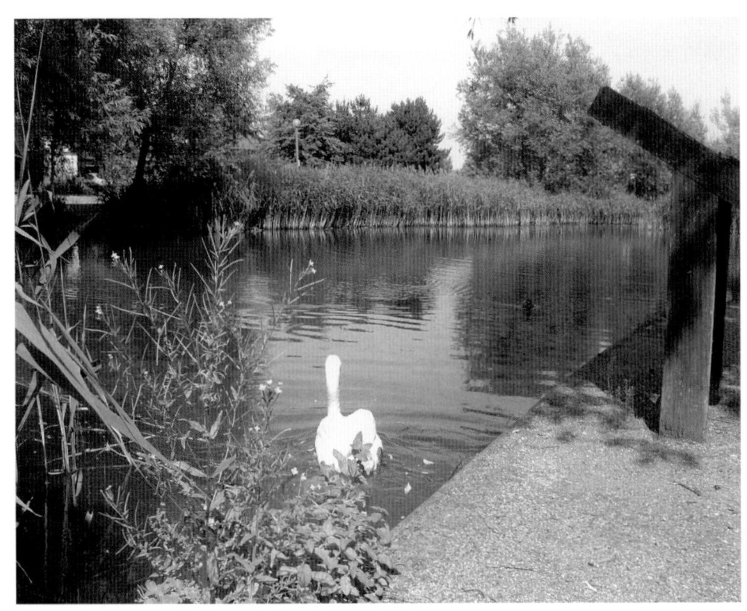

Gifford Lake marks a surviving remnant of the old Newport Pagnell Canal.

CAMPING

There are few opportunities for camping in this section. The two main sites are:

- Lovatt Meadow, London Road, Newport Pagnell (01908 610858) – *open March to December, a 2.75-acre open meadow site by a river, forty pitches for touring caravans only*
- Emberton Country Park, Nr Olney (01234 711575) – *open April to October, a 175-acre leisure park with 200 pitches for caravans, tents and motor homes. Full watersports, fishing, pitch & putt, climbing crag and so on*

The nearest camping supplies outlets in this section are:

- Ellis Brigham Mountain Sports, Avebury Boulevard, Milton Keynes (01908 609122)
- The Outdoor Shop, Xscape Centre, Milton Keynes (01908 200388)
- Silvertrek, Central Milton Keynes (01908 200388)
- Pennine Way Outdoor Adventure, Secklow Gate East, Milton Keynes (01908 669841)

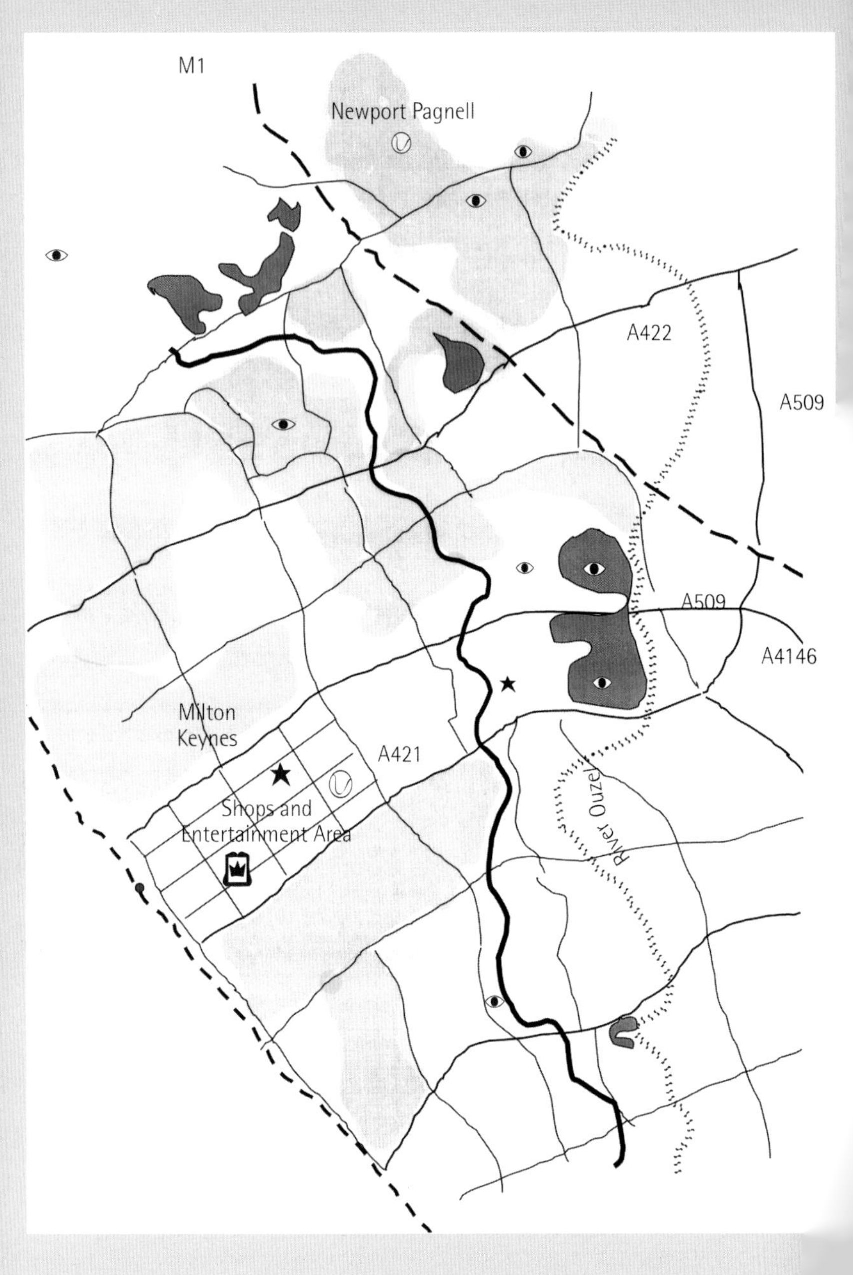
M1
Newport Pagnell
A422
A509
A509
A4146
Milton
Keynes
A421
Shops and
Entertainment Area
River Ouzel

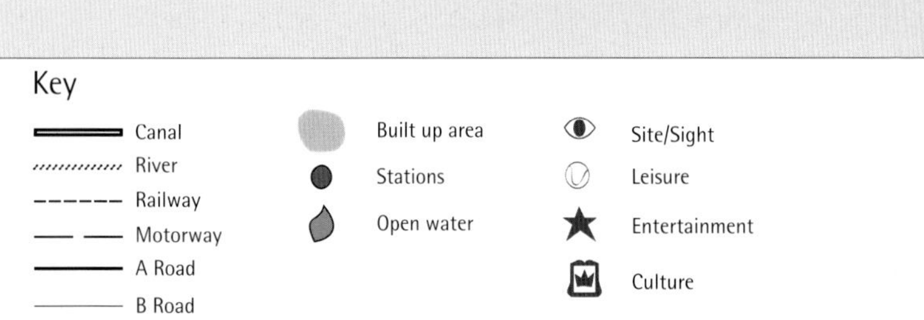
Key
Canal
River
Railway
Motorway
A Road
B Road
Built up area
Stations
Open water
Site/Sight
Leisure
Entertainment
Culture

SEEING AND DOING

INTRODUCTION

This section is less for traditional sightseeing and more for exploring and contrasting the available historic sites in the north and south with the more modern attractions of the new town of Milton Keynes. The latter is rapidly evolving into a major regional centre for the arts, as well as a national centre for some sports. From humble beginnings, and in a relatively short space of time, Milton Keynes has added considerably to the cultural and entertainment options to people in the region.

SIGHTS

Perhaps the best place to start to get a flavour of the history of Newport Pagnell is the church of St Peter and St Paul, which looks down on the meadows of the River Ouzel. The area around the church provides a reminder of the town's main role as a fortification.

Just down the road is Tickford Bridge, a Grade II listed ancient monument, built in 1810 to a design by Thomas Wilson. The bridge is an iron masterpiece sitting on two stone abutments, and it is the latter, combined with the fact that all the bridge's joints are pegged and are in compression, that gives the bridge its remarkable strength. The original Toll House also sits alongside the bridge and is worth taking in.

> Components for Tickford Bridge were cast by Walkers of Rotherham, and then shipped by canal and sea to London, where they again took the canal route before covering the final stretch by road.

Newport Pagnell is also the home of Aston Martin Lagonda, which holds occasional charity open days. The factory building itself originally produced coaches for the nobility, continuing in this trade until the Second World War.

While in the area, it may be worth making a slight detour north of Newport Pagnell to Olney, to visit the Cowper and Newton Museum (01234 711516), which celebrates the lives of the poet and musicians responsible for, among others, the hymn 'Amazing Grace'.

Moving on to Milton Keynes, if it's museums you're after, then the Milton Keynes Museum (01908 316222), located in the grounds of a Victorian model farm, gives a good introduction to the life of this area before the bulldozers moved in, focusing on North Buckinghamshire as a whole rather than simply Milton Keynes.

In a similar vein, the City Discovery Centre in Bradwell Abbey (01908 227229) is housed in seventeenth-century farm buildings, but here the accent is very much on the coming of the new town. If you really have to, this is also the best place to find Milton Keynes' famous concrete cows. Created in 1978, these rapidly became an icon of the city, although they are perhaps less so today.

Given its recent history, Milton Keynes is not blessed with many historical buildings – although you may be surprised to catch the odd thatched house that survived the developers, such as the Old Rectory Farmhouse behind the Peartree Marina which houses the Inter-Action Riding Stables (see Sampling). Much of

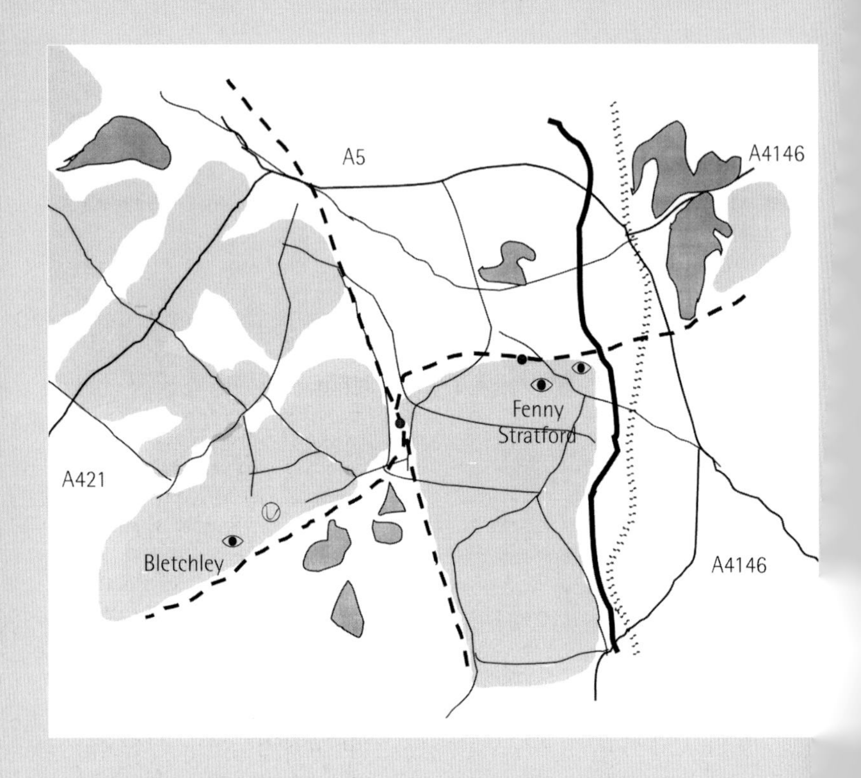
A5
A4146
Fenny
Stratford
A421
Bletchley
A4146

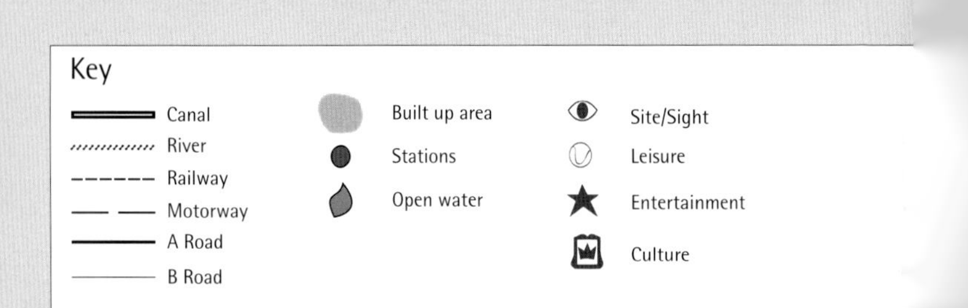
Key
Canal
River
Railway
Motorway
A Road
B Road
Built up area
Stations
Open water
Site/Sight
Leisure
Entertainment
Culture

the city's attraction lies in how it was put together and its surroundings. While the city's planners may not have got everything right, their desire to please and to make room for innovation, along with their willingness to acknowledge more ancient antecedents, cannot be doubted. For example, the city is thought to lie on an ancient ley line and this is reflected in how the city centre's boulevards were set out. Prehistoric sites were also left untouched and preserved, and archaeologists were given free rein when the large lakes on the city's outskirts were dug.

These lakes are another good example of the wish to create a pleasant environment for people to live and work in. Utopia was never going to be possible, but that didn't stop the planners from trying! Now, over thirty years on, some of these features have bedded in and matured while others are perhaps showing their age. Milton Keynes is 'settling down', and the fact that not everything is new, and individuals have had a chance to mould their environment, has worked in the city's favour.

Both Willen and Campbell Parks are good examples of this. Each offers a pleasant open space and both contain their own Art Trails. These consist of a number of – mainly (but not exclusively) – steel structures which sometimes just creep up on you, including one of a profile of a head and a gnomon – a stationary arm that projects the shadow on a sundial, and looks a bit like a giant cricket wicket.

A turf and bronze maze in Willen Park is an enlarged version of the Saffron Walden Rosicrucian Maze, while the Circle of Hearts Medicine Wheel, which takes the form of a North American 'medicine wheel', was created by local volunteers in conjunction with Landscape Town and Country as a meeting place for Milton Keynes residents to celebrate the New Millennium with wishes for global peace in the new century.

The Peace Pagoda in Willen Park was the first of its kind in the West. Built by the monks and nuns of the Nipponzan Myohoji, a spiritual non-violent movement, it holds sacred relics of the Lord Buddha presented from Nepal, Sri Lanka and Berlin. The Pagoda frieze, of traditional design, tells the story of Buddha, from his birth 2,500 years ago at the foot of the Himalayas, to his death at Kusinagara after fifty years of teaching. The Peace Pagoda is a working Buddhist temple with regular services.

You always know where you are in Milton Keynes.

Willen and Caldecotte Lakes, on the eastern edge of the city, are also pleasant places to linger, as are the various Linford Lakes to the north. Finally on this theme, the Ouzel Valley Park, which links the Willen and Caldecotte Lakes, provides a wide parkland corridor which has been richly planted with trees and hedges and is now a place where wildlife flourishes. Examples include old meadow wildflowers such as yellow rattle and pignut, while the pond near the car park off the H7 is home to a number of rare dragonflies.

It is best to view the rest of the city as one large architectural experiment, from the city's new cathedral to the glass monolith that is the Xscape centre, or the glass pyramid of The Point nearby. The shopping centre itself is unconventional, if for no other reason than it exists in, and as the heart of, the city; unlike more modern out-of-town developments.

Further south, the main things to see in Fenny Stratford are the High Street, which retains some of its distinct character, and the canal itself, not least Fenny Lock.

There is little to entice a tourist into the heart of Bletchley other than the Rectory Cottages, which were once owned by the de Grey family, and have a fine medieval hammer-beamed hall; and the church of St Mary's, which dates to the twelfth century.

Bletchley Park (01908 640404), on the outskirts, is the town's most obvious attraction. Described as a living museum where visitors are shipped back to 1942, the park celebrates the role of the people who worked here to crack the Nazis' Enigma Code using the giant computer Colossus. The exhibitions chart the development of electronic intelligence through a collection of computers, and there is also an assortment of costumes, toys and other memorabilia from the wartime period.

CULTURE AND ENTERTAINMENT

Once regarded unfairly as something of a cultural black hole, in recent years Milton Keynes has developed into a cultural hotspot, with the arts, music and theatre as well as more prosaic sports and entertainment pursuits all enjoying a high profile.

Milton Keynes Theatre (01908 606090) at Marlborough Gate Central, Milton Keynes, offers a busy and varied programme suited to all ages and tastes, while the nearby Milton Keynes City Orchestra has established itself at the heart of the city's cultural life. Formed in 1974, the orchestra comprises musicians who play regularly in the major London orchestras, and has made a number of recordings of unfamiliar works by lesser-known English composers, with a focus on exploring England's musical heritage. The area also has the Milton Keynes Chorale (01296 712472), which currently has almost 150 members and performs regularly in the Milton Keynes Theatre.

On the subject of music, a number of pubs and venues stage live music across the area. Examples include the Trekkers Pub in Milton Keynes (01908 670015), which stages open acoustic blues sessions most Mondays; the Cannon in Newport Pagnell (01908 610919), which holds folk sessions on Wednesday evenings; and the British Legion Club in Newport Pagnell (01908 613604), where there is more folk on the second and fourth Tuesdays of every month.

On a larger scale, the National Bowl on the outskirts of the city is a major outdoor entertainment venue with a national reputation. As its name suggests, it sits in a natural bowl and can hold 65,000 people. In 1992 a huge sound stage was added, which has enabled it to attract some major stars over the years, including David Bowie, Michael Jackson, Bon Jovi and Robbie Williams.

The Milton Keynes Gallery on Midsummer Boulevard (01908 676900), opened in 1999, presents six to eight exhibitions of contemporary art each year in the area that is becoming known as the 'theatre district' at the easternmost end of Midsummer Boulevard. The exhibitions cover all media including painting, sculpture, installation, print and photography, and it is possible to buy limited edition prints here.

If you like your entertainment less subtle and preferably with a strong back beat, the Xscape centre on Avebury Boulevard in the heart of Milton Keynes has a number of entertainment options under one (curved) roof. These

One of the newest cathedrals in the country, that at Milton Keynes.

include the Mid City Lanes (01908 295211) ten-pin bowling alley, which has regular 'glow sessions', that is bowling in the dark; a snow slope with real snow (0871 2225670); a sixteen-screen multiplex cinema (0871 2208000); the Silvertrek Climb Zone, with two fully supervised indoor walls (01908 200388); as well as a sports club, shopping outlets and places to eat. The Point, in the centre of town, is another multiplex cinema. Just off the canal by Bridge 81B, is Gullivers Land (01908 609001), a theme park for younger children which offers a good family day out.

Lacking a sporting heritage of its own, Milton Keynes has greedily snapped up any sporting infrastructure it could bid for, ranging from the relocation of Wimbledon professional football club, now known as the MK Dons (01908 609000), to national centres for hockey and badminton.

Bletchley bandstand.

For those looking for more casual sport, the Middleton Swimming Pool (01908 610477) in Newport Pagnell is a modern swimming complex offering a variety of swimming sessions in addition to normal public swimming.

The Shenley Leisure Centre in Milton Keynes (01908 340853) has a sports hall, squash courts and treatment rooms (and tanning studio), as well as floodlit artificial grass pitches and the Clock Inn Bar. The centre also has an arts and entertainment programme with professional and amateur theatre and comedy nights. This can be a good place to head if you're looking for something a little less formal.

Finally, Bletchley also has its own large Leisure Centre (01908 377251), which regards itself as the largest such centre in the area with a wide range of facilities.

If its nightlife you're after, the centre of Milton Keynes is probably the place to head for, where there are three nightclubs:

- Bar Central, Midsomer Boulevard (01908 609206)
- The Oasis Bar, The Point, Midsomer Boulevard (01908 661774)
- The Toad, Xscape, Avebury Boulevard (01908 251060)

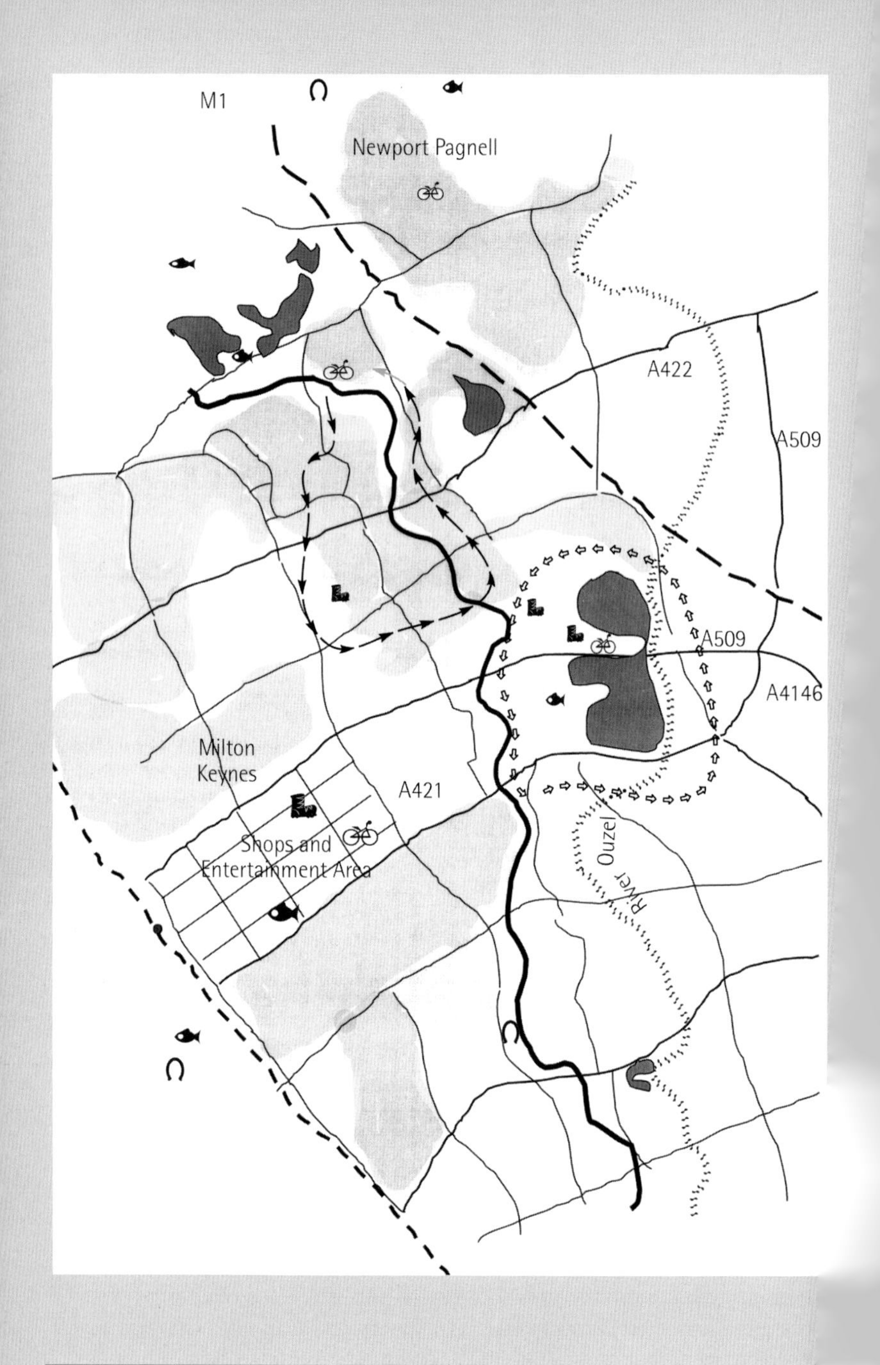
M1
Newport Pagnell
A422
A509
A509
A4146
Milton Keynes
A421
Shops and Entertainment Area
River Ouzel

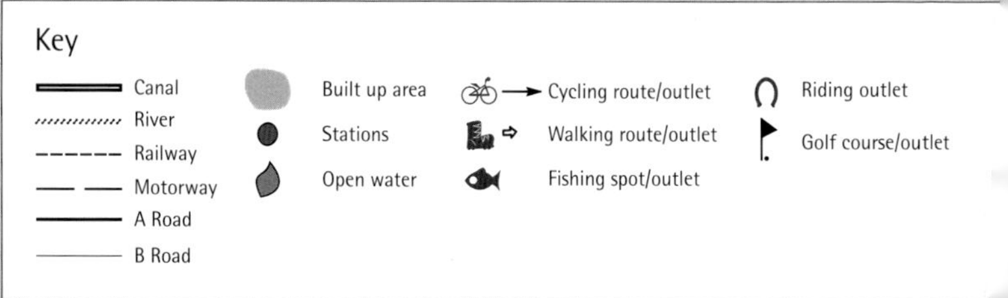
Key
Canal
River
Railway
Motorway
A Road
B Road
Built up area
Stations
Open water
Cycling route/outlet
Walking route/outlet
Fishing spot/outlet
Riding outlet
Golf course/outlet

SAMPLING

INTRODUCTION

Milton Keynes is definitely the town of the car but this does not mean that there aren't plenty of opportunities to sample the surrounding countryside. Once again, the city planners were determined that Milton Keynes should hang on to its rural heritage, and much effort has been made to allow the resident and visitor alike to enjoy it, whether by foot, horse or bike.

WALKING

The Midshires Way runs north/south along the western edge of the map, cutting across the heart of the town centre to the west of the shopping centre and railway station.

The Milton Keynes Boundary Walk describes the southern limit of the section while a number of public footpaths use the towpath as a jumping-off point into open countryside, notably towards the southern end of the section south of Caldecotte Lake, east of Fenny Stratford. There is also a warren of short paths to the east of the canal arund Woughton on the Green. Finally, the lakes to the north of the section offer further walking opportunities, with the Midshires Way reappearing just south of the Linford Lakes.

The city also promotes its Canalside Walk, identifiable by the line of trees laid out alongside the canal as it skirts round the outside of the built-up area and the generally good condition of the towpath. The path between the trees is suitable for easy walking or cycling, while the towpath is a little more challenging. There are a number of set pieces along the route, including:

- Linford Manor Park, an area of landscaped parkland with seventeenth-century buildings and the church of the Linford Estate off Bridge 77
- The Grand Junction Canal Trail, also off Bridge 77 at Linford Wharf, which takes in the route of the former Newport Pagnell Canal
- The Brick Kilns at Bridge 79
- Willen Lakes from Bridges 81A or 82
- Fenny Stratford Lock at Bridge 95A

Linford Woods is also another good place to walk. Sited just half-a-mile out from the city centre, this is ancient woodland covering about 100 acres with primroses and wood anemones in spring, followed by bluebells and early purple orchids. Linford Woods is a good place for bird-spotting with examples including marsh and willow tits, nuthatches, treecreepers and all three types of British woodpecker. Car parks serving the woods are at Breckland off H3 Monks Way and at V7 Saxon Street.

The Linford Lakes, along with those at Willen and Caldecotte that Milton Keynes is also blessed with, all make for delightful walking, often with information provided on things to look out for.

Walk A runs to the east of the towpath and allows the walker to sample not only a gentle stretch of the canal but also the delights of the reed-lined

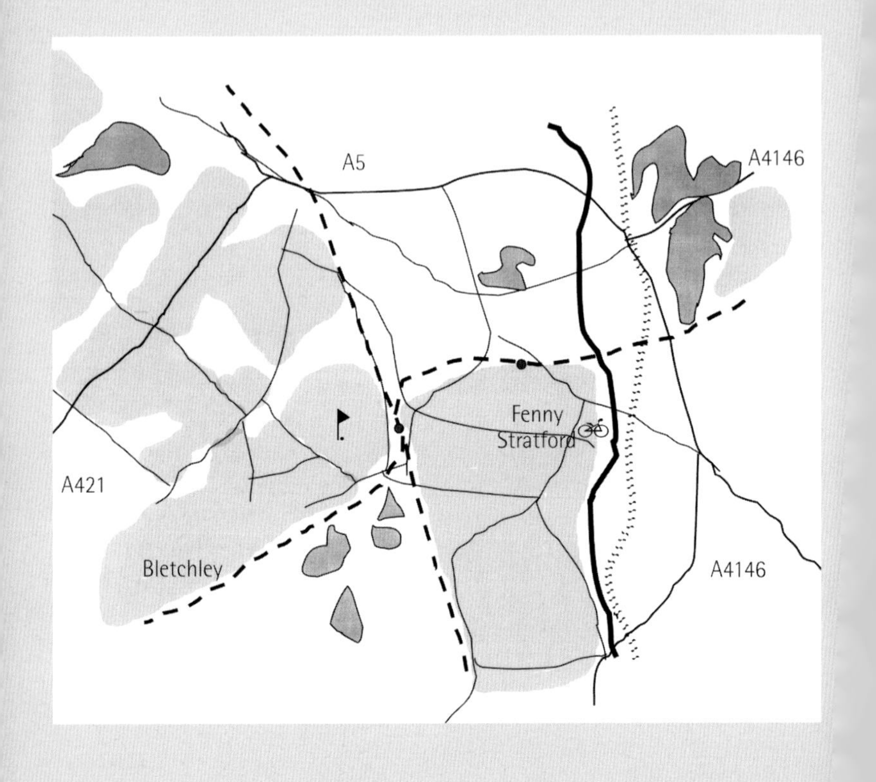
A5
A4146
Fenny
Stratford
A421
Bletchley
A4146

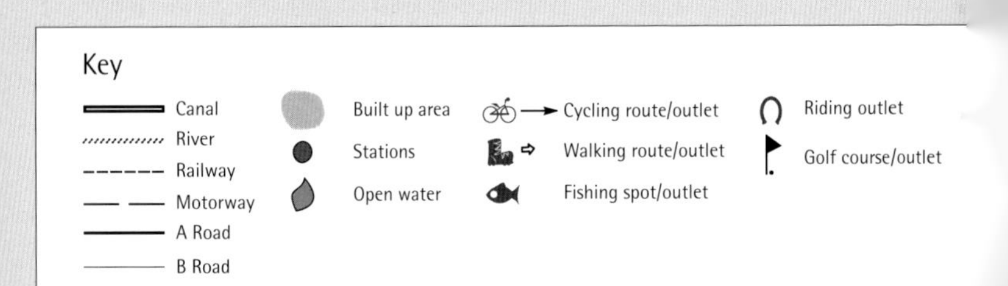
Key
Canal
River
Railway
Motorway
A Road
B Road
Built up area
Stations
Open water
Cycling route/outlet
Walking route/outlet
Fishing spot/outlet
Riding outlet
Golf course/outlet

River Ouzel and the wide-open expanses of Willen Lake. Effectively two lakes, this artificial waterway was constructed to provide not only active water-sports but also opportunities for the more gentle pastimes of bird-watching and angling.

SECTION A WALK

Willen Lake, The Canal and the River Ouzel

Description:	*A flat and easy walk taking in three types of water and a pagoda.*
Distance:	*5 miles*
Duration:	*2 hours*
Starting point:	*Grid Reference 406874, OS Explorer 192 (E)*
Nearest Refreshment:	*Either the Camphill Café near the start of the walk or The Barge Inn a little further on.*

Park in the car park marked Peace Pagoda, north of the intersection of the H5 and V10, and follow the red cycle path across a footbridge over a road, which leads you to the canal by the Camphill Café. Turn left and follow the towpath south to Bridge 83, where you pick up signs for the Ouzel Valley Walk. Pass to the right of the pub and bear right at the fork into open parkland. On reaching the Ouzel turn left, and follow the river until the end of some trees, where the path heads left up a short steep hill and emerges onto the southernmost of the two large Willen Lakes, bisected by the A509.

On reaching the road the Ouzel rejoins the route and leads you up to Willen Mill. Stick with the path round the northernmost fringe of the lakes until you reach the bottom of the path leading up to the Peace Pagoda, taking care to examine the board by the lake detailing the various wildlife that live there. The path beyond the pagoda crests a hill and brings you back to the car park.

Walking equipment outlets along this section include:

- Ellis Brigham Mountain Sports, Avebury Boulevard, Milton Keynes (01908 609122)
- Pennine Way Outdoor Adventure, Secklow Gate East, Milton Keynes (01908 669841)
- Silvertrek, Xscape Centre, Milton Keynes (01908 200388)

The Milton Keynes Peace Pagoda, inaugurated in 1980, was the first such edifice in the Western Hemisphere. It contains relics of the Lord Buddha presented by Nepal, Sri Lanka and, somewhat oddly, Berlin. One thousand cherry trees and cedars have been planted around the site in remembrance of the victims of all wars.

CYCLING

Milton Keynes planners had dreams of a population moving around their carefully laid-out metropolis on two wheels. Although this vision never quite came to pass, its legacy remains in the network of red asphalt cycle paths that criss-cross their way over and under the town's busy road, and the place remains extremely cycle-friendly. New formal routes are being added all the time, including a recent one from Woburn Sands to Kingston.

Sustrans National Cycle Routes 6 (Derby – Luton) and Route 51 (Oxford – Cambridge) pass through Milton Keynes, with the former following the canal through Great Linford, New Bradwell, Castlethorpe and onto Northampton, while the latter takes a westerly route from the centre past the Furzton Lake, through Furzton, Emerson Valley and then on a principally off-road surfaced track into Winslow. These two routes also make up part of the Millennium Circular Ride which loops around the city for approxmately 12 miles (see Learn More and Links).

One way to sample this section by bike is to start at the parking place south of Bridge 77 and head south until you pick up a redway taking you right and then shortly afterwards left (south), towards Linford Woods. Skirt these and pick up the redway, again heading right (east) towards Campbell Park.

Cross over the canal and head for Willen Lake, passing round the far side of the water and along the top, past the Peace Pagoda, until you once again pick up the canal. From here head right (north) along the towpath until you rejoin your starting point, a total of around 10 miles.

Cycle outlets along this section include:

- Roy Pink Cycles, High Street, Newport Pagnell (01908 210688)
- Action Bikes, Xscape Buildings, Milton Keynes (01908 395999)
- Chainey's Cycles, Shenley Church End, Milton Keynes (01908 504004)
- Whitecap Cycle Hire (01908 691620) – *cycle hire based at Willen Park*
- P&D Cycles, Fenny Stratford (01908 642203)

RIDING

Despite its reputation as an urban centre, Milton Keynes is in fact well endowed with formal bridleways and horse-riding paths. There is a network of around 50 miles of paths, some of which reinstate bridleways that disappeared when the city was first built.

The routes are marked with green horseshoe signs on white plaques, and have a variety of surfaces ranging from grassland to bark, and hard surface where the path may be shared by cyclists and walkers.

One of these trails, Swan's Way, goes from Goring to Salcey Forest, passing through the city from south to north. It is marked with signs depicting a swan within a horseshoe on a green directional arrow, linking up with the Three Shires Way (from Tathall to Grafham Water) near Hanslope.

There is also the Three Shires Way itself, a 37-mile-long route that spurs off Swan's Way and cuts across the top right-hand corner of the map toward Bedford via Olney.

Horse-riding establishments and outlets along this section include:

A Milton Keynes canalside sign.

- Addersey Farm Livery Yard, Newport Pagnell (01908 551122) – *close to Salcey Forest with an Olympic floodlit ménage*
- Loughton Manor Equestrian Centre and Saddlery, Loughton, Milton Keynes (01908 666434) – *tuition for all ages*
- P.J. Higgins, Newport Pagnell (01908 617199)
- Inter-Action Rectory Riding Stables (01908 230081) – *a small stables with a wide variety of horses and ponies. The stables are open to adults and children aged five and above of all abilities, and also offers riding for the disabled*

FISHING

There's no shortage of fishing opportunities along this stretch, whether in the lakes, the canal or local rivers. The Milton Keynes Angling Association (01908 691777) controls the fishing of lakes at Furzton, Caldecotte and Willen, as well as stretches of the Rivers Great Ouse, Ouzel and the canal – a total of around 50 miles of bank.

Further north, its worth contacting the Newport Pagnell Fishing Association (01908 610639), which controls local fishing in its designated area. Key venues along this stretch include:

- Great Linford Lakes, Milton Keynes (01908 237233) – *a series of lakes with carp a speciality*
- Gayhurst Lakes, north of Newport Pagnell (01908 640558) – *two estate lakes with carp, tench, bream and roach*
- Haversham Lake, Milton Keynes

(01908 607577)
- Lodge Lakes, Milton Keynes (01908 616534)
- Loughton Lakes, Milton Keynes (01908 616534)
- Newport Pagnell Gravel Pits (01908 610639) – *Emberton Country Park, includes five fishing lakes and some stretches of river*
- Vicarage Spinning Trout Fishery, Little Linford (01908 61227) *– a stocked pond with rainbows, browns and goldens, as well as pike*

Outlets selling fishing supplies along this stretch include:

- Great Linford Tackle, Milton Keynes (01908 237233)
- Milton Keynes Angling Centre (01908 374400)

OTHER

Golf courses tend to be scattered around the periphery of this stretch, with Section B supplying more promising territory. One course is easily accessible, but even this is slightly off the map to the west of Bletchley:

- Windmill Hill Golf Centre, Bletchley (01908 631113) – *flat parkland championship course of Henry Cotton design. 18 holes, 6,773 yards. Also a twenty-three-bay-covered floodlit driving range and seven grassed bays*

SECTION B

MILTON KEYNES TO MARSWORTH

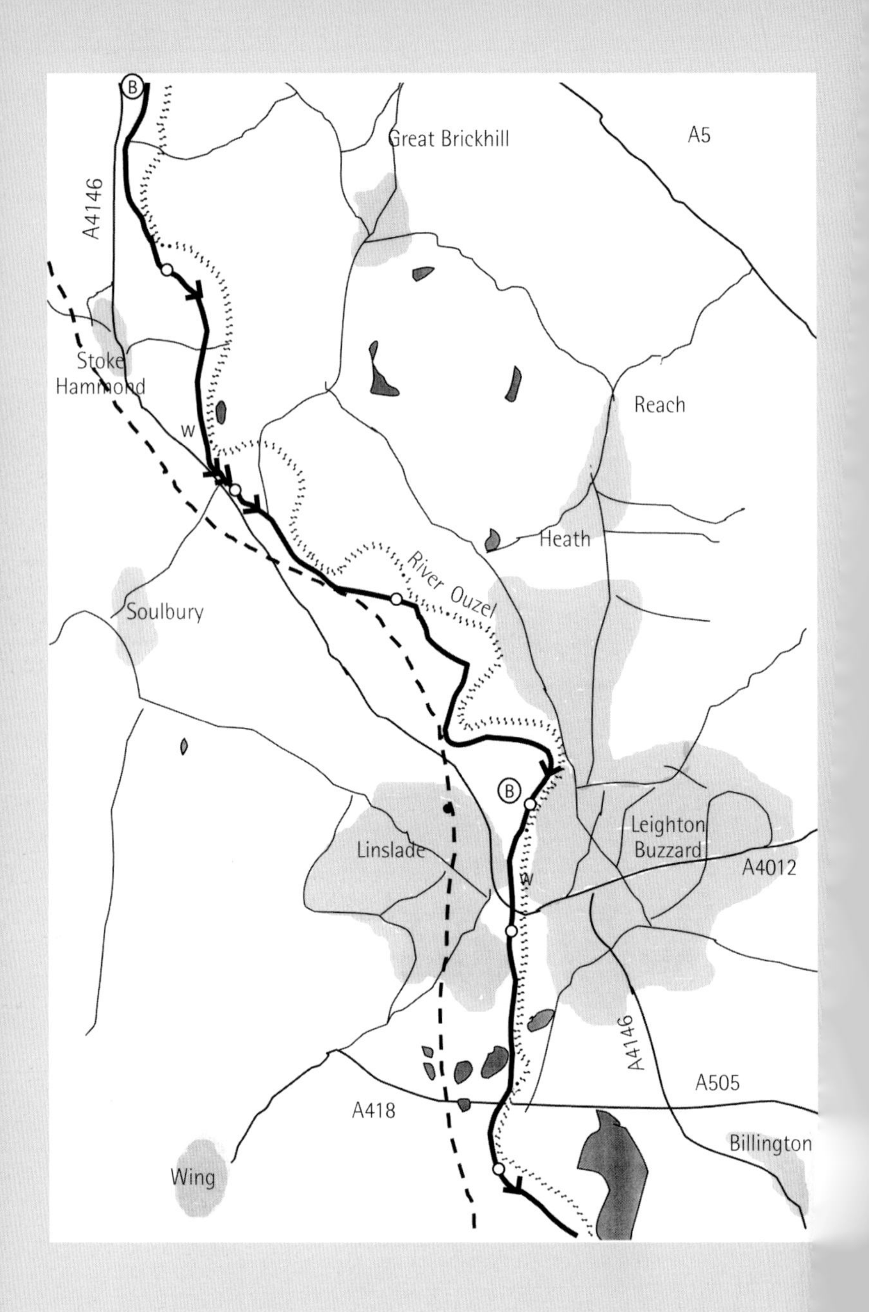
B
Great Brickhill
A5
A4146
Stoke
Hammond
W
Reach
Heath
River Ouzel
Soulbury
B
Leighton
Buzzard
A4012
Linslade
W
A4146
A505
A418
Billington
Wing

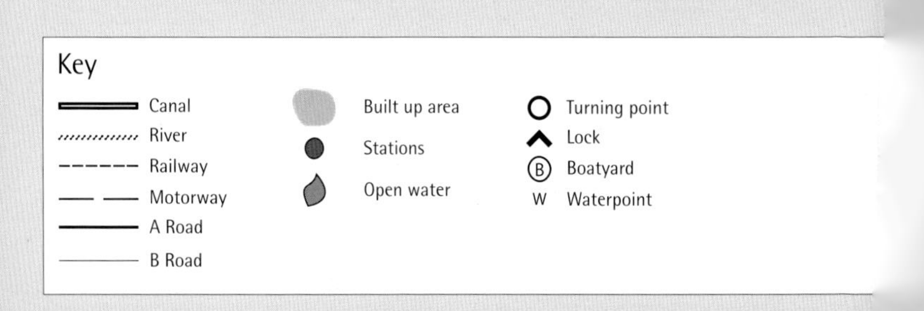
Key
Canal
River
Railway
Motorway
A Road
B Road
Built up area
Stations
Open water
Turning point
Lock
B Boatyard
W Waterpoint

SHAPERS

THE CANAL ON THIS STRETCH

KEY FACTS

LENGTH: 11.5 miles

BOATYARDS: 3
- Willowbridge Marina
- The Wyvern Shipping Company
- Pitstone Wharf

WATER POINTS: 4
- Soulbury
- Leighton Buzzard
- Slapton Lock
- Marsworth

TURNING POINTS: 8
- Stoke Hammond
- Soulbury
- Old Linslade
- The Wyvern Shipping Co.
- Linslade
- Grove Lock
- Slapton Wharf
- Marsworth

LOCKS: 16
- Stoke Hammond (6ft 11in)
- Soulbury Three Locks (3) (20ft 3in)
- Leighton Lock (6ft 8in)
- Grove Lock (7ft 6in)
- Church Lock (6ft 9in)
- Slapton Lock (7ft 1in)
- Horton Lock (6ft 9in)
- Ivinghoe Locks (2) (14ft 3in)
- Seabrook Locks (3) (20ft 4in)
- Marsworth Locks (2) (14ft 4in)

With Milton Keynes now firmly to the north, the canal adopts a steady southward direction, with Leighton Buzzard providing the single truly built-up area, the remainder being mainly scattered villages, many of which can be readily accessed from the towpath. The Ouzel valley dominates the north of the section, while Dunstable's Downs pick up the challenge to the south. This is a pleasant stretch of canal with a generally good towpath and lots of mooring.

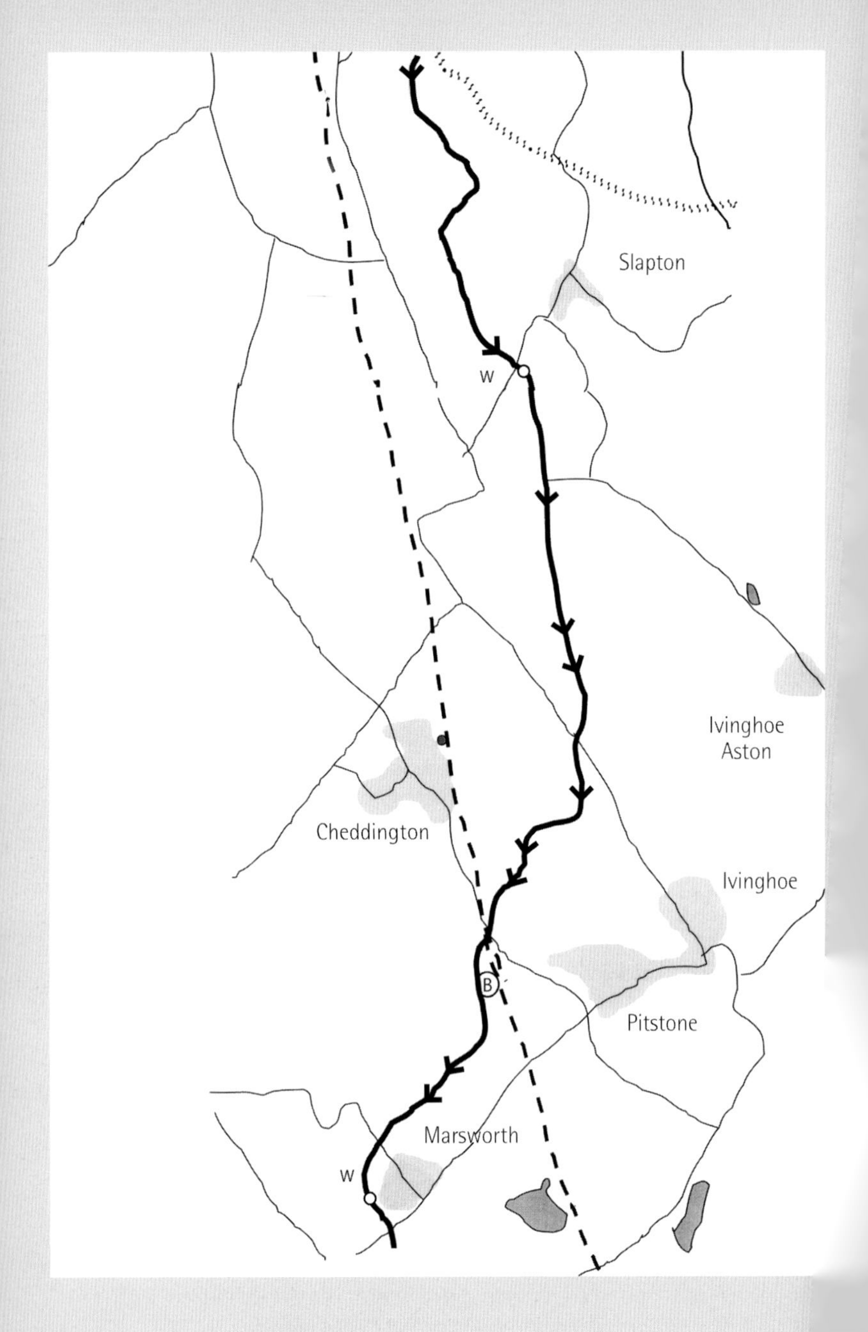
Slapton
W
Ivinghoe
Aston
Cheddington
Ivinghoe
B
Pitstone
Marsworth
W

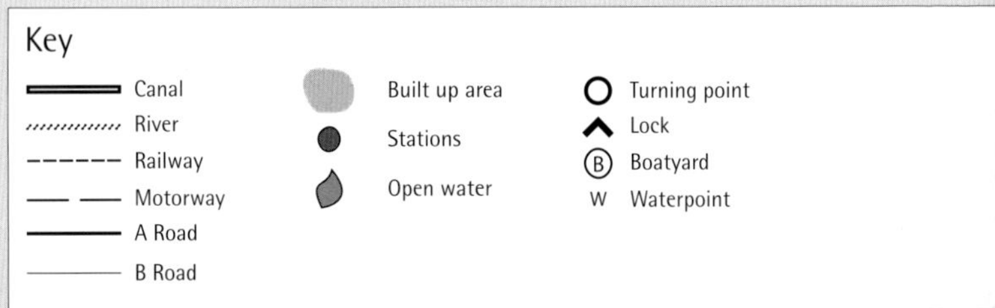
Key
Canal
River
Railway
Motorway
A Road
B Road
Built up area
Stations
Open water
Turning point
Lock
B Boatyard
W Waterpoint

It is time to begin the fall south through the heart of the Home Counties and the canal seems to shake itself ready for the task with a little wiggle just after Willowbridge Marina, and then stretches out into a modest straight section leading up to Bridge 102. Here the Stoke Hammond road practically touches the canal on the non-towpath side before the water curves off to the left and winds gently down to Bridge 104 and the pretty Stoke Hammond Lock. There is also a winding hole just before the bridge.

An old swing bridge, which looks as if it has swung its last, follows soon after, and the towpath crosses sides at Bridge 106. Further twists and turns follow and before long the River Ouzel, never that far away, comes alongside on the non-towpath side, and evidence of its presence is clear in the wide valley below, which is used as a golf course. The towpath remains in good condition, and after another curve the highly photogenic location that is Soulbury Three Locks and its adjacent pub comes into view. Understandably, this is a popular spot and boaters might want to grab a mooring if there's one going. There is a water point just before the locks, as well as refuse disposal, although, confusingly, Soulbury itself is a good mile away to the south-west along road not well suited to walkers.

The stretch between Soulbury and Bridge 111 offers plenty of mooring opportunities; the banks are mostly well reinforced, either with concrete or steel, and the sides are well dredged. Overnight mooring is less tempting as the railway line passes overhead on an embankment, and the train drivers seem to delight in sounding their horns as they go by.

The Ouzel's valley is now defining the surrounding landscape, with its edge topped with the Greensand Ridge, named after the lower greensand rock which run from here across Bedfordshire. The towpath is in good condition and this is a good stretch of canal to form a walk round. Old Linslade Manor sits in the crook of a bend just after Bridge 110, but little of it is visible from the canal.

The delightful Globe Inn north of Linslade, much beloved by photographers, heralds the start of a wide sweep into the Linslade/Leighton Buzzard area, with Leighton Lock perhaps the 'official' beginning. Houses begin to gather on the far bank shortly after this, and the Wyvern Shipping Co., a major base for hire boats, soon looms, and there is a winding hole here.

Over to the left the Ouzel reasserts its presence once again and, after a slight kink in the course, a run of long-term permit mooring leading up to Bridge 114 marks the entrance into Linslade proper. These collapse down into a short run of 2-hour only 'Shopping Stop' moorings, with a Tesco supermarket alongside. There is access to the various delights of Linslade and Leighton Buzzard from here and 2 hours may not always be enough.

Visitors' moorings follow, but boaters should not worry too much if they fail to secure a spot as there are plenty of bankside moorings on the other side of the bridge. The towpath crosses over a hump-backed bridge the other side of Bridge 114, where there is often a colourful day boat moored opposite, and it is possible to get a good view of the spire of Leighton's All Saints church through a gap to the left through the commercial buildings that follow.

There are a number of disused greenhouses on the right, but it is the industrial units that dominate the scenery on both sides on the path out of Leighton Buzzard. These don't last too long and soon the Ouzel reasserts itself, running alongside the canal for a while by the towpath, which gets much bumpier here. While attempts have been made to stiffen up the muddier parts of the path with plastic matting, these have only been partially successful.

Tall trees on the bank confirm that the town has been passed and this stretch becomes pleasantly quiet, but noise from the road means the illusion of being in the middle of nowhere can never totally take hold. For a brief while, willows dominate both banks, but after passing under the A505 the landscape on the right opens up to reveal the canal's near-constant companion, the railway, in the middle distance.

Although still possible, for the first time in a while mooring becomes much less formal in the run-up to Grove Lock, although there is the compensation of a pub, its pink exterior standing out proudly in the scenery. The views remain long and open to the right and the canal widens out considerably here, twisting and turning like a lazy river. The canal has clearly broken its banks along this stretch, with old sidings still visible to the walker and a major hazard to helmsmen.

Along this stretch and the run-up to Church Lock, the towpath becomes decidedly less even and reeds populate the bank. The path crosses over to the other side at Bridge 116 by the pretty white cottage marked as being constructed in 1916, and at last there is a chance to catch the view over to the left, which is one of rising downs in both the near and far distance. The church from which the lock gets its name is modest, and has long since been decommissioned.

The towpath gains a fresh lease of life here, although reeds continue to dominate. Meadows give way to fields as the canal cuts a gentle path through the countryside, almost doubling back on itself in the run-up to Bridge 118. Although the towpath soon reverts to turf, it remains solid and easy going. This largely bridgeless run is pleasantly quiet with good moorings in the final stretch to Slapton Lock. There are more long-term moorings here on the opposite bank, and also a water point, with Bridge 120 providing an access point to the nearby Carpenters Arms.

A high hedge obscures the view to the right but on the other side the downs reassert themselves, as do the reeds in the approach to Horton Lock and Bridge, which has an unusual double arch. The Keeper's Cottage here is two years younger that that at Church Lock, but is just as attractive. A farm now occupies the wharf that once stood here, after which there is a long straight stretch leading up to the Ivinghoe Locks and Bridge 122.

The three Seabrook Locks follow, after which there is a swing bridge, an unusual sight on this canal and one which can catch boaters out. All of a sudden, as if from nowhere, the railway appears and loops away to the left. Just after that, Bridge 126 provides convenient access to services at Pitstone to the south, and while Cheddington to the north is a little further, it does have a pub. The boatyard below the bridge is mainly dedicated to canal trips, and there is some good public parking just north of the bridge.

After a sharp turn to the right there is a grand grey timbered boathouse on the opposite bank that looks like it might be more at home at Cape Cod than on the canal. Look up and over to the left and if you're lucky you may spot white flecks circling in the air – these are gliders coming off Dunstable Downs. The two Marsworth Locks follow and there is now a steady run in to Marsworth Junction, with the towpath typically busy with boats. There is access to Marsworth itself at Bridge 130, and a water point just before the turn to the right down the Aylesbury Arm by the abandoned BW yard.

THE AYLESBURY ARM

Although not covered in this Guide, the Aylesbury Arm of the Grand Union spurs off to the west at Marsworth, starting with a staircase lock, the only one of the Grand Union. The Arm is a mere six miles long but manages to pack sixteen locks into this short distance. The route is remarkably straight and ploughs through open fields in its determination to reach its destination in as short a time as possible.

This apparent desire to avoid unnecessary detours is understandable as Aylesbury sits in a hollow, which explains the number of locks as well as one of the reasons why the canal was to have a relatively short life. Water was a scarce commodity here so close to the canal's summit, and the Arm needed to justify its constant 'borrowing' of this valuable resource.

The Arm passes close to only one village, Wilstone, shortly after Marsworth, and most boaters will be tempted to take the 4-hour journey into the town centre without stopping. Heavily reed-lined banks can make mooring difficult, but these, combined with the practice of managing the 200-year-old hedgerow through the traditional practice of hedge-laying, means that this can be something of a haven for wildlife. Noctule and Daubenton's bats live here during the summer months, while flowers such as arrowhead and meadowsweet exist alongside the more usual yellow flag and willowherb.

On reaching Aylesbury the good folk of the local canal society, who have a lease on the wharf, are very welcoming, and will usually help arrange a short-term mooring. Those less dependent on finding a spot by the water (see Basics) can wander into the county town which offers the full range of services.

PRINCIPAL TOWNS AND VILLAGES ALONG THIS STRETCH

GREAT BILLINGTON:

Perched on the A4146, Great Billington is overlooked by the church of St Michael and All Angels on top of a hill. Like many similar villages, Billington has historically earned its living off the land, but these days, although there are still working farms, many of the old agricultural buildings have been converted to domestic use.

Great Billington has only recently had its greatness restored, after a campaign by locals to restore its prefix.

CHEDDINGTON:

Sitting just off the railway, Cheddington has seen some recent but sympathetic development that has helped it to survive as a thriving community. An ancient village dating back to the Domesday Book, Cheddington was known for centuries for its orchards, with plums being a speciality, although none remain today. West End Hill, south-west of the village, is designated as a local landscape area. The village also has its own railway station with a service into London Euston.

It was at Cheddington that the Great Train Robbery took place during the early hours of 8 August 1963.

GREAT BRICKHILL:

Sitting on top of a hill, Great Brickhill has the advantage of some stunning views, most notably from a Georgian-style house in the centre, but the downside of this is that the village is scattered and, although picturesque, with a range of building styles in evidence, it has little to hold the casual visitor.

HEATH AND REACH:

The few remaining older properties around Heath Green, including the Duke's Head pub, make it just about possible to imagine what this village once looked like. Successive waves of building have led to the village losing its sense of focus, although it pretty much retains a separate identity.

IVINGHOE:

Perhaps best known for its Beacon, the hill where this sits just outside the village is the site of an Iron Age hill fort. The village has several good examples of Tudor architecture, especially around the village green, known locally as the Lawn.

> Sir Walter Scott named his novel *Ivinghoe* after the Bucks village of the same name.

IVINGHOE ASTON;

A small hamlet consisting of four farms and a variety of houses, Ivinghoe Aston has a pub owned by the local community. Set out along the road, the village has grown slowly over time and has one or two buildings of note, including the Old School House at the southern end.

LEIGHTON BUZZARD:

The centre of Leighton Buzzard is tucked away just off the A4146 and has much to offer. There is plenty of history here as well as a full range of shops, from national chain stores to local specialists.

LINSLADE:

Less than 100 yards separates Linslade from Leighton Buzzard, but it seems to sit firmly in the shadow of its larger neighbour. The town, if it can be called such as the two formally exist as one, seems to lack a centre if you discount the large Tesco by the canal, and perhaps the canal is its main defining feature. Otherwise there is a collection of un-enticing shops and a lot of housing, although Linslade does have the honour of having the railway station, and because of this Linslade is a popular commuter town.

MARSWORTH:

Best known for its reservoirs which feed the summit of the canal, Marsworth is centred around its junction with the canal and the two pubs there. Housing stretches out to the north-east of the B489 in the crook of the intersection of the Grand Union and its Aylesbury Arm.

PITSTONE:

Sitting at the foot of the Chiltern Hills, Pitstone was – until recently – dominated by its cement works, which was closed down and converted for residential and business use in the 1990s.

> Edward I spent five weeks over Christmas on the Pitstone estate in 1290, even holding Parliament here, the costs of his court being met by the local inhabitants, who no doubt spent most of his stay willing him to move on.

SLAPTON:

An area of rapid growth in recent years, with more modern building almost swamping the few remaining examples of older cottages. The village's pub is probably now its most distinguished building. Evidence of this growth can be seen in the number of footpaths that cut through the housing.

SOULBURY:

An eclectic mixture of cottages, both brick and thatched, sits alongside larger and more modern housing, with wide grass verges to the north of the village distancing the houses from the road. The village's name is Anglo-Saxon in origin, and means 'stronghold in a gully', which is perhaps appropriate.

The Disneys, distant relations of the famous Walt of that ilk, were once a significant family within Stoke Hammond.

Wing was once notorious as the proposed site of a new London airport. Campaigners, using the slogan 'Wings Off Wing Airport', succeeded in persuading the planners to expand Heathrow instead.

STOKE HAMMOND:

The local manor of Stoke Hammond was for many years owned by the Duke of Norfolk, but these days there is less to distinguish this pleasant but uninspiring village. The housing is mostly modern and uninspiring, and perhaps the most significant feature is the fact that there is a small stream running through the heart of the village

WING:

Wing owes its prominence to being on an ancient track linking the two centres of learning at Oxford and Cambridge. These days it is a moderately large village that seems to have grown like Topsy from a discrete centre. The A418 (Leighton Road) provides a boundary to one side, allowing the protection of some playing fields, but this road becomes busy and the village's side roads provide a number of 'rat runs' for impatient motorists.

HISTORY

This section sees the canal wandering along the border between Buckinghamshire and Bedfordshire and, in the process, drifting down to the outskirts of Hertfordshire. Being peripheral in county terms has had an impact upon the history of the towns and villages featured here. Some, such as Linslade, have even changed counties from time to time. Existing at arm's length from centres of power and patronage has, for many villages, allowed them to develop independently of outside influences, and it was not until the canal burst into their lives, followed closely by the railway, that these places were forced to change.

This is not true of all the places featured along this section, of course. Leighton Buzzard and its companion, Linslade, have been, and continue to be, vibrant market towns and, at times, even places of pilgrimage. The Romans' Watling Street passed to the north here, and the towns sat conveniently halfway between the two ancient centres of learning at Oxford and Cambridge.

As such, the focus here was as much north-east to south-west as it was south-east towards the capital. Ivinghoe stands at the junction of the Upper and Lower Icknield Way, a thoroughfare that gained its name from the tribe of the Iceni, and it is likely that Queen Boudicca of that tribe used this route to rally her troops.

Almost without exception, the towns and villages in this section existed at the time of the Norman invasion, with most having a record of some kind in the Domesday Book. There is also evidence of settlement before then, but this is sporadic, suggesting that this was an area of passage rather than of major settlement. Ivinghoe Beacon hosted an Iron Age hill fort, but given the prominence of that geographical feature, it would have been surprising if it had not have been utilised.

However, it is known that the Saxons chose to settle among these lands, attracted no doubt by the ready availability of woodland, water and the fertile soil. In some places, such as Great Brickhill and Billington, the attraction was similar to that at Ivinghoe, that is the strategic position offered by geography, with both of these settlements sitting on top of hills.

Furthermore, many of these settlements would have been comparatively prosperous. Wing, for example, still has one of the oldest Saxon churches in the country. This, the church of All Saints, was built by Aelfgifu, wife of the Saxon King Eadwig, in the tenth century, and has an unusually wide chancel arch. Equally, the names of many of the villages along here have Saxon roots. Slapton's name is thought to mean 'farm by a slippery place', while Linslade's name refers to a 'river crossing by a stream'.

Sir John Betjeman called Wing's All Saints church, 'the most important Saxon church in the country'.

Nearby Leighton had already grown to be a significant town by the time the Normans invaded, with the Domesday Book identifying it as belonging to the Crown and the largest Royal Manor in the county. In ecclesiastical terms the See, which extended as far as Billington and included the village of Reach, was transferred in 1075 to the Bishop of Lincoln, St Hugh.

In 1160, Leighton was classified as a 'peculiar parish' – an area within an archdeaconry, but outside the jurisdiction of either the archdeacon or the bishop. This status remained until the mid-nineteenth century.

Leighton remained in Royal hands, but the town gained little benefit from this association. Henry I gave away its annual rent of £56 to a Benedictine house in Normandy, the Abbey of Fontévrault, and in 1164 Henry II gave the manor itself to the Abbey, which until that point had not even had a cell in England – although it did so shortly afterwards, tellingly not in Bedfordshire.

A survey of the manor taken by Henry III suggested that the whole demesne, which included the manors of Clipstone and Reach, could support a total of 8 cart horses, 20 farm horses, 60 oxen, 80 cows, 200 lesser animals, 200 pigs and 4,000 sheep. Significant, but not enough to make the town stand out.

Having tutelage to a French Abbey proved to be difficult during the period of uneasy relations that followed, and ownership of the manor bounced between the Crown (the Abbess of Fontévrault gave it to Edward I's daughter for the term of her life) and back, although the house at nearby Grovebury was used as a Royal residence by Edward I himself during the thirteenth century.

Ownership disputes then became commonplace during the centuries that followed, with Leighton in particular often being used as a bargaining chip in deals ranging from promises of safe passage to France to wider land swaps. In between all this to-ing and fro-ing, the people who lived in these towns had to survive, and in 1251 Linslade was granted a royal charter to hold a weekly market.

The rationale behind this move was suspect, however, resting on the fact that Linslade was a place of pilgrimage due to the presence of a Holy Spring, which may have been the stream in its Saxon name. But it enjoyed this privilege for less than fifty years. The stream itself was unconsecrated, and therefore declared unholy of the Bishop of Lincoln in 1299. The poor clergyman who had instituted this early form of tourism was duly tried and executed as a heretic. The Royal Charter was removed soon afterwards.

Catesby and the other conspirators in the Gunpowder Plot of 1605 were apprehended in Little Brickhill, although their crime was too heinous to be heard in a mere assize

Elsewhere, life proceeded with less incident, with livings earned either from the land or occasionally through specialist activity. Little Brickhill, for example, had something of a reputation for making encaustic tiles in medieval times, with flues and ovens having been discovered in the grounds of the present Grange. This same village was also host to the local Assize Court for two centuries, until the reign of Charles I.

If the establishment of Saxon churches can be taken as a sign of settlement and relative prosperity before the Conquest, a fresh wave of building on and around these might indicate fresh confidence around the fifteenth and sixteenth centuries. Ivinghoe's church gained a fresh roof around this time, and Little Brickhill's a tower. During Elizabeth's reign the manors of Leighton were leased out to London-based merchants and it is around this time that church registers started to be kept. The local communities continued to till the soil, with wheat being a popular crop. Pitstone Mill, which today survives as the oldest extant post-mill in the country, dates back to 1624, and in the eighteenth and nineteenth centuries straw-plaiting was a significant local industry.

> The manor in Slapton was, for some time, owned by the Earl of Bridgewater. His family later became Dukes, the most famous of all being the father of the inland navigations.

Although the Civil War touched the area, it was transport in its various guises that finally opened the villages in this section to external influences. Coaches came first, with Little Brickhill in particular enjoying an advantage from sitting on Watling Street, something it exploited by having no less than fourteen inns. The canal followed, and was complemented and then replaced by the railway, which largely followed the same route.

Sand from this area is well regarded for its purity and range of colours – from white through to dark brown. Uses varied from foundry moulds to golf bunkers, which may help to explain the preponderance of courses in the surrounding area.

Marsworth benefited particularly from the canal, with coal, sand and wheat passing through it, while the otherwise sleepy village of Cheddington changed considerably when it gained its own station. It was the only village on the main Euston line, and one theory why it was granted this honour rests on the fact that it was convenient for carrying Lord Rosebery's racing horses when there was a meet on.

These days the canal and railway remain, with the former supplying character and a focus for the villages it passes through or near, while the latter carries many of the people who live nearby into London for work. Nowhere is this more true than in Leighton Buzzard and Linslade, which these days form one town, and largely a commuter one at that.

THE NATURAL LANDSCAPE

The Ouzel Valley is the defining geographical feature along this stretch. This natural cutting through the chalk is exploited by both the canal and the railway, with villages scattered about on the slopes on either side. At times, these slopes become hills and some of these villages, such as Great Brickhill and Great Billington, enjoy majestic views over the surrounding countryside. Hills also feature towards the south of the section, most notably around Ivinghoe, and to a lesser extent Marsworth, with the canal having to accommodate the rise up to the latter with a flight of locks.

> The River Ouzel comes from chalk springs that rise up from the north-facing scarp slopes of the Chiltern Hills, between Dunstable and Ivinghoe, and joins the River Great Ouse at Newport Pagnell.

Oolites tend to dominate the local geology, with greensands creeping in north of Leighton Buzzard, and chalk a prominent feature which helps to shape much

Signs mark out the Greensand Ridge Walk.

of the local topography towards the south of the section. In fact, it is hard to escape the chalk the further south you go, with the Whipsnade Lion a constant reminder of the underlying soil. Stockgrove Country Park to the north, and the Ashridge Estate to the south both provide plenty of woodland, while the Marsworth reservoirs, coupled with a scattering of disused gravel pits, provide water interest.

ACCESS AND TRANSPORT

ROADS

While the A5 clips the top right-hand corner of this section, it does not really make its presence felt. The main trunk roads linking the different towns and villages are the A4146, which runs roughly north–south, cutting through the top of Linslade and through Leighton Buzzard, and the A418, which spurs off this road south of Leighton Buzzard to connect with Wing, but becomes the busy A505 east of this junction.

Connections to the south of the section are mainly by B roads, but these tend to be in good condition, making for easy access. Indeed, the roads south of Leighton Buzzard almost deliver pleasant countryside driving conditions, of the sort more closely associated with leisurely Sunday afternoon runs, although it's as well not to get too carried away!

RAIL

Although the railway runs pretty much parallel with the canal for much of this section, there are only two stations for those wishing to access the surrounding countryside. These are at Linslade/Leighton Buzzard and Cheddington. The former is by far the larger of the two, although Cheddington enjoys an hourly service into London Euston.

The main train operator serving the area is: Silverlink (01923 207298) Otherwise, National Train Enquiries can be reached on 08457 484950.
In addition, Leighton Buzzard has an independent rail system, the Leighton Buzzard Railway (01525 373888) – (see Seeing and Doing).

BUSES

The following list sets out the main buses servicing this stretch, although it is advisable to check before using them as some buses only run on certain days and others may have been withdrawn since publication of this Guide:

- 10, 11 – *Leighton Buzzard to Milton Keynes (MK Metro)*
- 31 – *Leighton Buzzard to Luton (Red Rose)*
- 52 – *Leighton Buzzard to Milton Keynes (InMotion)*
- 52 – *Milton Keynes, Stoke Hammond, Leighton Buzzard, Soulbury, Stewkley (Easy Bus)*
- 61 – *Aylesbury to Luton via Ivinghoe (Arriva)*
- 63, 64 – *Aylesbury to Ivinghoe via Cheddington (Arriva)*
- 65 – *Aylesbury, Wing, Leighton Buzzard (Arriva)*
- 139 – *Leighton Buzzard to Woburn Sands (Litchfield Cars)*
- 152 – *Leighton Buzzard to Bletchley via Stoke Hammond and Great Brickhill (Red Kite)*
- 159 – *Leighton Buzzard to Stoke Hammond (Arriva)*
- 160/165 – *Bedford to Leighton Buzzard (United Counties)*
- 161 – *Aylesbury to Whipsnade via Marsworth, Pitstone and Ivinghoe (Easy Bus)*
- 162 – *Ivinghoe, Pitstone, Marsworth, Cheddington, Linslade, Leighton Buzzard (Easy bus)*
- 170 – *Tring, Ivinghoe, Pitstone, Marsworth (Arriva)*
- 171 Leighton Buzzard Circular *(Easy Bus)*
- 172 – *Dunstable, Slapton, Cheddington (Red Kite)*
- 173 - Ivinghoe, Slapton, Cheddington, Leighton Buzzard *(Easy Bus)*
- 175 – *Hemel Hempstead to Leighton Buzzard (Arriva)*
- 176 – *Ivinghoe, Pitstone, Marsworth, Cheddington, Slapton, Milton Keynes (Easy Bus)*
- 327 – *Hemel Hempstead Circular taking in Marsworth, Pitstone and Ivinghoe (Red Rose)*
- X15 –*Aylesbury to Milton Keynes via Wing, Leighton Buzzard and Heath and Reach (Arriva)*

Contact details for bus operators in this area are listed below, although Bedfordshire operates a single number service on 01234 228337, while Traveline (www.traveline.org.uk) on 0870 6082608 can give details of specific services between 7 a.m. and 10 p.m. covering Hertfordshire and Buckinghamshire:

- Arriva The Shires, Luton (01923 682262)
- Easy Bus, Aylesbury (0870 7288188)
- InMotion Travel, Dunstable (08707 444746)
- Litchfield Car Services, Woburn (01908 583766)
- Red Kite, Leighton Buzzard (01525 211441)
- Red Rose Travel, Aylesbury (01296 399500)

TAXIS

The following list gives a selection of the taxi operators in this section:

- AAA Taxis, Leighton Buzzard (01525 851000)
- D&R Taxis, Leighton Buzzard (01525 375588/378570)
- Dialacar Taxis, Leighton Buzzard (01525 850605)
- Prestige Taxis, Leighton Buzzard (01525 852113)
- Shireways Taxis, Leighton Buzzard (01525 373621)
- Steve's Taxis, Leighton Buzzard (01525 377777)
- Toddington Taxis, Leighton Buzzard (01525 851499)
- Cheddington Cars, Cheddington (01296 661666)
- Acme Cars, Wing (01525 385000)

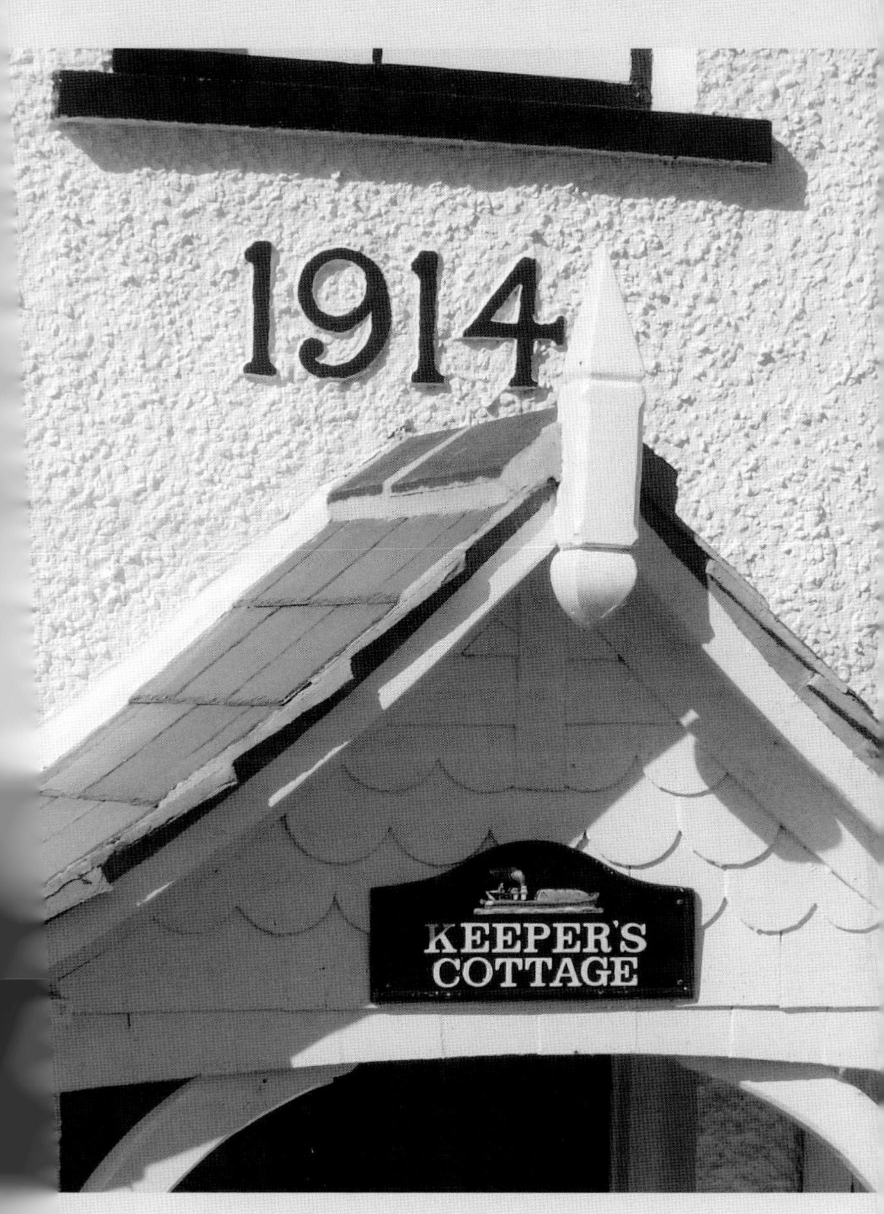

One of the many lock-side cottages along this section.

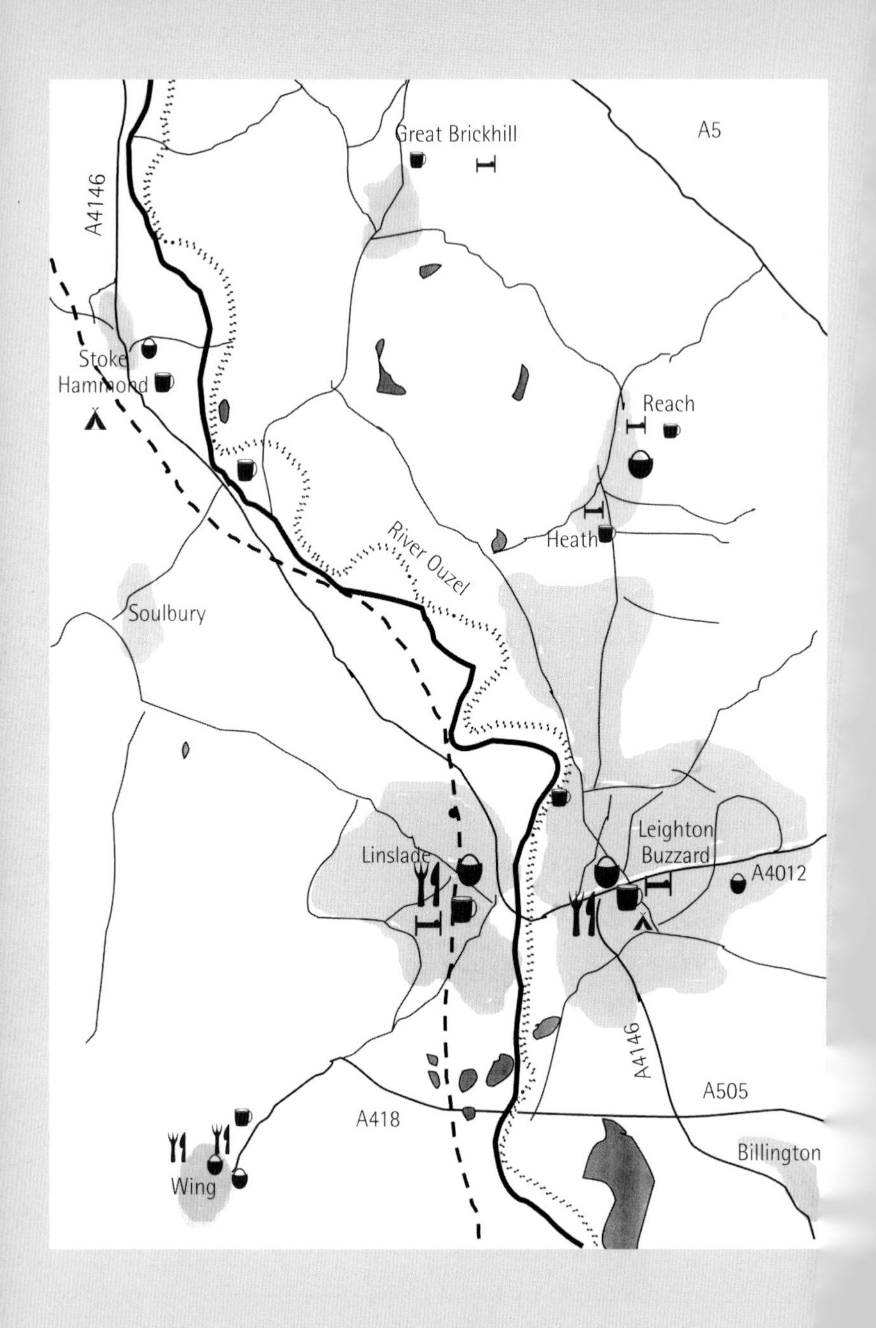
Great Brickhill
A5
A4146
Stoke
Hammond
Reach
Heath
River Ouzel
Soulbury
Leighton
Buzzard
Linslade
A4012
A4146
A505
A418
Billington
Wing

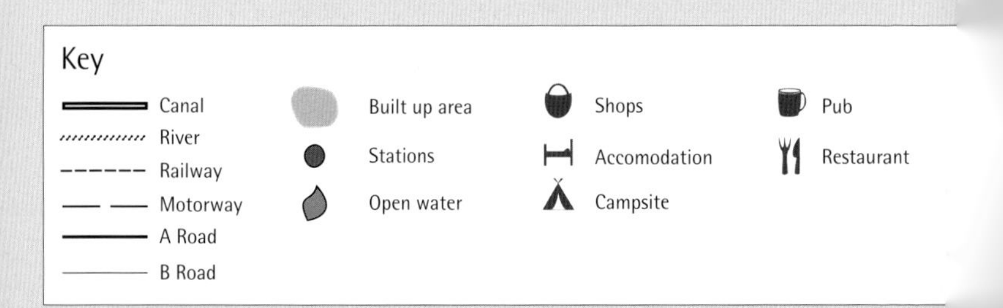
Key
Canal
River
Railway
Motorway
A Road
B Road
Built up area
Stations
Open water
Shops
Accomodation
Campsite
Pub
Restaurant

BASICS

INTRODUCTION

The combined towns of Linslade and Leighton Buzzard sit in the middle of this section and act as a focal point for most basic services. The outlying villages have minimal shopping, although they provide the occasional good alternative for those looking for somewhere to eat, drink or even sleep.

SHOPPING

The clear centre for shopping along this stretch is Leighton Buzzard, with the surrounding villages largely confined to local stores of varying levels of sophistication, with that at Stoke Hammond an example of one at the more comprehensive end of the scale.

There is a small parade of shops as you pass through Heath and Reach, but again, they cater very much to local needs, although there is a small Co-Op. Between them, Linslade and Leighton Buzzard have a range of supermarkets, from Co-Op and Iceland through to Waitrose, with a large Tesco neatly crammed in the space between the two towns.

The shops along the main road do not inspire a lot of confidence, with most looking like they could do with revamping. Leighton Buzzard claims to be the fastest growing town in Bedfordshire, and current evidence seems to suggest that the retail sector has struggled to keep pace with this growth. The Town Council seems to acknowledge this and, in late 2004, plans were announced to develop a section to the north of the town, with the local paper claiming the proposed centre would rival that of central Milton Keynes – a truly ambitious claim!

Although there is an impressively wide main street in the old part of town, the shops that line its side tend to be at the economy end of the scale. All the basics are here – the banks and building societies, newsagents, pharmacies and charity shops, as well as a post office off Church Square, but you have to look hard to find anything special. There is also the Waterbourne Walk arcade, built in the 1970s and refurbished twenty years later.

It is worth delving into some of the alleyways off the High Street, where you will find a good specialist bookshop and a delicatessen. The road linking the northern end of the old town with the main road is given over mainly to fast-food outlets, and coffee shops also seem to have undue prominence in this town. It is pretty much the same story along the main Leighton Road itself.

Perhaps some of the most interesting food-buying opportunities in this area are off the High Street. Buffalo House at Bury Farm in Slapton (01525 220256), for example, has a small visitors' centre displaying and selling goods from their buffalo herd, including, of course, mozzarella cheese.

Equally, Pecks Open Farm Shop (01525 210281), just east of Leighton Buzzard, sells farm-fresh milk and soft fruit in the summer. Leighton Buzzard also has a Farmers' Market every third Saturday and a WI Market every Tuesday in the

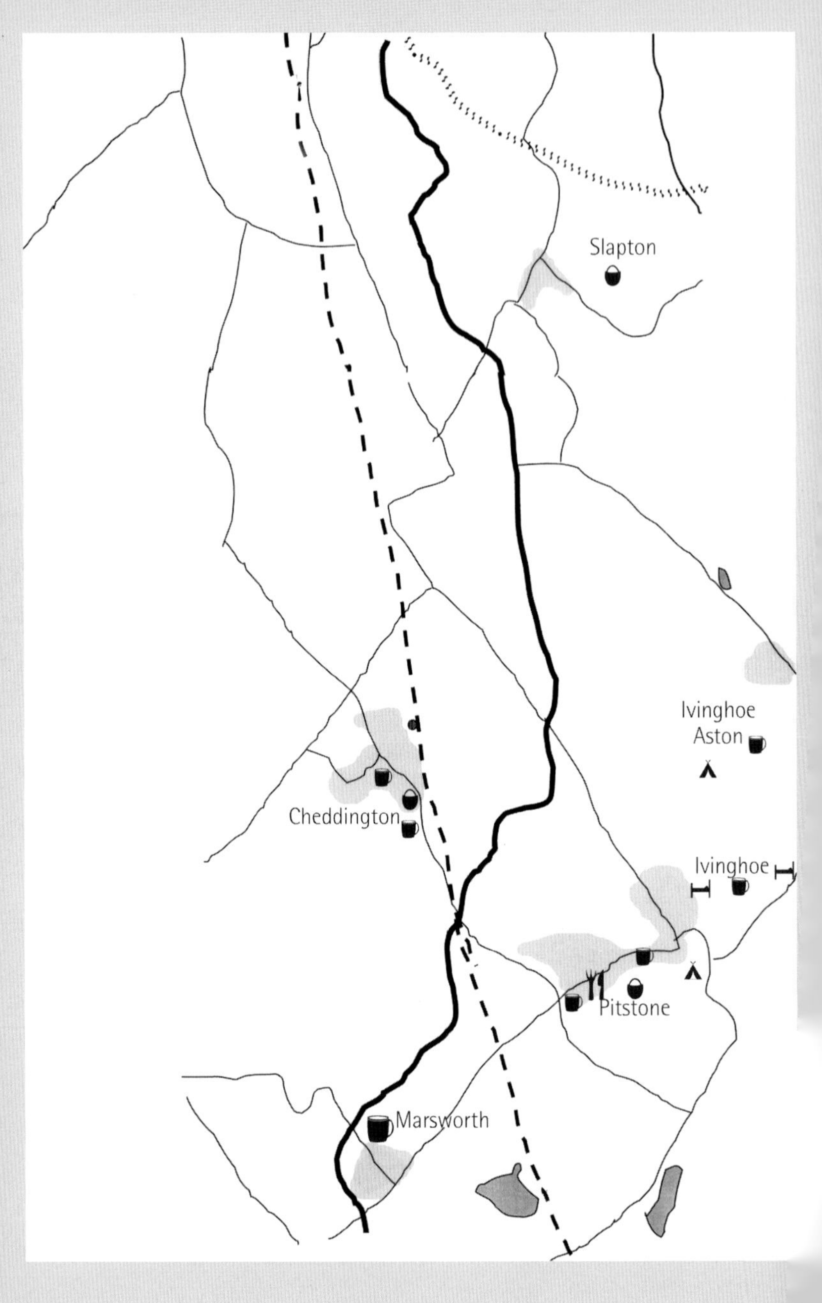
Slapton
Ivinghoe
Aston
Cheddington
Ivinghoe
Pitstone
Marsworth

Key
Canal
River
Railway
Motorway
A Road
B Road
Built up area
Stations
Open water
Shops
Accomodation
Campsite
Pub
Restaurant

Market Square. Another interesting non-conventional outlet is Mrs Huddleston's (01582 381621), a maker of luxury preserves, again outside Leighton Buzzard.

Wing has a Londis, while Cheddington has a fine example of a small village store with a sub-post office, as does Pitstone.

EATING AND DRINKING

PUBS

The following list covers many of the pubs in this section but cannot claim to be totally comprehensive. Many of those featured offer food, although serving times and menus will naturally vary:

The landlord of the Dolphin in Stoke Hammond once accused local schoolboys of stealing hens from villagers' backyards. He got his comeuppance when he was caught in the act himself, and went on to hang himself in shame.

- Old Red Lion, Great Brickhill (01525 261715)
- The Dolphin, Stoke Hammond (01525 270263)
- The Axe and Compass, Heath and Reach (01525 237394) – *friendly family pub*
- The Cock, Heath and Reach (01525 277390) – *pub and hotel*
- The Boot, Soulbury (01525 270433) – *garden to rear, recently refurbished*
- The Three Locks, Soulbury (01525 270592)
- The Globe Inn, Linslade (01525 850551) – *extremely welcoming canalside pub with large car park and an extensive menu*
- The Bedford Arms, Leighton Road, Linslade (01525 312103)
- The Black Horse, North Street, Leighton Buzzard (01525 381129)
- The Crown, North St, Leighton Buzzard (01525 217770)
- The Golden Bell, Church Street, Leighton Buzzard (01525 373330) – *tucked away off the main street*
- The Red Lion, North Street, Leighton Buzzard (01525 374350) – *small but friendly*
- The Roebuck, Hockliffe Street, Leighton Buzzard (01525 373206) – *unpretentious local*
- The Wheatsheaf, North Street, Leighton Buzzard (015252 374611) – *live bands on Friday and Saturday, large screen TV*
- The Grove Lock, Grove south of Leighton Buzzard (01525380199) – *once a lock-keeper's cottage but much extended; also a restaurant with extensive menu; very popular in the summer.*
- The Cock Inn, Wing (01296 688214)
- The Sportsman's Arms, Wing (01296 688254)
- Carpenters Arms, Slapton (01525 220-563) - *800 yards north of Bridge 120*
- The Old Swan, Cheddington (01296 668226)
- The Three Horseshoes, Cheddington (01296 688367)
- The Duke of Wellington – *just off the canal between Pitstone and Cheddington (01296 661402)*
- The Bell, Pitstone (01296 668078)
- Duke of Wellington, Pitstone (01296 661402)
- The Village Swan, Ivinghoe Aston (01525 220544) – *community-owned pub*
- The Kings Head, Ivinghoe (01296 668388) – *pub and restaurant*
- Anglers Retreat, Marsworth (01442 822250)
- Red Lion, Marsworth (01296 668366)

SECTION B

- The White Lion, Marsworth (01442 822325) – *waterside location, look out for the giant carp in the canal*

Cafés and fast-food outlets along the route and in surrounding areas include the following:

- Golden Star, Wing Road, Linslade (01525 371441) - *Chinese restaurant*
- The Barista Sisters, Lake Street, Leighton Buzzard (01525 383585) – *café*
- Barrington's Café, Leighton Buzzard (01525 851691)
- Muffins, Leighton Buzzard (01525 375080)
- Ocean Fish Bar, Leighton Buzzard (01525 374072)
- On A Roll, Hockliffe Street, Leighton Buzzard (01525 851177)
- Renoirs, Lake Street, Leighton Buzzard (01525 384777)
- Reubens Gourmet Sandwiches, Leighton Buzzard (01525 850344)
- Wing On, Wing (01525 371183) – *Chinese takeaway*

Indian and Italian outlets tend to dominate along this stretch. The following offer a selection of places to try:

- Linslade Balti House, Wing Road, Linslade (01525 374455)
- Raj Indian Restaurant, Linslade (01525 379319)
- Indian Ocean, Wing Road, Linslade (01525 383251) – *Indian restaurant*
- Akash, North Street, Leighton Buzzard (01525 372316) – *Indian restaurant*
- The Dragon Inn, Peking and Cantonese, North Street, Leighton Buzzard (01525 371045)
- Lots of Spice, Leighton Buzzard (01525 851212) – *Indian restaurant*
- Mama Rosa's, North Street, Leighton Buzzard (01525 375149) – *Italian restaurant*
- Mandarin House, Chinese Restaurant, North Street, Leighton Buzzard (01525 852228)
- Shan Shui, Chinese Restaurant, Leighton Buzzard (01525 850880)
- The Dove, Wing (01296 688258) – *Indian restaurant*
- The Queen's Head, Wing (01296 688268)
- May Fu, Marsworth Road, Pitstone (01296 661969) – *Chinese restaurant*

SLEEPING

This area is not terribly well endowed with places you can lay your head. The Swan in Leighton Buzzard dominates the hotel options, while there is a smattering of B&Bs in the surrounding areas.

HOTELS

- The Cock Hotel, Heath and Reach (01525 237390)
- The Swan Hotel, High Street, Leighton Buzzard (01525 372148) – *thirty-eight en suite rooms in an elegant Georgian building in the town centre.*

The White Lion at Marsworth.

The view looking out from Great Brickhill.

BED AND BREAKFASTS/GUEST HOUSES

- Partridge House, Three Locks Golf Club, Great Brickhill (01525 270470) – *two twin rooms and one double room*
- The Axe and Compass, Heath and Reach (01525 237394)
- The Bedford Arms, Leighton Road, Linslade (01525 312103)
- The Hunt Hotel, Church Road, Linslade (01525 374692)
- The Black Horse, Leighton Buzzard (01525 381129)
- Greenacres Farmhouse B&B, Leighton Buzzard (01525 277214) – *modern farmhouse near to the A505 with good views*
- Heath Park House, Heath Road, Leighton Buzzard (01525 381640) – *large Victorian house*
- River House, Leighton Buzzard (01525 376084) – *private house with outdoor swimming pool; close to the canal; two double rooms, one single*
- Bull Lake B&B, Ivinghoe (01296 668834) – *one double room, one single room, one twin room*
- The Old Forge, Ivinghoe (01296 668122) – *four double rooms, two twins rooms*

Those considering visiting the Aylesbury Arm may wish to consider the following:

- Little Venice B&B, Aylesbury (01296 339242) – *one family room, one double room in family home*
- Hartwell House B&B, Aylesbury (01296 747444)
- Holiday Inn Garden Court, Aylesbury (01296 398839) – *thirty-nine rooms and an indoor pool*

CAMPING

There is a Youth Hostel at Ivinghoe (0870 770 5884), housed in a magnificent Georgian mansion that was once the home of a local brewer.

Camping is also possible at the Old Dairy Farm, Orchard Mill Lane, Stoke Hammond (01908 274206). As the name suggests, this is a farm site set in 26 acres of open grassland. You can also camp at the Silver Birch Café on the Upper Ickneild Way in Pitstone (01296 668348).

The nearest camping supplies outlet in this section is:

- Millets, Waterbourne Walk, Leighton Buzzard (01525 371623)

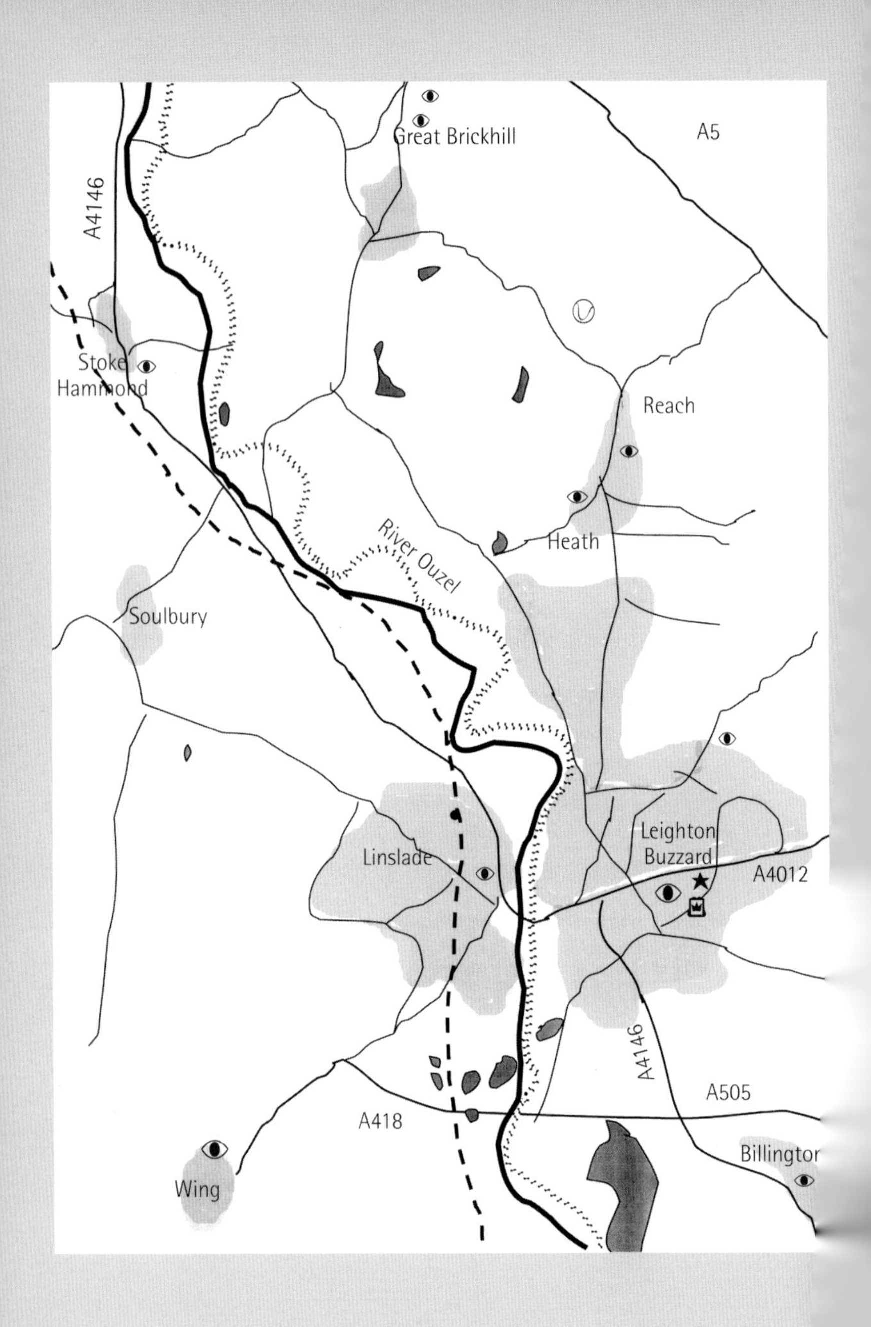
Great Brickhill
A5
A4146
Stoke Hammond
Reach
Heath
River Ouzel
Soulbury
Leighton Buzzard
Linslade
A4012
A4146
A505
A418
Billington
Wing

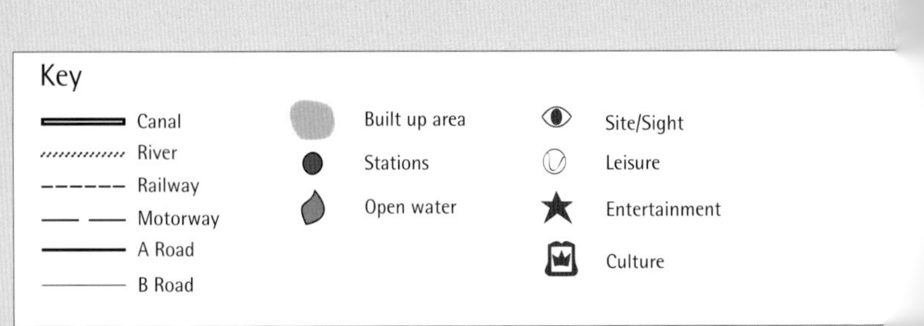
Key
Canal
River
Railway
Motorway
A Road
B Road
Built up area
Stations
Open water
Site/Sight
Leisure
Entertainment
Culture

SEEING AND DOING

INTRODUCTION

This is a deceptive area for seeing and doing, with most of the smaller villages rewarding a visit, as nearly all enjoy a long history with legacies in various shapes. These vary from memories of a tyrannical Victorian local squire in Billington to Second World War bombers in Marsworth. In between, Linslade and Leighton Buzzard, which acts as a sort of cultural capital for the area, makes up for its lack of excitement in the shopping stakes by having a detailed town trail.

SIGHTS

If you are in the area, Great Brickhill can reward a visit, both for the stunning views enjoyed from its eyrie-like position, and for the diversity of building styles on view. The Cromwell Cottages to the south of the village offer a fine combination of brick-filled half-timbered construction with thatch. Opposite the church of St Mary the Virgin there is an unusual metal-studded wooden door in the house know as 'The Castle'.

The church itself is a Grade II listed building, with parts dating back to the thirteenth century, although it was heavily restored in the mid-nineteenth century. It is possible to walk down to the Ouzel from Great Brickhill (see Sampling), but it's a long way back! The village is also notable for the high brick wall that surrounds the 70-acre park of Great Brickhill Manor, which was demolished in 1937. The Duncombe family, who were lords of the manor, now live in the Old Rectory near the church.

> The Old Rectory in Great Brickill is shielded from the site of the old manor by a folly wall, built by an ancestor who disliked the vicar so much that he did not want to see him or his home.

The most prominent feature in Stoke Hammond is probably St Luke's church, although the manor was once owned by the Duke of Norfolk. Soulbury has two manor houses, Chelmscote Manor and Liscombe Park. The latter dates to the sixteenth century, and is set back behind gates on the Soulbury to Leighton Buzzard road. It is built in soft red brick in the Elizabethan style. Its oak-panelled rooms are not open to the public (unless you wish to get married there) as it remains a family home. However, the stable block has been converted to a leisure and health complex, and there is also a polo field.

Look out for the village pump in Heath and Reach, which was donated in 1830. Nearby there are the private grounds of Rushmere Park, which include 200 acres of pine forest and a paintball centre (see below). The local church, St Leonards, was originally a private chapel belonging to Heath Manor House, and was given to the people of the village in 1705.

Leighton Buzzard Railway (01525 373888), to the north of the town, is a narrow-gauge railway built nearly a century ago to carry sand. The track is only 2ft-wide, and copes well with the various sharp curves and steep gradients

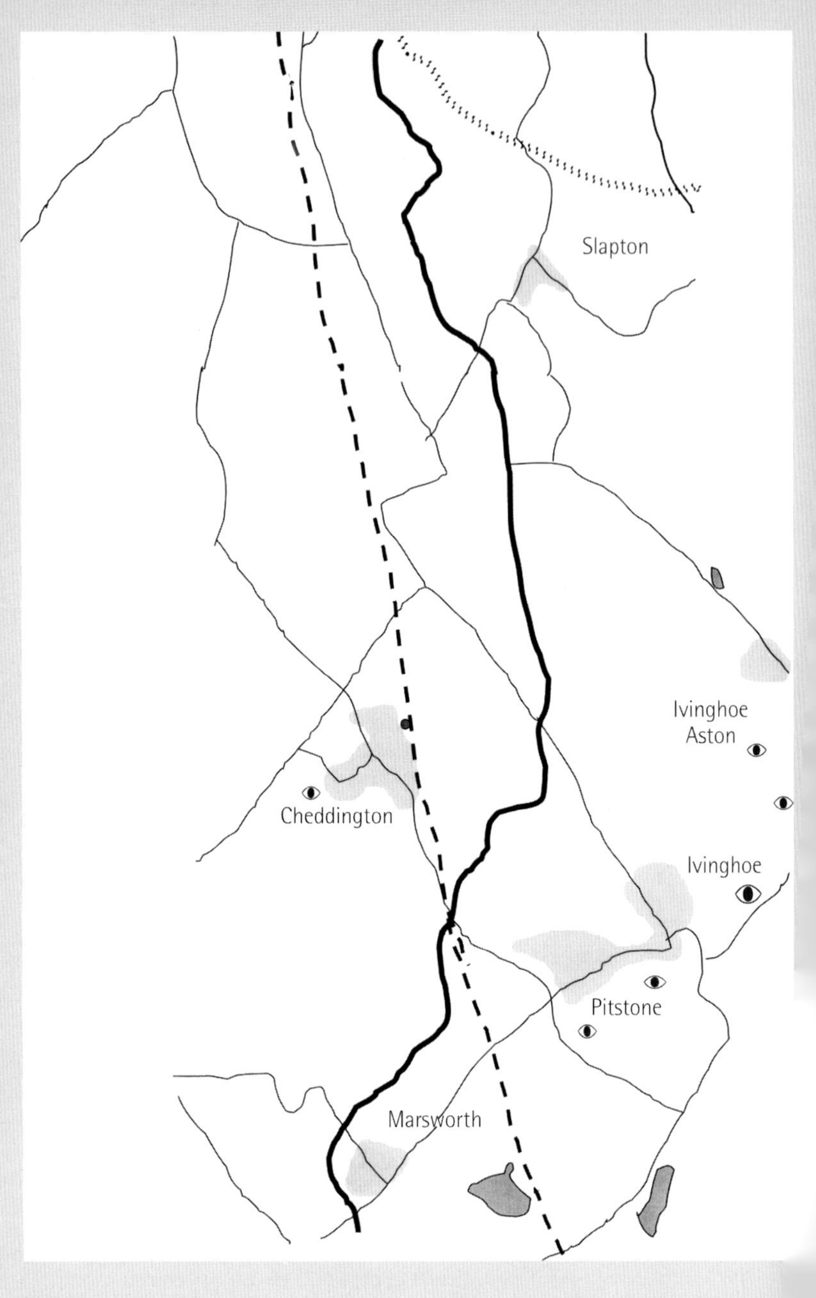
Slapton
Ivinghoe
Aston
Cheddington
Ivinghoe
Pitstone
Marsworth

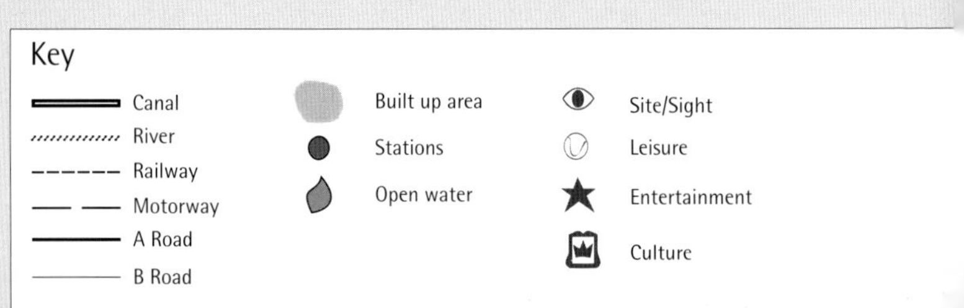
Key
Canal
River
Railway
Motorway
A Road
B Road
Built up area
Stations
Open water
Site/Sight
Leisure
Entertainment
Culture

along the 70-minute round trip. Trains run mainly at the weekend from April to October, with a few Christmas specials thrown in.

A bad fire nearly destroyed All Saints church in 1985, when the belfry and ten bells were wrecked, although the oldest bell, 'Ting-Tang', fell into the lower altar and escaped the flames.

In Leighton Buzzard itself, the spire of All Saints church is hard to miss, with the building itself built out of the local sandstone. The tower has clunch dressings, triple arcades on each face and an octagonal broach of limestone decorated with narrow lights. There is a set of five sundials around the church, and the font inside has been in use for more than 700 years.

Standing outside the church in Church Square is an impressive war memorial, which is thought to be unique on account of its being the largest single block of granite every quarried in these isles. It is 25ft high and over 3ft square, and weighs a total of 22 tons. It was first quarried in 1870 and brought here in 1920, with its erection taking three days to complete.

Still in Church Square, the building that is now the post office was built in 1790 as a School House, becoming Pulford School. The Golden Bell next door is supposed to get its name from the fact that it was convenient for the bell ringers. Opposite is The Cedars, the childhood home of Mary Norton who wrote the children's book *The Borrowers*. Originally built by a Quaker family in 1856, it is now part of Leighton Middle School.

The custom of beating the bounds is maintained every May, when an unfortunate choir boy is chosen to stand on his head in front of the almshouses to listen to extracts from the donor's will.

Other places scattered around the town include the Friends Meeting House, also built by Quakers in 1789, and the Black Horse pub, the only remaining original thatched house in the town. The Almshouses in North Street stand out, and were built in 1630 for eight elderly poor people on the condition that the bounds be beaten every Rogation Monday.

The Market Cross in the High Street cannot be missed, and can be dated back to the late fourteenth or early fifteenth century. Around 27ft high, the upper of two tiers has five figures in niches: the Christ, the Madonna and child, a bishop, a king and St John. The town hall opposite is not as old, being built in 1851 where an earlier building stood. The building has had a variety of uses over the years, from parish meeting house to fire station, and still seems to be seeking a full role today.

Peacock Mews, one of the highlights of local shopping, is named after the Peacock Inn, which is the second oldest building in the town, dating back to 1645. The Swan Hotel meanwhile has all the hallmarks of a coaching inn. Try spotting the original fire insurance sign under the eaves.

It is hard to appreciate that the Tesco superstore in Linslade sits on an historic site. Look up and you will see a 'Vimy Bomber' weathervane, as a factory once stood here making parts of this aircraft during the war. In Vicarage Road you will see St Barnabas' church, which is dressed in Bath stone. Built in 1849 due to the town's growing population, the interior has a hammer-beam roof sitting on plain stone corbels, and windows which include examples of both Kempe and William Morris.

Wing suffers from the lack of a by-pass, with heavy traffic passing along its outskirts. It is easy to miss the middle of the village, where there are a few older buildings, including some Almshouses founded in 1596, some cottages and the

Old Rectory. Wing has the air of a village waiting to shrug off the yoke of the car and re-discover itself. One recent victory saw the villagers successfully stopping the last open field in the village being sold for housing, and it is now a recreation area.

Outside Wing sits Ascott House (01296 688242), a National Trust property acquired by Leopold de Rothschild in 1874 as a hunting box, and subsequently transformed into a centre for a remarkable collection of works of art, the nucleus of which was inherited from his father, Baron Lionel de Rothschild.

From 1941 to 1947, a group of Chelsea Pensioners lived at Ascott, after the Royal Hospital in Chelsea was bombed.

Great Billington's church of St Michael, on top of Billington Hill in the middle of the village, is thirteenth century in origin, although the arch of the west window of the nave and the piscine of the chancel are the main evidence of this. Modest in design, the octagonal bell tower has a single bell. Nevertheless, this church is worth a visit if you are in the area.

An Iron Age fort and settlement once occupied the site where the church now sits in Billington.

Mead Open Farm (01525 852952) in Billington is an open farm with traditional animals offering a range of seasonal activities. In the 1880s, large areas of Billington were bought by Arthur Macnamara, who transformed it into a Victorian model village, including the building of a school halfway up the hill, although this has since closed. Many of the cottages still have the 'AM' cipher on them, a brand that the eccentric, and much feared, Macnamara, scattered liberally around the village.

Squire Macnamara was frightened of thunder, and an underground suite of rooms was furnished at Billington Manor, where he would disappear at the slightest threat of a storm.

Many instances of Macnamara's cruelty have been recorded. It is said that at his burial, when the blacksmith came to erect the iron railings round his grave, the spikes were turned in to stop him escaping the grave, rather than the usual custom of turning the spikes out to keep the devil out. This story cannot be verified as the railings were removed as part of the war effort.

Slapton has seen a lot of change in recent times and many of its older buildings have been sacrificed in the name of progress. Now mainly a commuter village, there are one or two cottages worth looking out for, but they do not merit a detour.

Should you be wandering near Slapton, don't be surprised if you come across some buffalo roaming in one of the fields, as one of the local farms has turned its hand to raising these beasts and even hosts regular open days for the public to learn more.

Also closed to the public is Cheddington Manor, whose half-timbered red brick structure and tiled roof, along with its gardens and lakes, are thought by many to be one of the best examples of a Manor House in the county. This is one of three large houses in the village, the others being The Rectory and The White House. Cheddington also has a Millennium Green and seat.

Ivinghoe Aston has an Old School House, dated 1869, on the main road. This once housed a public elementary school which itself was founded in 1876. Attendance was said to be poor when it first opened, as most of the young children were employed in the local industry of straw-plaiting, although the rapid decline of this activity in the 1880s saw more children coming through the doors.

Beacon Hill (233m high), site of the famous Ivinghoe Beacon, can be reached from a car park in the Ashridge Estate, although there is a marked lack of signage pointing you in the right direction. The terrain can be rugged and sturdy footwear is advised. The hill is the highest of a series of soft chalk hills stretching out from Ivinghoe. If evidence of this is required it is possible to gain an excellent view of the chalk Whipsnade Lion from the car park.

Cheddington used to be prodigious in its production of fruit, in particular plums. At the height of production up to a ton of fruit would be sent by cart to Covent Garden every day, mostly prune damsons, used in jam.

St Mary's church in Ivinghoe has fifteenth-century poppy-end bench ends, one of which is carved in the shape of a mermaid carrying a looking glass. The town hall in the village hosted a Saturday market until around 1900, selling mainly straw-plait goods from the ground floor of the building. The upper floor is now the village hall, but used to hold a Court of Petty Sessions every third Saturday in the month.

An imposing thatch-hook on the churchyard wall at Ivinghoe was once used to pull burning thatch from houses to prevent the spread of fire.

The imposing Georgian building facing the green (known locally as 'The Lawn') used to be the home of the local brewery manager, but it is now a youth hostel. On a clear day it is possible to see Mentmore Towers from the green, once (in)famous as the home of the Transcendental Meditation Movement when it was sold to the Maharishi Mahesh Yogi, and later as the headquarters of the Natural Law Party that briefly livened up the British political scene in the 1980s and 1990s. Now privately owned, there are views of Mentmore Towers from the golf course east of Wing.

Ivinghoe's Town Hall, which dates to 1795, was recently restored, and now hosts the village library.

Pitstone grew exponentially with the coming of Pitstone cement. Although now closed, the quarry has left its legacy in an active community. Its antecedents go back much before then, the most notable evidence of which is the Pitstone Windmill, the oldest surviving post-mill in the country. This sits in splendid isolation in the middle of a field, but can be viewed.

The farm which owns the field also hosts the Pitstone Green Museum. The museum celebrates rural life with buildings representing how a farm would have looked in 1831. It houses examples of local trades and professions as well as farm machinery, and also has a science and vintage radio room.

For those more interested in contemporary history, there is also a full-size section of a Second World War Lancaster bomber. The museum's collection can only be viewed on occasional open days and it is best to check ahead first on 01296 668083. Outside the entrance to the museum there is a large steel support roller, which was originally installed in Pitstone Cement works in 1936.

These days, Marsworth is a canal village, but during the Second World War another form of transport dominated. The RAF flew Wellington bombers out of here, and later, the USAF flew Fortresses and Liberators – including a leaflet squadron. The airfield had a dining hall that could sit 1,000 people and even its own theatre, the stage of which was later donated to the village hall. Churchill often stopped here on his way to Chequers, and General Patten also visited once.

An old cement grinder in Pitstone.

Those considering visiting the Aylesbury Arm may wish to consider the following:

- Bucks County Museum and the Roald Dahl Children's Gallery (01296 331441), *a hands-on gallery of everything to do with Roald Dahl and his books.*

CULTURE AND ENTERTAINMENT

This section is not particularly well blessed with cultural opportunities. Leighton Buzzard has a thriving theatre in its centre (01525 378310), which acts as the focal point for most of the performed arts. This is effectively the only theatre and cinema in the area, the attractions of Milton Keynes to the north and Luton to the east perhaps overshadowing those available locally.

Also in Leighton Buzzard there is the Shades Nightclub in Lakes Street (01525 852959), and some pubs act as live-music venues, notably The Cock in Heath and Reach (01525 852395), where there is folk music on the second Sunday evening of every month, and The Wheatsheaf on North Street (015252 374611), which hosts live bands on Friday and Saturday.

The Red Lion on North Street (01525 374350) also acts as a live-music venue, as does the Carpenters Arms on Wing Road (01525 240272), which has live entertainment on Monday evenings and an open-mike session on the last Friday of the month.

Those looking for something more active may head for Rushmere Park north of Heath and Reach, which has the Great Adventure Game (01234 266266) – a paintball centre, while the Tiddenfoot Leisure Centre, Mentmore Road, Linslade (01525 375765), has two indoor swimming pools; two squash courts; an all-weather sports pitch; tennis and netball courts; sports hall; roller skating; badminton; a fitness training centre; and a bar/café.

Finally, there are a number of children's play areas and other public open spaces around this section. One worth particular mention is the Memorial Playing Fields in Mentmore Road, Linslade. This has a children's amusement area; pavilion; bowls green; cricket table; football pitch; and tennis courts.

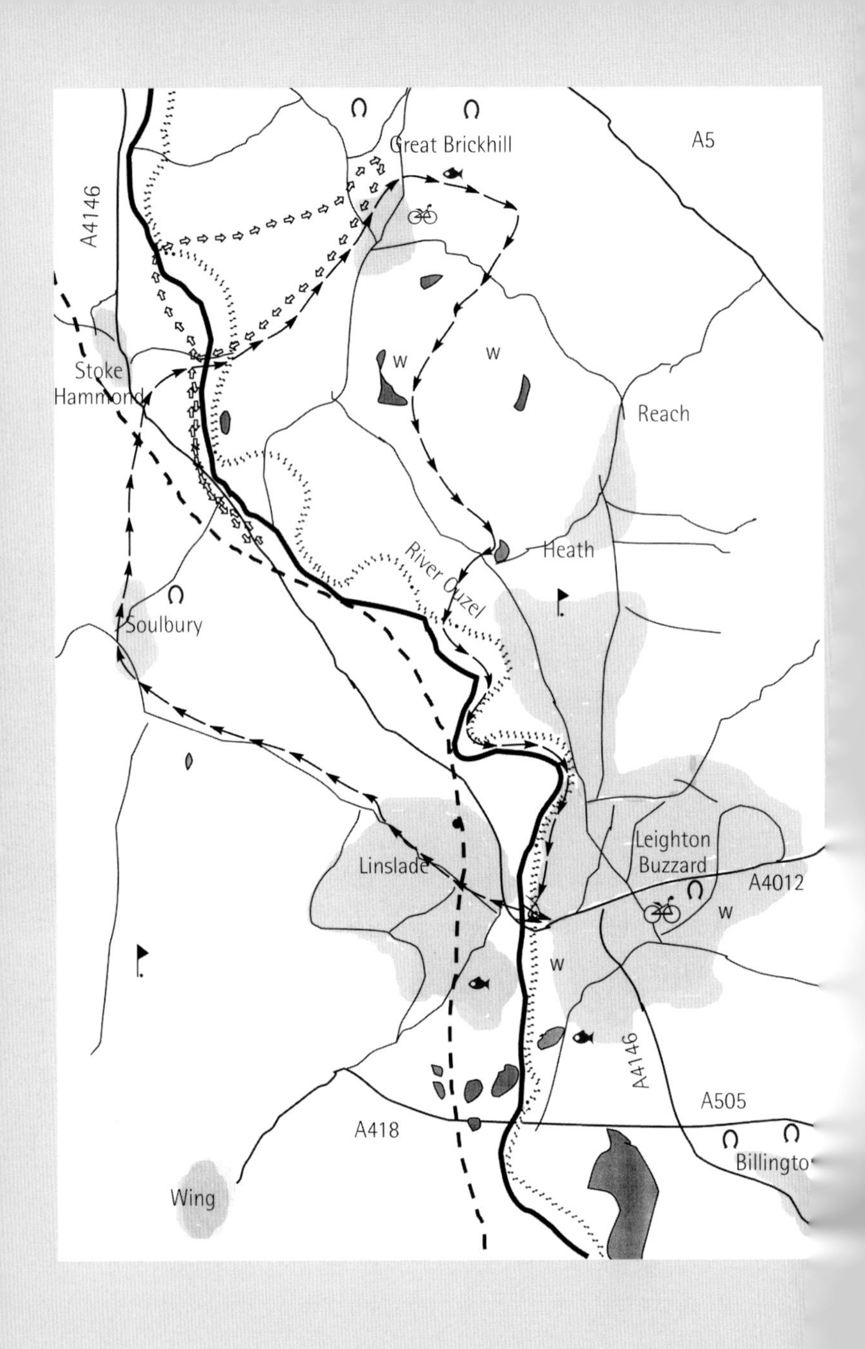

Great Brickhill
A5
A4146
Stoke
Hammond
Reach
w
w
Heath
River Ouzel
Soulbury
Leighton
Buzzard
A4012
Linslade
w
w
A4146
A505
A418
Billingto
Wing

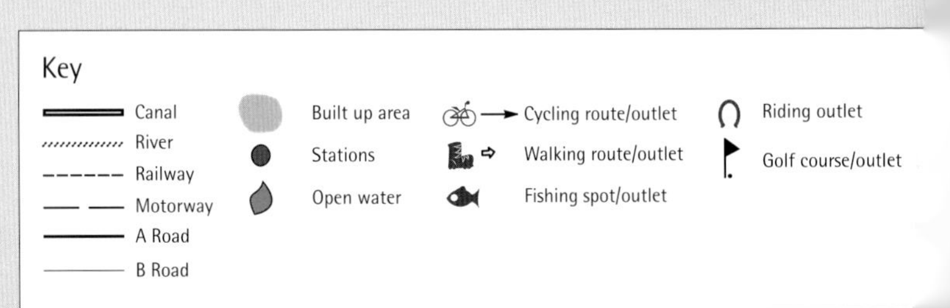

Key
Canal
River
Railway
Motorway
A Road
B Road
Built up area
Stations
Open water
Cycling route/outlet
Walking route/outlet
Fishing spot/outlet
Riding outlet
Golf course/outlet

SAMPLING

INTRODUCTION

The Ouzel valley makes this a pleasant stretch of canal to saunter through with a number of easy access points for the canal. There is formal parking just north of The Three Locks at Bridge 108, and by the Globe Inn at Linslade by Bridge 111 as well as between Pitstone and Cheddington at Bridge 126 and at Marsworth. The Stockgrove Country Park between Heath and Reach and Great Brickhill offers another good place to leave the car and delve into the countryside or maybe have a picnic.

WALKING

With the exception of Leighton Buzzard and its near neighbour/putative suburb Linslade, which sit either side of the canal halfway down this section, this is an open and rural part of the canal given colour by a number of small, but interesting, villages. As a consequence, there is no shortage of footpaths which allow the walker to sample the local area, many of which run alongside fields.

The Cross Bucks Way runs south of Soulbury before petering out on the Bedfordshire border, while the Two Ridges Link starts at the towpath west of Slapton and offers some strenuous walking up to Ivinghoe Aston and beyond, before joining up with the Ridgeway national trail east of Pitstone. The second ridge referred to is the Greensand Ridge, which can be picked up in Leighton Buzzard.

The Greensand Ridge is a 40-mile walk named after the lower greensand rock which forms a narrow ridge across Bedfordshire and gives Leighton Buzzard its sandy soil. It begins at the Canal Bridge in Linslade by the Globe pub, and follows the River Ouzel before passing through the Woburn Estate before ending in Gamlingay east of Bedford.

> The iron in the Greensand Ridge accounts for the orange-brown stone used in the construction of many of the local buildings.

Ivinghoe lies on the edge of the Icknield Way, a 105-mile walk which has strong claims to be the oldest road in England. It stretches from here to Knettishall Heath in Norfolk.

Stockgrove Country Park, north-west of Heath and Reach, offers a wide variety of habitats in a relatively condensed 80 acres, including an oak woodland that has been designated a Site of Special Scientific Interest, and a hand-dug lake fed by natural springs. A number of paths cut across the park and there are also parking and picnic sites. Finally, the River Ouzel, which runs alongside the canal until dashing off to the east just south of Leighton Buzzard, also provides a pleasant walking companion along much of this stretch.

Slightly further west is Linslade Wood, 14 acres of woodland off the Stoke Road which is known locally as the 'Bluebell Wood'. Pathways here lead through privately owned land planted with spalings, with the idea of creating a new community woodland.

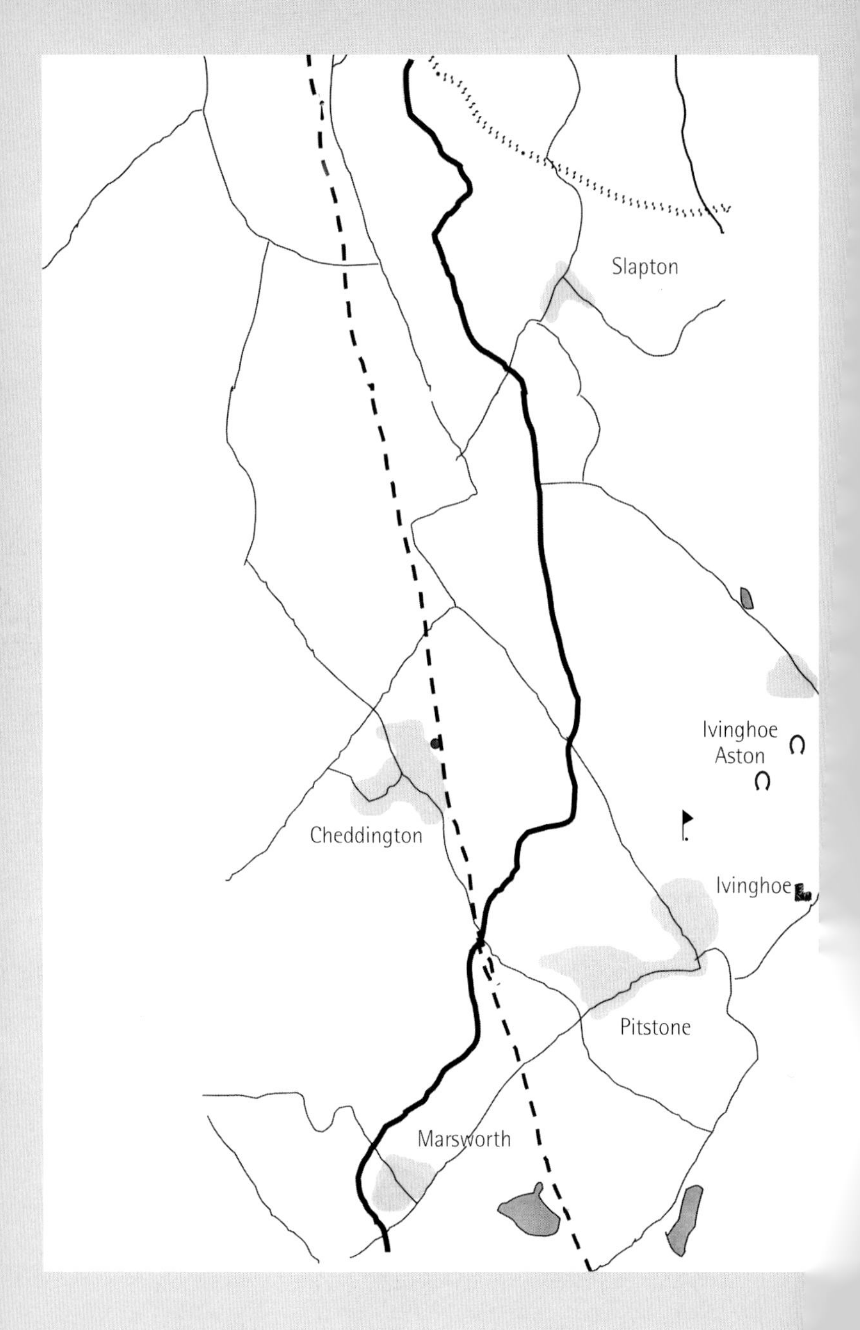
Slapton
Ivinghoe
Aston
Cheddington
Ivinghoe
Pitstone
Marsworth

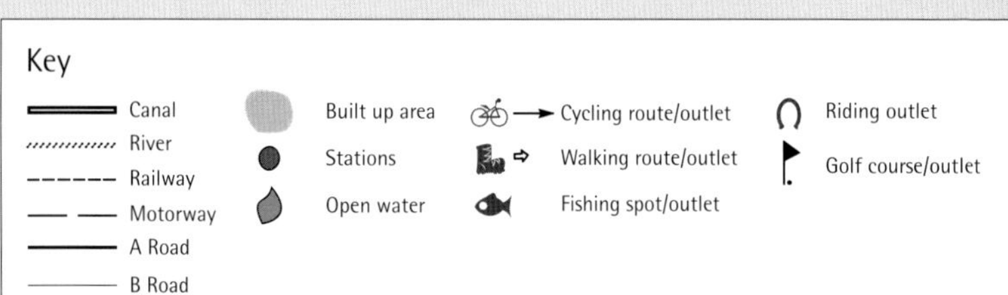
Key
Canal
River
Railway
Motorway
A Road
B Road
Built up area
Stations
Open water
Cycling route/outlet
Walking route/outlet
Fishing spot/outlet
Riding outlet
Golf course/outlet

The nearby Tiddenfoot Waterside Park, off the Mentmore Road, is a much bigger area with a lake and car parking, as well as some newly laid footpaths and cycleways. It is also possible to fish in the lake.

The Ouzel can be enjoyed at Ouzel Meadows, just off Lock 27. Bought by the town council in 1999, this land had been virtually abandoned, but by re-introducing cattle-grazing the council have been able to encourage the growth of meadow flowers and other native wildlife. A pretty area full of pollarded willows, it is exclusive to walker as both fishing and cycling are prohibited.

Walk B has been designed to allow the walker to experience the twin delights of the canal and the river, following a climb up into Great Brickhill to give a vantage point over the Ouzel valley.

SECTION B WALK

Soulbury Three Locks and Great Brickhill

Description:	*Towpath and field-side walking incorporating a steady climb into and out of Great Brickhill, although there is a pub here where you can pause*
Distance:	*5.75 miles*
Duration:	*2.5 hrs*
Starting point:	*Grid Reference 891282, OS Explorer 192 (E)*
Nearest Refreshment:	*The Three Locks pub at the start and finish of the walk or the Old Red Lion in Great Brickhill.*

Park in the layby outside The Three Locks pub, which is on the A4146 south of Stoke Hammond. Find the towpath and head north, leaving the locks behind you, and past the attractive Stoke Hammond Lock where the river comes alongside a little further down. Just before Bridge 102, head through the small gap up some steps and turn right onto a minor road. You now cross over the river via a trio of stone bridges. On reaching Westfield Farm, take the footpath on your right and cross the field diagonally to the opposite boundary and a small wood planted to commemorate the Queen's Golden Jubilee in 2002.

Turn left at the corner of the field, keeping the derelict wall to your left, and bear right at the wooden fence. At the apex of the field, take the footpath on your left up a narrow track. On reaching a road, bear left and head up to the War Memorial and into Great Brickhill. Bear right and take the chance to look out over the valley before heading right at the Old Red Lion into Ivy Lane, and then right again into Stoke Lane. At Haines Farm, follow the track to the left and downhill through some trees. On reaching Paper Mill Farm, bear right and head towards a pair of picture-postcard bridges over the Ouzel. Stay with this road which brings you back to Bridge 102, where you re-trace your steps to the pub.

Walking equipment outlets along this section include:

- Millets, Waterbourne Walk, Leighton Buzzard (01525 371623)

A raised platform over a boggy stretch of the Greensand Ridge Walk.

CYCLING

The towpath and surrounding footpaths provide plenty of opportunities for cycle routes, and there is a strong tradition of cycling here, with at least two clubs in the Bossard Wheelers (01525 758732) and the Buzzards Mountain Bike Club (01525 381593), the former based in Linslade and the latter in Leighton Buzzard.

A good way to sample this section on two wheels is to set out from Great Brickhill and head south down Ivy Lane, turning right at the Old Red Lion down Heath Road, and then right again to join up with a short section of bridleway which then becomes a footpath. Follow this through woods until you link up with the Greensand Ridge walk. Follow this south, round the edge of Rushmere Park, until you reach Rushmere itself.

Here you pick up the road and head south-west until you link up with the canal. Follow this south (right), through its various twists and turns, until you reach Bridge 114 in Linslade. Turn right here, following the B4032 uphill to Soulbury. Take the minor road through the other side of Soulbury, heading for Great Brickhill. Here you can either head to where you started or pick up the short stretch of bridleway on the left after a couple of hundred yards, which will take you into Stoke Hammond.

On reaching the A4146, turn left, and just before the Dolphin pub turn right, heading slightly downhill towards the canal again. Cross over the canal at Bridge 106 and pick up the bridleway just after the stream. Take the spur to the left and follow this back into Great Brickhill – a (slightly challenging) total of around 11 miles.

Cycle outlets along this section include:

- Dorvic's Cycles, Leighton Buzzard (01525 373060)
- Chainey's Cycles, Leighton Buzzard (01525 852400)

RIDING

Many of the routes described in the walking section are also suitable for riding. In particular, much of the Ridgeway, the Icknield Way and the Greensand Ridge Walk are also bridleways. Elsewhere, Great Brickhill and Soulbury are connected by a bridleway south of Moat Farm House, but otherwise this is not an area particularly well blessed with public paths.

> Great Billington used to have its own point-to-point course, with Edward VII, when he was Prince of Wales, once breaking his collarbone in a fall during a race.

Horse-riding establishments and outlets along this section include:

- Bryerley Springs Farm, Great Brickhill (01525 261823)
- RB Equestrian, Saddlery and Tack Shop, Lower Rectory Farm, Great Brickhill (01908 365335)
- Liscombe Park Riding School, Soulbury (01296 689090)
- Blackbarn Stables, Leighton Buzzard (01525 852176)
- Ryecroft Stables, Billington (01525 377173)
- W. Edwins, Great Billington (01525 373359)
- Nicolette Morris Stables, Grove Farm, Ivinghoe Aston (07946 238544)
- Rocklane Riding Centre, Ivinghoe Aston (01525 222402) – *Riding lessons can also be arranged at the Village Swan community pub*
- Just off the map there is also the Bow Brickhill Trekking Centre, Bellow Hill Farm, Woburn Sands Road, Bow Brickhill (01908 373046)

FISHING

Opportunities for canalside fishing are complemented by others alongside lakes, many of which are the result of previous extraction industries. The canal is controlled mainly by the Luton Angling Club (01582 728114), and the Leighton Buzzard Angling Club (01525 379099).
Lakes include:

- Alders Farm Fishery, Great Brickhill (01525 261713) – *two purpose-built trout lakes, each around 3 acres, set in a wooded valley. These are both trout lakes with rainbows and browns up to 2lb, with some larger fish in Alders Pool. Day tickets available*
- Rackley Hills, Grovebury Road, Leighton Buzzard (01582 696759) – *a lake in the midst of some industry but with two sides looking onto woodland and fields. Some large catfish and carp, with the latter growing up to 20lb, as well as roach, bream, perch, gudgeon, pike and tench*

The popular Grove pub outside Leighton Buzzard sits in glorious isolation.

- Tiddenfoot Lake, Mentmore Road, Leighton Buzzard (01582 696759) – *Tiddenfoot is within a council-run countryside park and has one shallow side and three deeper sides. Catfish and carp are again evident, but there is also tench, roach, rudd and bream*

Outlets selling fishing supplies along this stretch include:
- Terminal Tackle, Leighton Buzzard (01525 370779)

OTHER

Golf courses begin to spring up wherever there is a possibility from here on into the outskirts of London. Local courses include:

- The Three Locks Golf Club, Great Brickhill 01525 270050 – *a picturesque course nestled in an area of outstanding natural beauty, visible from the towpath. With the River Ouzel nearby, water hazards are abundant. 18 holes, 6,400 yards and a practice ground*
- Leighton Buzzard Golf Course, Plantation Road (01525 373812) – *18 holes, 6,101 yards*
- Mentmore Golf Club (01296 662020) – *slightly off the map but worth mentioning. Two courses, The Rothschild (6,700 yards) and The Rosebery (6763 yards), with a driving range*
- Aylesbury Vales Golf Club, Wing (01525 240196) – *gently undulating course with water hazards. 18 holes, 6622 yards and a 10-bay driving range*
- Ivinghoe Golf Club (01296 668696) – *a carefully landscaped parkland course in the shadow of Ivinghoe Beacon. 9 holes, 4508 yards*

SECTION C

MARSWORTH TO HEMEL HEMPSTEAD

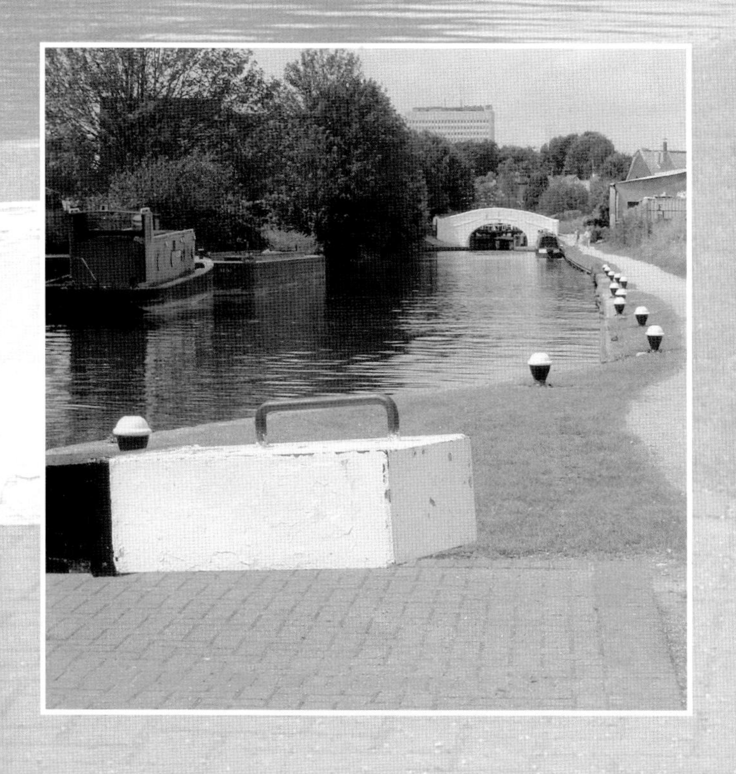

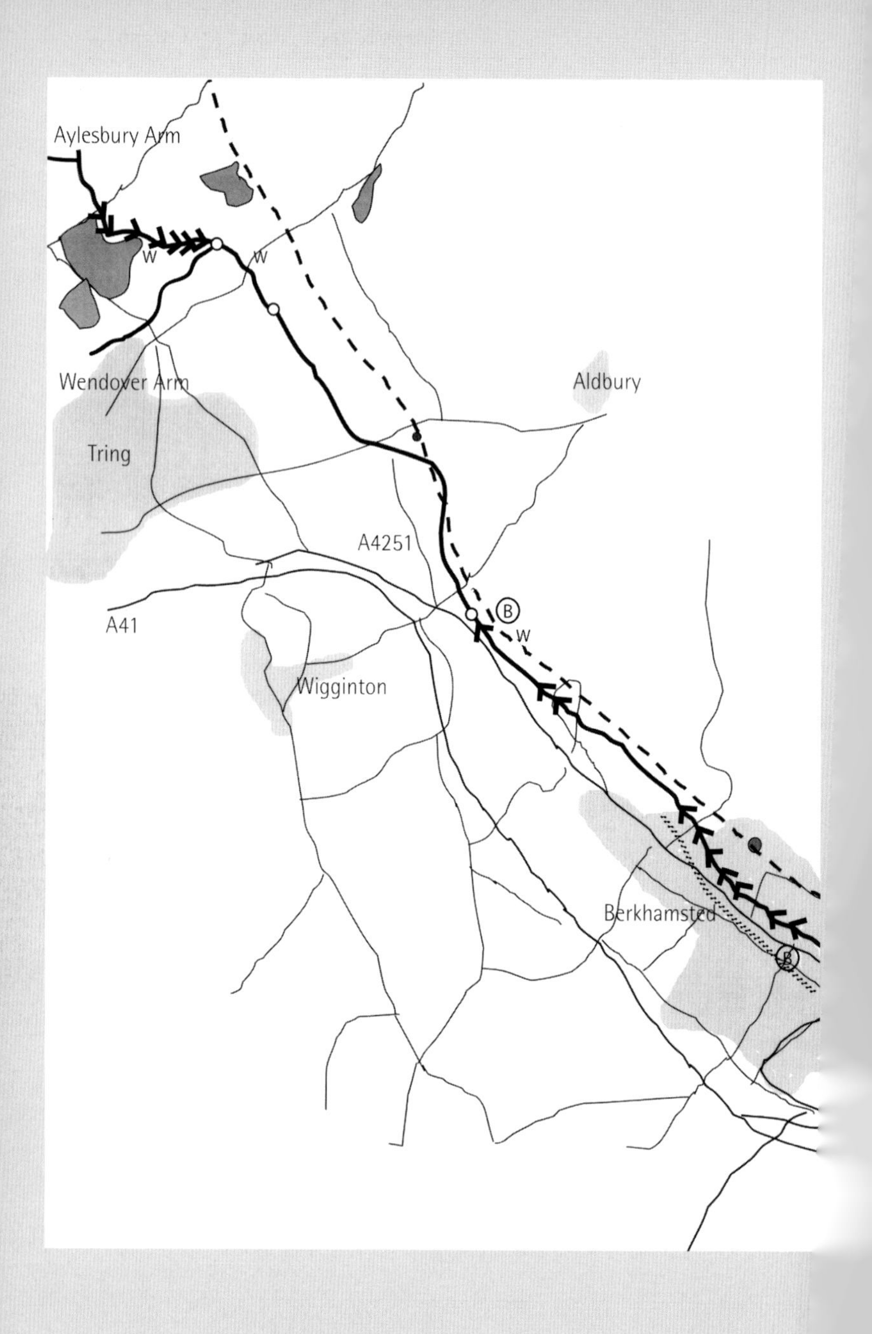
Aylesbury Arm
W
W
Wendover Arm
Aldbury
Tring
A4251
B
W
A41
Wigginton
Berkhamsted
B

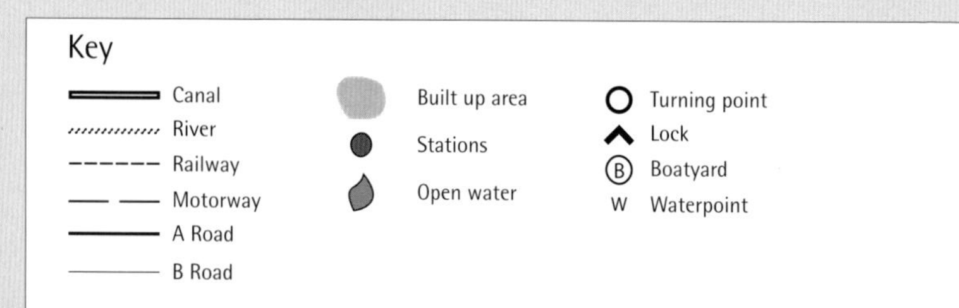
Key
Canal
River
Railway
Motorway
A Road
B Road
Built up area
Stations
Open water
Turning point
Lock
Boatyard
W Waterpoint

SHAPERS

THE CANAL ON THIS STRETCH

KEY FACTS

LENGTH 10.75 miles

BOATYARDS: 3
- Cowroast Marina
- Bridgewater Boats
- Middlesex and Herts Boat Services

WATER POINTS:5
- Startop's End
- Bulbourne
- Ravens Lane, Berkhamsted
- Cow Roast
- Port of Berkhamsted

TURNING POINTS: 5
- Wendover Arm Junction
- Upper Icknield Way Bridge
- Tring Station
- Cowroast
- Winkwell

LOCKS: 25
- Marsworth Locks (7) (42ft 3in)
- Cowroast (6ft)
- Dudswell Locks (2) (13ft 4in)
- Northchurch Locks (4) (26ft 11in)
- Berkhamsted Locks (3) (16ft 10in)
- Bourne End Locks (3) (29ft 4in)
- Winkwell Locks (3) (13ft 7in)
- Boxmoor Top Lock (6ft 8in)
- Fishery Lock (7ft 1in")

Although on paper a relatively built-up part of the canal, for long stretches the waterway almost seems to hide from 'civilisation' here. The deep cutting outside Tring aids this sense of anonymity, while the waterway seems to positively shy away from Hemel. It is left to Berkhamsted to embrace the water, something it does with alacrity, making this a fitting mid-point for the section.

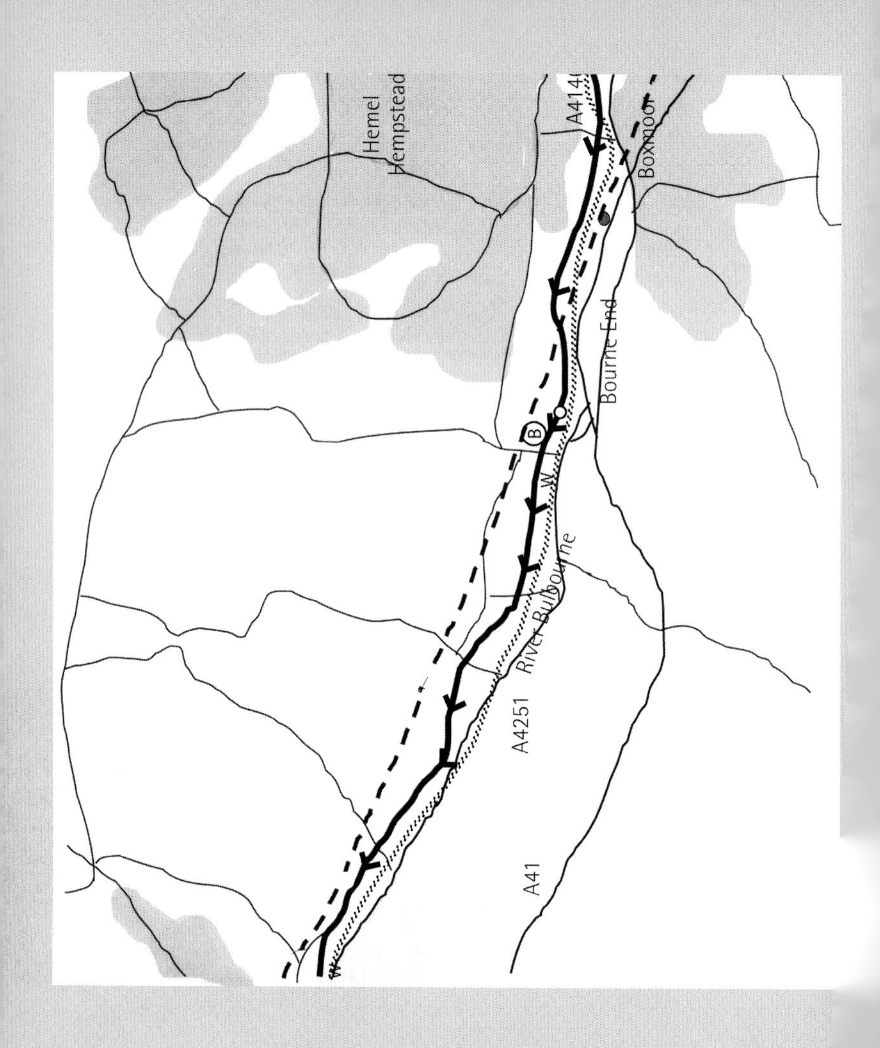
Hemel Hempstead
A414
Boxmoor
Bourne End
B
W
River Bulbourne
A4251
A41

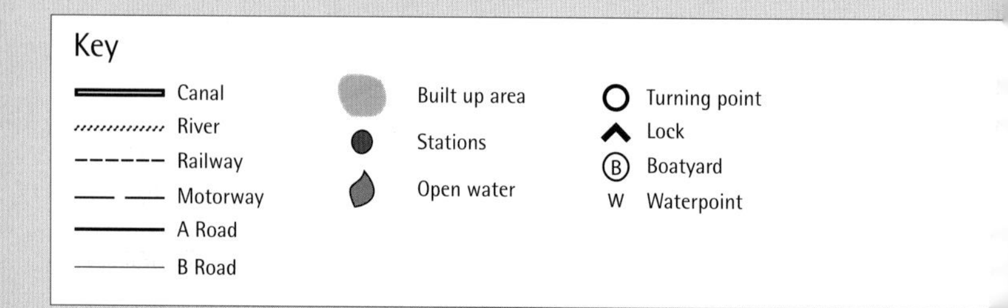
Key
Canal
River
Railway
Motorway
A Road
B Road
Built up area
Stations
Open water
Turning point
Lock
B
Boatyard
W
Waterpoint

The Marsworth flight of seven locks starts at Bridge 132. These are well spread out and the network of the Marsworth and Tring reservoirs, which feed the summit of the canal, flanks the first of them. The reservoirs and the canal are popular with fishermen, whose tents line the bankside. The towpath runs either side throughout the length of the flight, and at the top lock a sign indicates that there is only 38.5 miles left to Brentford. The sign also signals a turn right down the Wendover Arm, 6.75 miles of canal currently under restoration.

The towpath is excellent here, although trees either side hide the view. Mooring is possible between some of the locks, but there is rarely trouble finding a berth along the next mile, even in the height of summer. The canal is now at its summit and a long run of formal moorings follows, which even has its own designated BBQ spot.

BW's old Bulbourne workshop follows on the right, with the Grand Junction Arms a convenient watering hole alongside a watering point. Just after this there is a winding hole and a long run in which the canal seems to accept the embrace of nearby trees as it proceeds down a deep cutting. This was a particularly difficult part of the canal to dig due to the soft Hertfordshire sandy soil, and bricks had to be brought up by canal from Southall for reinforcement.

For many years, Bulbourne Workshops acted as the source for many of the lock gates used on the UK's canals. Today the site has a sad, derelict air, with the large crane in the yard rusting and impotent.

The towpath crosses over to the other side at Bridge 134, doing so via a steep path. Yet more moorings follow and this spot is particularly conducive to peace and quiet. A metal road bridge heralds an approach to the convenient Tring railway station, as well as the Ridgeway long-distance path. There is also a sign giving details of the Aldbury Millennium Walk and other local facts.

There are more formal ringed-moorings a little further down just before Bridge 156, although these look out onto some commercial units, after which the trees begrudgingly begin to part to reveal occasional glimpses of the hills to the south. Moored boats start to accumulate in earnest along the run-up to Cowroast Lock and Marina, a spot that has won a number of awards for its well-kept neat gardens. A blue metal arched bridge takes the towpath over the entrance to the marina itself, where there is a good view out to the north-east. Shortly after there is a mooring for access to services such as water. It is possible for boats to turn around here. At Cowroast there is access to the nearby pub, and petrol station which sells basic supplies, with boaters having their own set of (rather slippery) steps on the non-towpath side. Another long straight stretch precedes the two Dudswell Locks, the first of which has a solitary lock-keeper's cottage, and the second, a short run of picturesque houses. These locks start the descent down towards Brentford. The towpath now crosses back over to the right at Bridge 138, which is something of a relief as prior to here it deteriorates into a rather uneven track.

Cowroast boasts its own apiary, and sells honey. The place gets its name from Cow Rest, rather than any kind of barbeque connection. Drovers bringing cattle from the Midlands to London used to pause here.

After the bridge things improve and this is a pleasantly un-built-up area, with a high hedge to the right and the railway flanked by rising hills to the left. Northchurch Lock starts a run of nine through Berkhamsted, bringing a rapid descent from the summit. For the first time in a while, the landscape becomes more suburban, with both housing and commercial property lining both banks. The towpath is clearly defined and really more of a pedestrian route through the north of Berkhamsted. The town itself can be accessed from Bridge

SECTION C

Berkhamsted is the home of sheep dip. A small factory was opened here by William Cooper of Clunbury, who had experimented with arsenic and sulphur to produce the perfect mix.

140, although it is much better to use one of the many access points further down. There is also a station here just off the canal to the north.

A wooden footbridge and a comprehensive children's play area complete with car park (Canal Fields) is as good a place as any to define the centre of Berkhampsted from a towpath traveller's point of view. There is ample mooring and the town is canal-friendly, with a long run of information boards dotted along the route. The often hidden River Bulbourne flows alongside the canal, which adds to the sense of serenity. The towpath crosses back to the left at Bridge 141 and this marks the first of three consecutive pubs and an area known locally as the Port of Berkhamsted.

There is another water point at Bridge 142, and a pub. The towpath crosses over again at the next bridge, and the town soon fades into memory as the canal regains its former languid pace. Bottom Side Lock (No.58) is rather appropriately followed by the 'in-elegantly'-named Sewer Lock, which in turn precedes the three Winkwell Locks, which end with the magnificent sight of the Three Horseshoes canalside pub. Here, there is access to Bourne End, the last village before the much larger town of Hemel Hempstead.

The death certificate of Joseph Buck, the Winkwell lock-keeper, in 1898, cites his cause of death as 'drowning in his own lock, although there is no evidence to show by what means the deceased fell into the water.' What is not recorded is that the death took place on Christmas Day, and he was on his way back from the Three Horseshoes, so we can take a reasonable guess.

SECTION C

Immediately after the Three Horseshoes and Winkwell Swing Bridge, there is the small Winkwell Dock, and after that, Lock 61, an equally diminutive marina tucked in on the non-towpath side. A good run of mooring follows (watch out for weed) before the concreted-in Stephenson ironwork railbridge, where the railway crosses the canal in order to link up with the station on the edge of town.

Throughout this section the towpath is solid and easy to use, and a long, straight stretch of it follows, taking in Boxmoor Top Lock. The River Bulbourne comes alongside once again, and is sandwiched between the canal and the railway, before disappearing off into a channel along the bottom of some housing on the left, although a stream does remain on the towpath side.

There are more good moorings before Fishery Lock, which are convenient for the Fishery Inn, which marks the beginning of metropolitan Hemel. The river crosses back, unsure whether it wants to be part of the canal or not, before retreating off to the right to make up its mind. This leads to some wide meadows with the canal defining the northernmost limit.

Winkwell Dock was used to offload manure and timber from London, and coal from Leicester, for local use.

THE WENDOVER ARM

The Wendover Arm sweeps off the Grand Union at the end of the Marsworth locks, under a grand bridge. At the moment it is navigable for only less than a mile, although the local Wendover Arm Trust is active in restoring the canal both in tangible terms and in terms of money raising. The annual Tring Canal Festival held every spring Bank Holiday is the trust's big event, and they have already been successful in opening a further 500 yards of the 6-mile stretch.

From a walker's perspective, the towpath is firm and takes you into Wendover itself, past the RAF Halton air-training establishment. This is a walk well worth doing, with a number of interesting bridges and some excellent wildlife-spotting opportunities.

PRINCIPAL TOWNS AND VILLAGES ALONG THIS STRETCH

ALDBURY:

A scattered community dispersed on the sides of a hill and bordered to the east by large tracts of common land. Recent infill-housing sits side by side with half-timbered and converted farm workers' cottages. A significant proportion of the cottages are painted a variety of pastel colours. The church of St John the Baptist dominates the centre, along with a traditional village green.

BERKHAMSTED:

This has a prominent place in this country's history, with its castle the home of a number of monarchs. Sitting on the Roman Akeman Street, the town positively oozes history, and has adopted both the canal and the railway as a natural part of its growth. In recent times, the town has developed to the south along a spur of the Chiltern Hills, while the area to the north has remained undeveloped and open for the use of residents and visitors alike.

Bourne End's stream used to be much more spasmodic, earning it the reputation of being a 'woe water', its appearance being seen as a portent of war.

BOURNE END:

A small village clinging to the side of the valley leading up from the canal, and sandwiched between the Bourne Gutter chalk stream and the A41 trunk road. The stream was once a watercress bed and the village's mill that used it is now a small hotel. Road (Akeman Street), canal and railway all utilise the gap in the Chiltern Hills, and the village co-exists successfully with all three.

BOXMOOR:

The area clustered around the railway station outside Hemel Hempstead, which has largely lost its sense of being separate from its larger neighbour. The area is probably better known for its namesake, the Boxmoor area of common land.

The station at Boxmoor was originally the first stop out of London from Euston, and the coming of the railway was largely responsible for the development of Boxmoor village itself.

When Hemel's 'Magic Roundabout' opened in 1973, traffic stuttered to a halt and backed up to Berkhamsted while drivers tried to figure out how it worked. Thirty years on, it still catches the odd visitor by surprise!

HEMEL HEMPSTEAD (WEST):

The western approach to Hemel Hempstead is dominated by the single office block built as the European Headquarters of the photographic giant Kodak. The town was identified as a 'New Town' after the war, and these days has two distinct parts: the now slightly aged-looking centre, and the much more attractive old town. Hemel's other main claim to fame is its 'magic roundabout' traffic system.

SECTION C

HEMEL OLD TOWN:

Situated to the north-west of Hemel, this area retains much of its charm, with original buildings and St Mary's church perched on the side of the High Street on a hill surrounded by open ground.

NORTHCHURCH:

This small village on the outskirts of Berkhamsted used to be known as Berkhamsted St Mary's until a second church (St Peter's) was built to the south. The village has many examples of fifteenth- and sixteenth-century half-timbered houses, including the George and Dragon pub and some church almshouses. One cottage was originally a school for teaching children how to plait straw. These days, Northchurch is more or less a suburb of Berkhamsted.

> Northchurch churchyard contains the grave of Peter the Wild Boy, who was brought to England by Queen Caroline in 1725, after he was found wandering wild in the forests of Germany. He was looked after by a local farmer, and given a dog collar with his address on it.

TRING:

Cocooned as an apparent outpost of Hertfordshire, Tring appears to be largely self-sufficient, with its High Street and its older heart running along the southern edge of town, and most of the more recent housing to the north and west. This said, Tring Wharf and the New Mill towards the canal define the northern limit, while the train station sits a mile out of town to the east. By-passed by the busy A41, Tring continues to cling to its market town antecedents, driven largely by the fact that it sits on an intersection of Akeman Street and the Icknield Way, and has a market to this day.

WIGGINGTON:

Wiggington sits high on top of a hill, and the approach to the village is somewhat marred by a rather ugly telephone mast on the summit. Otherwise, the village's two most distinguishing features are the church of St Bartholomew, and the fact that it acts as the main portal for the original Champneys Health Club.

HISTORY

Most of the towns and villages in this area can trace their antecedents back to the Domesday Book, although there is evidence that people lived and died here for some time before then.

The graves of Bronze-Age dwellers have been discovered in Aldbury, and they were followed by Iron-Age settlers who devoted considerable energy to the construction of dykes on the north-west boundary of the parish. Both Tring and Hemel can also trace their history back to ancient times, with the area then largely covered by dense forest.

Tring and Berkhamsted owe much to their position on key trading routes, with the latter sitting on the Roman Akeman Street, which itself was built on a much older Belgic road, and Tring sitting on the junction of this and the much more ancient Icknield Way. As such, it should come as no surprise that as the forest were slowly cleared, both these centres developed as market towns servicing th local area.

Hemel Old Town, a world away from the nearby malls.

The Romans were active in the area, which at that time looked east towards the city of Verulamium (modern-day St Albans), with this impressive walled-city acting as a focus for trading. Raw materials excavated from the area, along with food, were traded for some of the finer things in life such as pottery, wine and cloth, and there is evidence that some Romans chose to build extensive villas in the area – a place in the country perhaps?

The Romans were followed by the Saxons, although their influence was not strong. It is from this time, however, that settlements became more established and a charter dated 705 records that Offa, King of the Saxons, granted land in the district of 'Hamele' to the Bishop of London. Today's pronunciation of Hemel Hempstead is clearly recognisable in the Saxon name of 'Hamelhamstede', meaning 'homestead of Hamele'.

It is Berkhamsted, however, that was the dominant settlement around this time, and the town has a special place in the next significant phase of the country's history, being the spot where the Norman Conquest was effectively completed. It was here that Edgar Atheling finally submitted to William the Conquerer, and offered him the crown. William declared a preference to be crowned in London, but took the keys to the capital as collateral.

> Just as Verulamium was once briefly the Roman's centre of government, locals claim that through this surrender, 'Berko', as they know it, has also been the nation's capital.

In 1086 the manor of Berkhamsted passed to Earl Mortain, William's half-brother, and it was he who decided to stablish a castle here. Mortain's tenure was brief, and when his son rose up gainst the new king, Henry I, the castle was granted by the king to his chancellor, Randulph, who set about building the castle up to such a condition that within twenty years Henry was able to hold court there.

In 1155 Henry II passed the castle to Thomas Beckett, and further lavish spending saw the castle's keep and walls strengthened. A symbol of the town's growing significance around this time was the granting of a Royal Charter freeing the merchants of Berkhamsted from all tolls and dues.

In 1189 the castle passed into royal hands, namely those of Prince (later King) John, brother of Richard the Lionheart. Although it fell briefly to Prince Louis of France, by 1255 it was back in royal hands, and further expenditure followed. Revenge against the French was gained a century later, through the imprisonment of King John of France, here after the Battle of Poitiers.

Hemel's early history largely replicates this pattern, with 'Hamelhamsteade' having been held by King Harold's brother, and thus passed to Mortain, who held it as part of his Honour of Berkhamsted. Along with the castle, ownership of Hemel passed among a line of royal lords and bishops until Edmund, King John's grandson, who was born at the castle, gave the Manor of Hemel Hempstead to a group of monks known as the Bonhommes, along with a monastery at Ashridge, in the second half of the thirteenth century. This state of affairs was to last for 250 years.

Berkhamsted's peak probably occurred in the late fourteenth century. Edward III carried out extensive repairs to the fabric of the castle, and in 1361 the Black Prince honeymooned there with his wife, Joan, the Fair Maid of Kent. Soon after, the castle and its estates passed to the Duchy of Cornwall, with the poet Geoffrey Chaucer at one time the Clerk of Works there.

In 1469 Edward IV gave the castle to his mother and, following her death thirty years later, it fell into a period of decline. When Sir Edward Carey, Keeper to the Jewels to Queen Elizabeth, was granted the manor in 1580, he decided to use the remaining stonework to build a new mansion at Berkhamsted Place, thus sealing its fate.

It was in Tudor times that the balance of power underwent a subtle shift from Berkhamsted to Hemel. In 1539, Henry VIII granted a Charter of Incorporation to the town and, following its dissolution as a monastery, Ashridge became a favourite haunt of Elizabeth. It was also Elizabeth who gave the lands around Boxmoor to Robert, Earl of Leicester, who in turn conveyed the land to the people of Hemel in the form of a trust.

Meanwhile, Tring maintained its position as a market town, although it had suffered greatly from the Black Death and the subsequent enclosures. Like Berkhamsted and Hemel, the manor of Tring had spent many years in royal ownership, and remained so until the death of Charles I's wife, Henrietta. The manor passed into the hands of Charles II's Clerk to the Treasury, Henry Guy, who had a mansion designed by Sir Christopher Wren built in the park, thereby laying the foundations for much of the town's later history.

In subsequent years Tring Park was the home of the Reverend Lawrence Washington, the great-great-grandfather of the first President of the United States, but it was in the nineteenth century that things really began to change. In 1872 the banker and MP, Lionel Rothschild, bought the estate for his son, Nathaniel. Known as 'Natty', the new owner arranged a water supply to the town and built new homes in the traditional half-timbered style, many of which remain scattered about the town today.

It is Natty's son, Lionel, who is best remembered, for it was he who had an interest in natural history and established the museum for which the town is renowned today. As well as collecting exotic species, Lionel introduced them to his estate, so that around this time it was not unusual to spot kangaroos or giant tortoises wandering around the quintessentially English landscape.

The turn of the eighteenth century and the subsequent Victorian period were also good for Berkhamsted. First the canal and then the railway saw the town become something of an industrial centre, with William Cooper's Sheep Dip a famous export. Hemel also prospered around this time, with the railway providing direct access to London markets, although the town itself was to remain the private property of the Halsey family until it was acquired by the Hemel Hempstead Development Corporation.

Today, the three main towns along this stretch all retain evidence of the history that has shaped them. Protected by its valley and by-passed by the A41, Berkhamsted has been allowed to prosper without being spoiled. It is the same story with Tring, stuck out on a limb in, but not necessarily of, Hertfordshire. Old Hemel has also survived, but needs to be uncovered from under the shadow of its more dominant modern namesake. Linking all three is the canal, winding its way down from its summit, and beginning the long descent into the outskirts of London.

THE NATURAL LANDSCAPE

This western outpost of Hertfordshire is not that typical of the rest of the county, both in terms of topography and 'feel'. Looked at dispassionately, Tring could sit in either Hertfordshire, Buckinghamshire or Bedfordshire, and this is reflected in the range of post and telephone codes used by the surrounding villages. Equally, Hemel Hempstead seems to sit on its own, in the same family, but not really a close relative of either St Albans to the east or Watford to the south.

BW's old Bulbourne Workshops, where lock gates were once made.

SECTION A MILTON KEYNES

Top: *Not an ancient pyramid, but the home of Bletchley Leisure Centre.*
Above: *The Point in central Milton Keynes continues the pyramid theme.*

Opposite: *An old bridge sign at Fenny Lock, a location that has won prizes for its upkeep.*

NOTICE.
This
BRIDGE
Is insufficient to carry a
HEAVY MOTOR CAR
The Registered Axle.weight of any axle of which exceeds
THREE TONS
or the Registered Axle Weights of the several
axles of Which exceed in the aggregate
FIVE TONS
or a Heavy Motor Car drawing a
TRAILER
if the Registered Axle.Weights of the several Axles
of the HEAVY MOTOR CAR and
Axle.Weights of the several
TRAILER
Exceed in the
FIVE

The Greensand ridges so typical of the previous section now begin to give way to chalk, which in turn provides a source for the various chalk streams which flow through this stretch and often join up with the canal. Perhaps the most defining feature of the local landscape here is the high ridge of hills to the south, which are often quite steep and consequently offer some quite stunning views, with particularly good examples to be had at Wigginton.

The canal winds its way through a gap in these hills, but they remain a dominant characteristic of the view throughout. The woods glimpsed around Ivinghoe in the last section now come into their own, with the Ashridge estate dominating the northern part of the section and extending down as far as Northchurch to the south, reaching east across Berkhamsted Common and into the fringes of Hemel Hempstead.

After an abundance of lakes in the previous section, pools of water are thin on the ground here, although the River Bulbourne, and the streams that feed it off the hills such as the Bulbourne Gutter, remain a fairly constant companion to the canal along here, with the River Gade flowing down the centre of Hemel Hempstead to join them.

ACCESS AND TRANSPORT

ROADS

The A41 exerts a noisy presence along this stretch, although its effects are rarely heard from the towpath. Both Tring and Berkhamstead sit to the north of the road, as does Hemel Hempstead, while the A4251 acts as a more sedate local artery linking the three. This latter road also passes through Bourne End and Boxmoor, and clings to the same valley as that occupied by the canal.

Hemel Hempstead acts as a magnet for more major A-roads linking the town to St Albans to the east, and points north. Otherwise, a network of local roads bring places such as Aldbury and Wiggington into the scene.

RAIL

This is a section well endowed with railway stations. That at Tring is close to the canal but a decent walk away from the town, while that at Berkhamsted is to the north of the town, again convenient for the canal, and also, as it happens, for the castle. Hemel Hempstead's station is in Boxmoor, very close to the canal and a fair distance from the modern part of the town, although a brisk walk from the old town. As elsewhere, trains run on the Euston line, linking London to the Midlands.

The main train operator serving the area is: Silverlink (01923 207298)
Otherwise, National Train Enquiries can be reached on 08457 484950.

BUSES

The following list sets out the main bus routes servicing this stretch, although it is advisable to check before using them, as some buses only run on certain days and others may have been withdrawn since publication of this Guide:

- 11 – *Hemel Hempstead Train Station to town centre (Arriva)*
- 30, 31 - *Hemel Hempstead to Berkhamsted via Aldbury*

Right: *The Bridgewater Monument, a pilgrimage spot for any canal enthusiast. (see* Seeing and Doing*)*

and Tring (Arriva)
- 61 - *Links Tring with Aylesbury and Luton (Arriva)*
- 63, 64 – *Aylesbury to Ivinghoe via Cheddington (Arriva)*
- 161 – *Aylesbury to Whipsnade via Wendover and Tring (Easy Bus/Country Rider)*
- 170 – *Tring to Marsworth (Arriva)*
- 207 – *Long Marston to Hemel Hempstead via Tring and Wiggington (Dacorum CVS)*
- 327 – *Hemel Hempstead Circular (Red Rose)*
- 387 – *Tring to Aldbury (Red Rose and Lutonian)*
- 500 – *Aylesbury to Watford via Tring, Berkhamsted and Hemel Hempstead (Arriva)*
- 501 – *Aylesbury to Watford via Tring and Hemel Hempstead (Red Rose)*
- 607 – *Tring to Watford via Northchurch and Berkhamsted (Arriva)*
- 873 – *Wiggington to Berkhamsted (Arriva)*

Contact details for bus operators in this area are listed below, although Traveline (www.traveline.org.uk) on 0870 6082608 can give details of specific services between 7 a.m. and 10 p.m.:

- Arriva The Shires, Luton (01923 682262)
- Dacorum CVS (01442 253935)
- Easy Bus/Country Rider (0870 7288188)
- Lutonian Buses (01582 492913)
- Red Rose Travel, Aylesbury (01296 399500)

TAXIS

The following list gives a selection of the taxi operators in this section:

- AAA Line Taxis, Tring (01442 890288)
- Aky Cars, Tring (01442 891234)
- Barrington Cars, Wiggington (01442 823263)
- Berkhamsted Cab Services, Berkhamsted (01442 877899)
- Bevs Cars, Tring (01442 824105)
- Choice Yellow Cabs, Berkhamsted (01442 875100)
- Choice Yellow Cabs, Hemel Hempstead (01442 246000)
- Diamond Cars, Tring (01442 890303)
- Gates Cars, Berkhamsted (01442 874747)
- Hemel Cars, Hemel Hempstead (01422 232353)
- Jeff's Taxis, Hemel Hempstead (01442 233392)
- Lynx Cars, Hemel Hempstead (01422 266644)
- Mike's Private Hire, Tring (01442 826161)
- TC Cabs, Wiggington (01442 875757)
- T.J. Taxis, Hemel Hempstead (01442 389090)

pposite above: *One of the many elegant sweeps the canal takes as it traces a path round Milton ynes.*
pposite below: *The Peace Pagoda in Milton Keynes' Willen Park was the first of its kind in the west.*

p: *Linford Lake is one of the many expanses of water created to add character to the fringes of Milton ynes.*
ove left: *Long stretches of tree-lined paths run alongside the towpath in Milton Keynes.*
ove right: *Milton Keynes' grid-road system allows for the creation of a number of wide boulevards.*

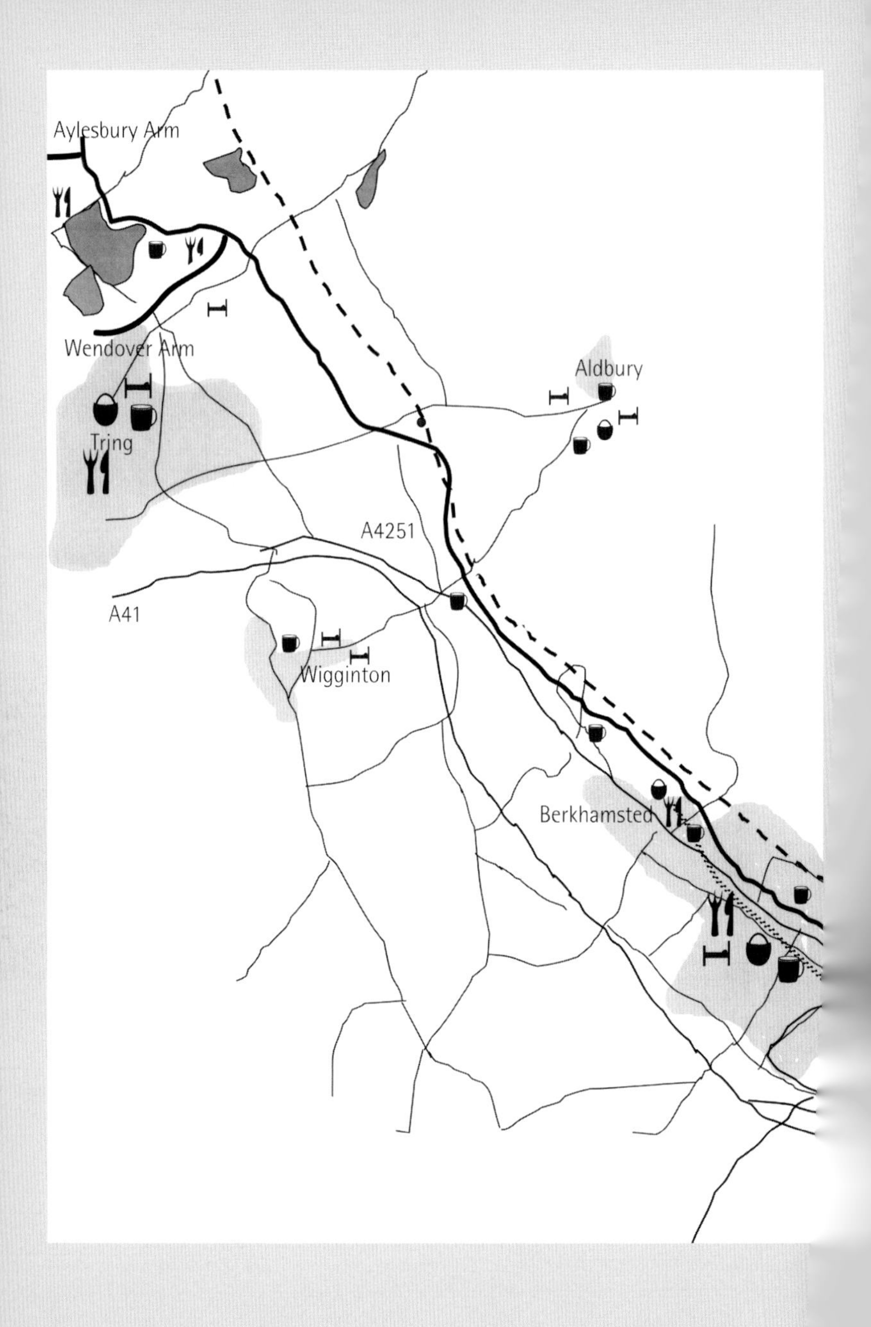
Aylesbury Arm
Wendover Arm
Tring
Aldbury
A4251
A41
Wigginton
Berkhamsted

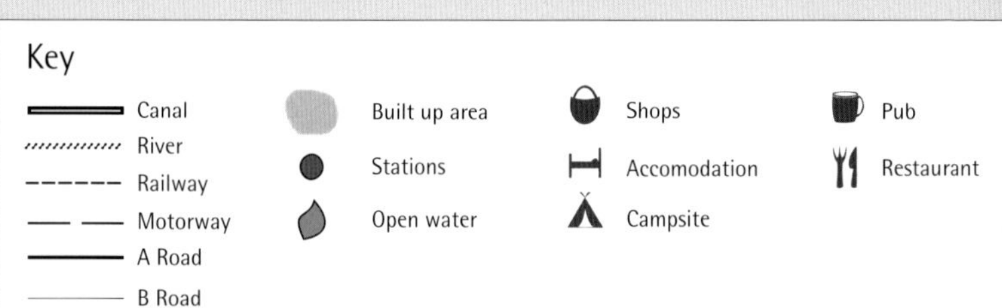
Key
Canal
River
Railway
Motorway
A Road
B Road
Built up area
Stations
Open water
Shops
Accomodation
Campsite
Pub
Restaurant

BASICS

INTRODUCTION

Both Tring and Berkhamsted were the subject of major re-vamps in the 1990s, and by and large these have been successful, although the latter remains a major traffic bottleneck, to the extent that enjoyment of the town can be spoiled by the sheer number of cars passing through.

Tring, on the other hand, has traffic-calming measures and a semi-pedestrianised feel to it, which is appropriate as its focus is on being a modern market town with a proud historical heritage. Both have a good mix of the familiar and the surprising, which, for those who have got used to the same old High Street names, can come as a refreshing change.

Old Hemel (the centre of the new town is covered in Section D) also has a pleasant High Street, with the added advantage that the big name stores do not impose their presence here, allowing local family-run shops full rein.

SHOPPING

Shopping opportunities in Tring are concentrated in the traffic-calmed High Street, although there is also a run of shops out along the western end of the B4365, consisting mainly of takeaway food shops and local shops. There is also a Londis in the northern end of the town, in the New Mill area.

The High Street itself has all the major banks and a full range of services, including a post office, with a Budgens in the centre and a large Tesco on the eastern fringe of the town. There is a small mall just off the High Street called Dolphin Square.

Many of the outlets along the High Street are independent, offering a dash of serendipity to the shopping experience. For example, there is not one but two ironmongers of the old school. This is also the older end of town, and it is worth looking up to take in some of the architecture and to admire some of the elegant street furniture.

There is a Farmers Market every second Saturday in Brook Street in Tring. The town also boasts a baker in Western Road (C.P. Atkins 01442 823392) that supplies bread made from locally milled flour, and Broughton Pastures based in The Silk Mill (01442 823993), which is reputed to be the UK's largest supplier of organic fruit wines.

Aldbury, outside Tring, has a village store with a sub-post office, while Northchurch, on the approach into Berkhamsted from the west, has its own shops including a butchers, an off-licence and a One Stop convenience store with sub-post office. There is a further run of shops in the stretch between Berkhamsted at Northchurch.

Berkhamsted itself has a long and varied shopping centre with a Waitrose supermarket sandwiched between the High Street and the canal, where there is also a Woods gift and garden centre. For those looking for supermarkets there is a Co-Op on the High Street, along with a Tesco metro.

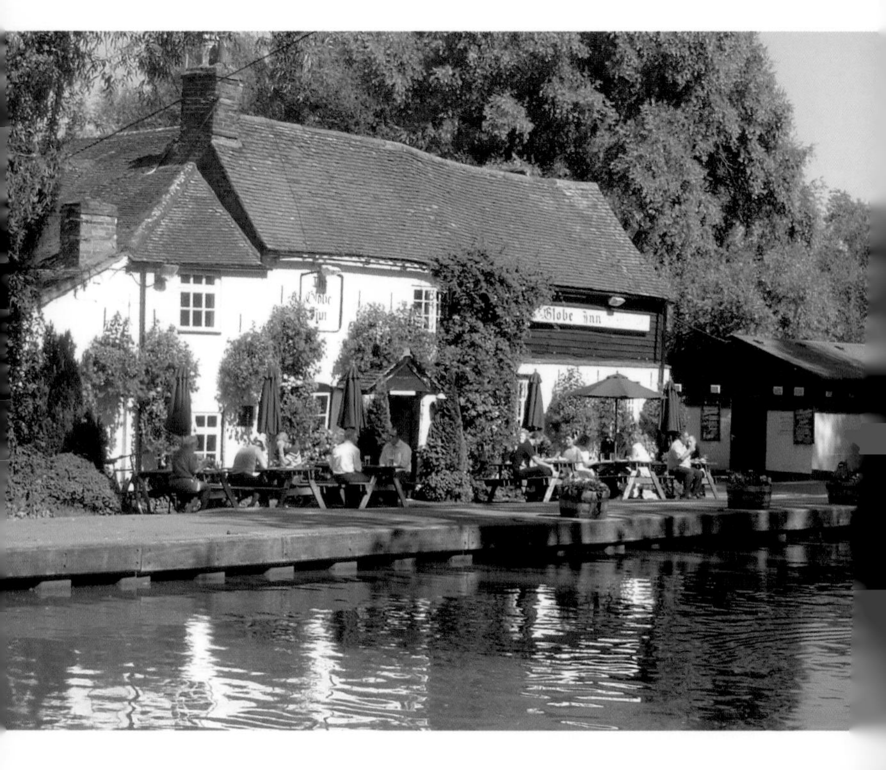

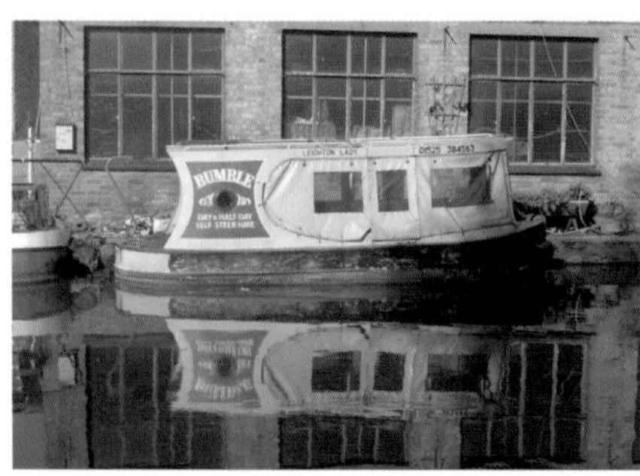

SECTION B MILTON KEYNES TO MARSWORTH

Top: *The Globe Inn at Linslade – a favourite photographer's spot.*
Above left: *The Bumble day-boat is a regular sight in and around Leighton Buzzard.*
Above right: *The Three Locks at Soulbury is the epitome of a canalside pub.*

Opposite above: *Cows grazing gently near Church Lock, just south of Linslade.*
Opposite below: *Bridge 1 on the Aylesbury Arm looks up at the Staircase Locks that form the ent to this canal.*

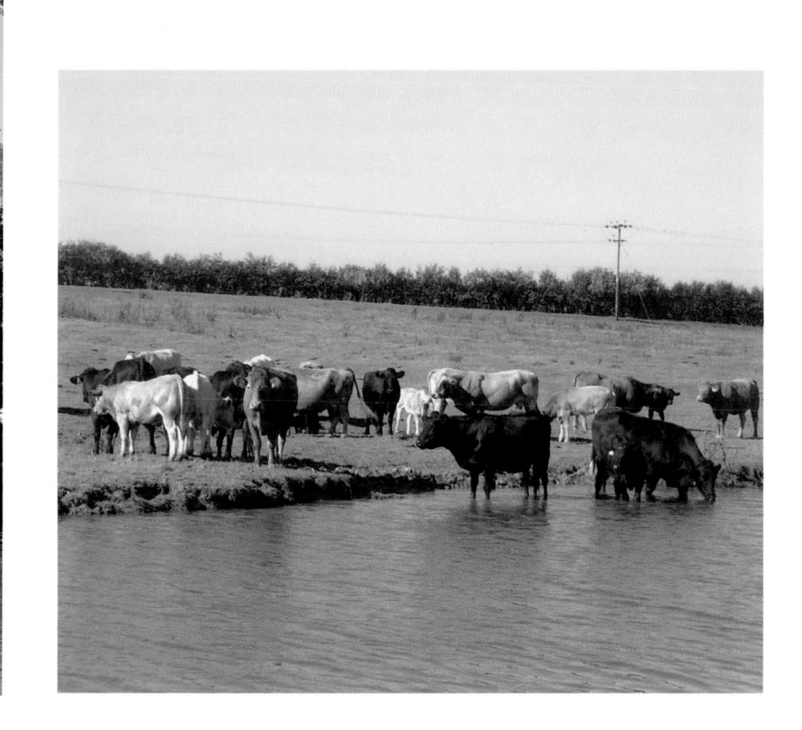

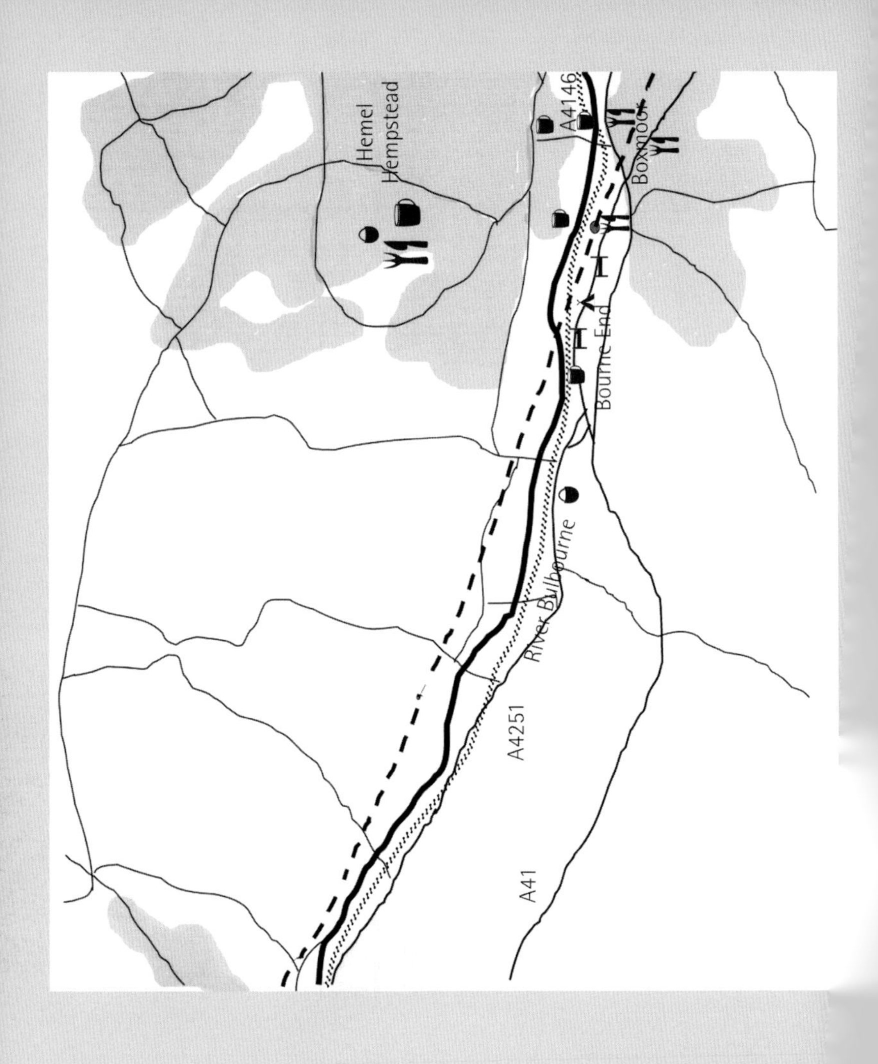
Hemel
Hempstead
A4146
Boxmoor
Bourne End
River Bulbourne
A4251
A41

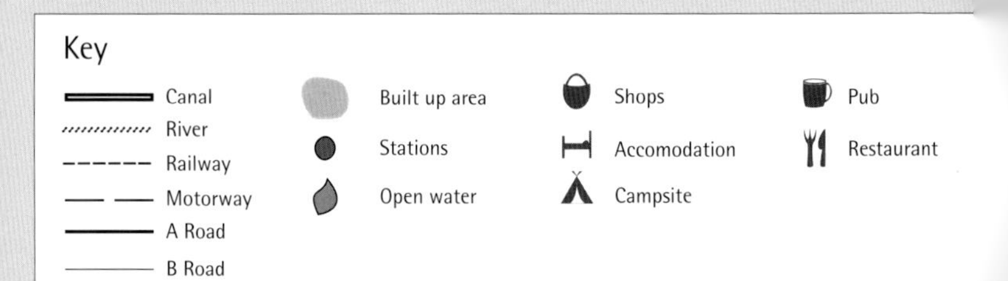
Key
Canal
River
Railway
Motorway
A Road
B Road
Built up area
Stations
Open water
Shops
Accomodation
Campsite
Pub
Restaurant

All the major banks are here and representatives of many of the larger High Street chains, but in among them are more unusual specialists, ranging from health-food shops to an outlet dealing simply in dolls' houses. There is also an old-style chemist and optician, and an arts-and-crafts shop, as well as local booksellers and a specialist kitchen shop. Curiously, there is even a shop for surfers in the town. Berkhamsted Farmers Market takes place in the High Street place every third Sunday of every month.

Bourne End has a large camping-supplies shop but little else, and Boxmoor's shopping experience is mainly confined to takeaway food outlets. Shopping in Hemel Hempstead is broken down into three areas: the Marlowes shopping mall and outdoor pedestrianised area; less fashionable but still useful shops along Marlowes Street, where there is also a covered market; and thirdly Hemel Old Town.

The first two of these are covered in the next section, while Hemel Old Town is a mixture of the often quite up-market through to the more prosaic, including the House of Elliot which sells antiques and collectables, a guitar shop and a delicatessen.

EATING AND DRINKING

PUBS

The following list covers many of the pubs in this section but cannot claim to be totally comprehensive. Many of those featured offer food, although serving times and menus will, naturally, vary:

- The Grand Junction Arms, Bulbourne (01442 890677) – *large family pub by Bridge 133, often offering BBQs in the summer*
- The Anchor, Tring (01442 823280) – *on the Western Road out of town.*
- The Bell Inn, Tring (01442 828357) – *on the High Street*
- The Robin Hood, Tring (01442 824912) – *on the eastern fringe of the town*
- The Black Horse, Tring (01442 890066) – *in the town centre just off the High Street*
- The New Mill, Tring (01442 825153) – *at the northern end of town near the Wharf*
- The Greyhound, Aldbury (01442 851228) – *an ivy-clad village-centre pub*
- The Valliant Trooper, Aldbury (01442 851203)
- The Greyhound Inn, Wigginton (01442 851228)
- The Cowroast Inn, Cowroast (01442 822287) – *a short stroll up from Bridge 137*
- The George and Dragon, Northchurch (01422 864533)
- The Boat, Berkhamsted (01442 877152) – *canalside pub on the edge of town*
- The Bull, High Street, Berkhamsted (01442 870364) – *canalside beer garden*
- The Crown, High Street, Berkhamsted (01442 863993)
- The Crystal Palace, Station Road, Berkhamsted (01442 862998) – *on the canal*
- The George, High Street, Berkhamsted (01442 862950)
- The Goat, High Street, Berkhamsted (01442 866936) – *specialises in folk music sessions*
- The Lamb, High Street, Berkhamsted (01442 862615)
- The Rising Sun, George Street, Berkhamsted (01442 864913)
- The Anchor, Bourne End (01442 866220) – *sixteenth-century timber-framed building*

Registered at Brentford. No 567
GRAND UNION CANAL CARRYING Co Ltd
London E.C.4

SECTION B MILTON KEYNES TO MARSWORTH

Opposite above: *St Mary the Virgin at Great Brickhill, a village with spectacular views.*
Opposite below: *The name of the Grand Union Canal Carrying Co. crops up time and again when you pass down this canal.*

Top: *Beacon Hill, Ivinghoe, stands out against the landscape, and was once an Iron-Age hillfort.*
Above: *The unusually named Heath & Reach lies just to the north of Leighton Buzzard.*

- The White Horse, Bourne End (01422 863888)
- The Swan, Boxmoor (01422 270488) – *also sells takeaway Thai food. A short walk from the canal*
- The Steam Coach, St Johns Road, Hemel Hempstead (01422 244480) – *across the cricket ground from the canal*
- The Fishery Inn, Hemel Hempstead (01442 261628)
- The Old Bell, Hemel Old Town (01422 252867)
- The Old Kings Arms, Hemel Old Town (01422 255348)
- The Rose and Crown, Hemel Old Town (01422 395054)

Cafés and fast-food outlets along the route and in surrounding areas include the following:

- Bluebell Café, Marsworth (01442 891708) – *homemade cakes sit alongside arts and crafts.*
- Banani, Frogmore Street, Tring (01442 827527)
- Chinatown, Akeman Street, Tring (01442 824831) – *Chinese takeaway*
- The Fish Shop, Akeman Street, Tring (01442 826296)
- P.A.M.S. Sandwich Bar, High Street, Tring (01442 824262)
- The Plaice, Dolphin Square, Tring (01442 828248)
- Sandwich Plus, Dolphin Square, Tring (01442 828296)
- Tringfellows, Parsonage Place, Tring (01442 825350)
- Proctors Plaice, Northchurch (01442 862460) – *fish and chips*
- Café Uno, High Street, Berkhamsted (01442 874856) – *on the ground floor of Berkhamsted Town Hall*
- Lots of Rice, Holiday Street, Berkhamsted (01442 865033) – *Thai/Sczechan takeaway*
- Berkos Kitchen, High Street, Berkhamsted (01442 876988) – *advertises itself as offering 'good old traditional English grub'*
- Kacey's Café Bar and Brasserie, Berkhamsted (01442 877066) – *garden terrace and internet access*
- McCoys, High Street, Berkhamsted (01442 866839) – *Fish and chips*
- Magoos, High Street, Berkhamsted (01442 870101) – *Wine and coffee house*
- Unicorn, High Street, Berkhamsted (01442 862369) – *Chinese takeaway*
- Way Inn, Berkhamsted (01442 864751) – *Christian centre with a restaurant and bookshop*
- Yeovil Café, Berkhamsted (01442 877663)
- The Coffee Cup Café, Hemel Old Town (01422 214443)
- Indian Hut, Boxmoor (01422 242700) – *Indian takeaway*

Tring is particularly blessed with Italian restaurants, while Berkhamsted has representatives from national chains as well as independent restaurants and hotel dining. There are one or two more unusual cuisines on the outskirts of Hemel Hempstead and in the Old Town. In addition, there is a mix of Chinese, Indian and Thai restaurants across the different towns and villages in this section.

The following list offers a selection of places to try:

- Balti Curry House, Tring (01422 827788)
- Da Vinci, Frogmore Street, Tring (01442 891300) – *Italian trattatoria*

- Forno Vivo, High Street, Tring (01442 890005) – *Italian restaurant*
- Francescos, High Street, Tring (01442 827258) – *Italian restaurant*
- Kristal Spice, High Street, Tring (01442 827032) – *Indian restaurant*
- Jubraj, High Street, Tring (01442 890386) – *Indian restaurant*
- Mighty Bite Pizzeria, Akeman Street, Tring (01442 823554)
- Brooke's Brasserie, Berkhamsted (01442 877211)
- Tamarinds Takeaway, Berkhamsted (01442 822333) – *Indian takeaway*
- Cape Fish, High Street, Berkhamsted (01442 879988) – *seafood restaurant*
- La Fiorentina, Lower Kings Road, Berkhamsted (01442 863003) – *Italian restaurant*
- Monsoon, High Street, Berkhamsted (01442 879829) – *Indian restaurant*
- The Orange Grove, London Road, Berkhamsted (01442 862370) – *Greek and Lebanese*
- New Akash, High Street, Berkhamsted (01442 865263) – *Indian restaurant*
- Pink Orchid (01442 878899) , Berkhamsted – *Thai restaurant*
- Punjab Brasserie, Berkhamsted (01442 863314) – *Indian restaurant*
- Regal of Berkhamsted, High Street, Berkhamsted (01442 865940) – *Peking cusine*
- Thai Cottage, Berkhamsted (01442 870808)

Chain restaurants operating along the High Street in Berkhamsted also include Ask (01442 878287), Café Rouge (01442 878141), Pizza Express (01442 879966) and Pizza et Pizza (01442 876366).

- Harvester, Boxmoor (01422 260515) – *near the station*
- Albertos, Hemel Old Town (01422 250063)
- Aragon Restaurant, in the Old Town Hall, Hemel Old Town (01422 228094)
- Cas Amigos, St. Johns Road, Hemel Hempstead (01422 264846) – *Mexican steak house a short*

Right: *An old town house in Castle Street, Berkhamsted.*

Below: *Castle Street in Berkhamsted has much to delight those with an eye for architectural detail.*

SECTION C MARSWORTH TO HEMEL HEMPSTEAD

Above: *Cowroast Marina on the edge of the rolling Dunstable Downs.*

Opposite above: *Berkhamsted's War Memorial in the heart of the town.*
Opposite below: *Seemingly wild horses prowl the common land at Boxmoor.*

Boats line the towpath at Winkwell.

walk north from the canal over the cricket ground

- Cochin, Hemel Old Town (01422 233777) – *South Indian coastal cuisine*
- The White Hart, Hemel Old Town (01422 265863) – *traditional restaurant*

SLEEPING

There is a wide variety of places to lay your head along this stretch, ranging from four-star luxury to basic B&Bs. The hotel chains also begin to exert a presence here, although these tend to be more at the budget-end of the spectrum. Camping, however, is difficult, as there are no formal sites.

HOTELS

- Pendley Manor Hotel, Tring (01442 891891) – *four-star hotel just up from the canal, located in 35 acres with full leisure facilities*
- Rose and Crown Hotel, Tring (01442 824071) – *twenty-seven rooms including family rooms and suites with four-poster beds*
- Travel Inn, Tring (0870 1977254)
- Stocks Country House Hotel, Aldbury (01442 851341) – *small hotel and country club enjoying spectacular views*
- Kings Arms Hotel, Berkhamsted (01442 866595) – *a Rothschild hotel with four-poster rooms and a fitness club*
- Penny Farthing Hotel, High Street, Berkhamsted (01442 872828) – *twenty rooms based in the centre of the town near the canal*
- The King's Arms, High Street, Berkhamsted (01442 866595)
- The Goat, High Street, Berkhamsted (01442 866936)

- The Watermill Hotel, Bourne End (01422 349955) – *A forty-nine-room hotel built around an old flour mill*
- Boxmoor Lodge Hotel, Boxmoor (01442 230770) – *family-run hotel and restaurant based in a seventeenth-century gatehouse*
- Hemel Hempstead Travel Inn, Bourne End (0870 2383309) – *in the A41 service area, sixty-four bedrooms*
- Southville Hotel, Hemel Hempstead (01442 251387) – *nineteen rooms, just off Old Hemel*

BED AND BREAKFASTS/GUEST HOUSES

- Catalpa Cottage, Tring (01442 826638) – *ground-floor double room with own parking*
- Cholesbury House, Tring (01442 758156) – *self-contained accommodation attached to a family home*
- The Gables, Tring (01442 828327) – *one double room*
- 16 Stoneycroft, Aldbury (01442 851294) – *one double room, one twin*
- Livingstone's B&B, Aldbury (01442 851527) – *one double room, two twins, in a private home in a conservation area*
- Stocks Farmhouse, Aldbury (01442 851397) – *two double rooooms, two twins*
- The Greyhound Inn, Wigginton (01442 851228) – *various accommodation*
- Rangers Cottage, Wigginton (01442 890155) – *Rothschild house set high up in Tring Park with excellent views*
- 305a High Street, Berkhamsted (01442 865136) – *three rooms*
- Broadway Farm B&B, Berkhamsted (01442 866541) – *one double room, two twins, on a working farm*
- Laurel Cottage, Berkhamsted (01442 851527) – *self-contained 'granny flat'*
- Ringshall Bed and Breakfast, Berkhamsted (01442 843396)
- Winnow Cottage, Berkhamsted (01442 873474) – *two twin rooms, one single*
- Alexandra Guest House, Hemel Hempstead (01442 242897)
- Bayview Guest House, Hemel Hempstead (01442 392828) – *seventeenth-century building that once housed Hemel's first bank*

CAMPING

There are no formal camping sites along this stretch. Despite this, there is a comprehensive camping shop in Bourne End, The Complete Outdoors Camping Shop (01442 873133).

BAILIWICK
OF
HEMEL HEMPSTEAD
THIS MARKET PLACE
WAS FORMED AND
THESE BUILDINGS
ERECTED BY
THE BAILIFF
AND THE
TOWN IMPROVEMENT COMMITTEE
A D 1888
MATTHEW LENO HIGH BAILIFF
JOHN ROBBINS D.D. VICAR
COMMITTEE
S STALLON CHAIRMAN
WILLIAM WHITE | W H CRANSTONE
ADAM J CHENNELS | FREDERICK MASON
GEORGE LOW F.R.I.B.A.
W. RALPH LOW A.R.I.B.A.
ARCHITECTS

posite above: *Hemel Old Town is a gem hidden away behind the more utilitarian modern centre.*
posite below left: *This lamppost/drinking fountain was erected in 1835 to mark the third tenary of the printing of the English Bible.*
posite below right: *Hemel Old Town's market place owes its existence to a Victorian Town rovement Committee.*

ve: *Signs outside the Old Bell in Old Hemel offer rousing advice.*

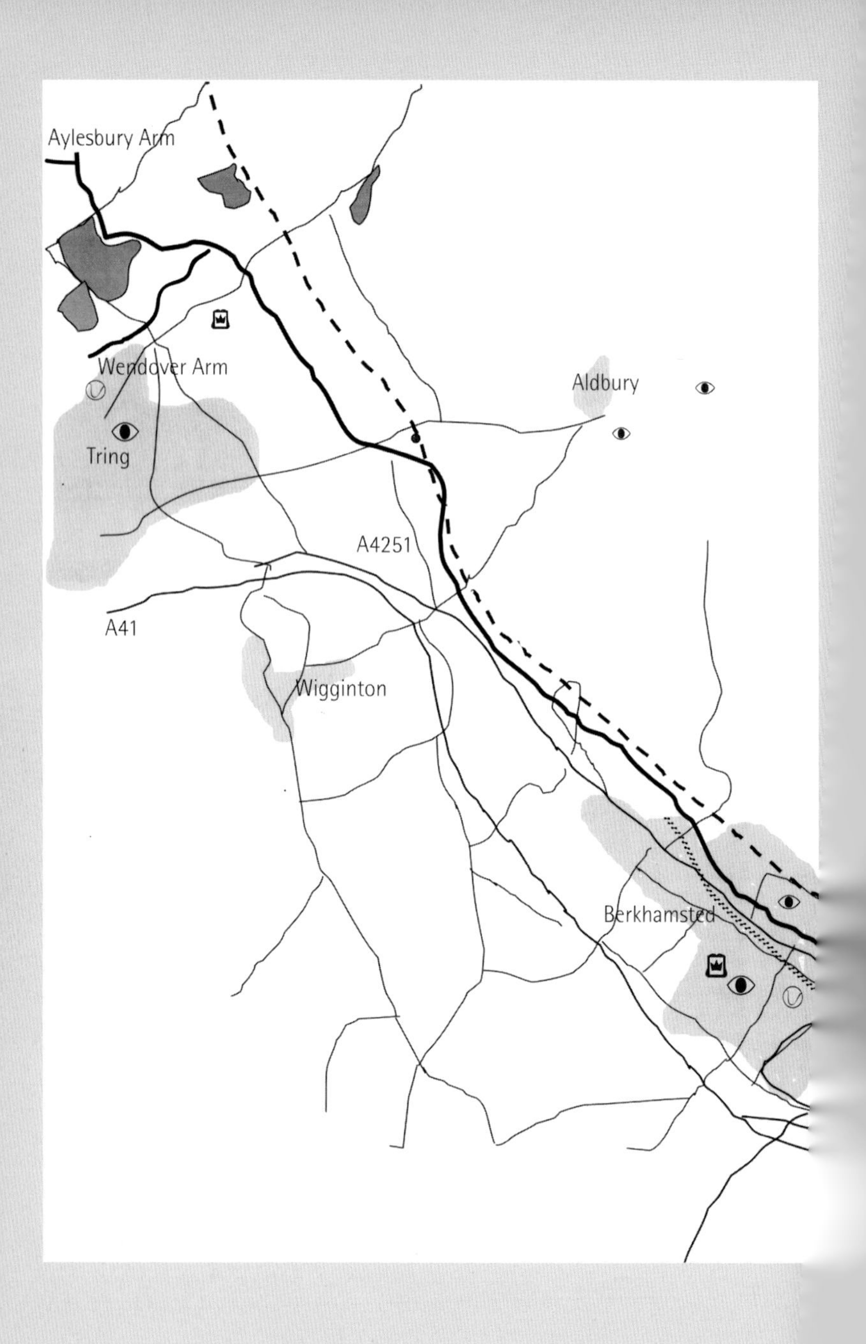

Aylesbury Arm
Wendover Arm
Tring
Aldbury
A4251
A41
Wigginton
Berkhamsted

Key
Canal
River
Railway
Motorway
A Road
B Road
Built up area
Stations
Open water
Site/Sight
Leisure
Entertainment
Culture

SEEING AND DOING

INTRODUCTION

Tring and Berkhamsted are both substantial market towns with a long history which they display proudly, making this a section only the foolhardy would rush through. The section ends on the outskirts of Hemel Hempstead and includes the older part of that town, an area that includes most of the history and cultural opportunities, if not the more modern attractions of sports and nightlife.

SIGHTS

Tring offers much to the casual visitor. A stroll along the High Street can reveal a range of building styles, although beware, as all may not be as it seems. The Rose and Crown opposite the church, for example, may appear to be a classic example of an Elizabethan half-timbered inn, but was built in this style in 1905 after the original was demolished.

Visitors are also advised to follow the wall-painted sign taking them up Akeman Street towards the Walter Rothschild Zoological Museum, which houses an excellent collection of stuffed mammals, birds and reptiles as well as insects. Bequeathed to the nation in 1937, the collection is now part of the Natural History Museum. Look out in particular for the dodo, while children always seem to enjoy the sharks.

> In 1902 Walter Rothschild introduced the Glis Glis, or Edible Dormouse, to Tring Park. They look like a small grey squirrel and are something of a nuisance to locals within the 25-mile radius of Tring, where they live, as they often choose to hibernate in roof-spaces and are a protected species.

Just beyond the museum on the corner with Park Road are the Louisa Cottages, almshouses built in 1893 for retired workers from the Rothschild Estate. Appropriately enough, these enjoy excellent views out onto Tring Park, which belongs to Tring Mansion, now an arts educational school.

A 300-acre park managed by the Woodland Trust, Tring Park was planted and landscaped in the eighteenth century, and walkers can access a number of monuments such as Nell Gwyn's Obelisk and a summer house. The obelisk's name is a reference to the fact that Henry Guy, Clerk to Charles II's Treasury, built the manor and allowed Nell Gwyn to live here, which must have constituted a smart career move. There is also an avenue of lime trees planted by the Rothschilds, who bought the estate in 1872.

Tring's parish church of St Peter and St Paul dates mainly from the fifteenth century, although parts of it are older. The walls were built using flints and Totternhoe stone, and the tower's walls are 5ft-thick. The tower is topped off with a 'Hertfordshire spike'. Inside, there are fourteen stone corbels in the arches of the nave cut into the shape of animals and unusual creatures, including a clawed monster with the head and body of a woman, which casts some concerns over the state of mind of the original carver. Back on the High Street, look out for Church Square, opened up as part of the early 1990s improvement measures, and the Memorial Gardens at the eastern end of town.

Top: *Look up to spot the unusual architecture on show in Tring.*
Above: *Although only ruins remain, Berkhamsted Castle was once one of the most famous royal residences in the kingdom.*

Opposite above: *This self-explanatory sign hangs above a house in a Tring side-street.*
Opposite below: *The Louisa Cottages in Tring have an excellent view out over the park.*

SPIDERS

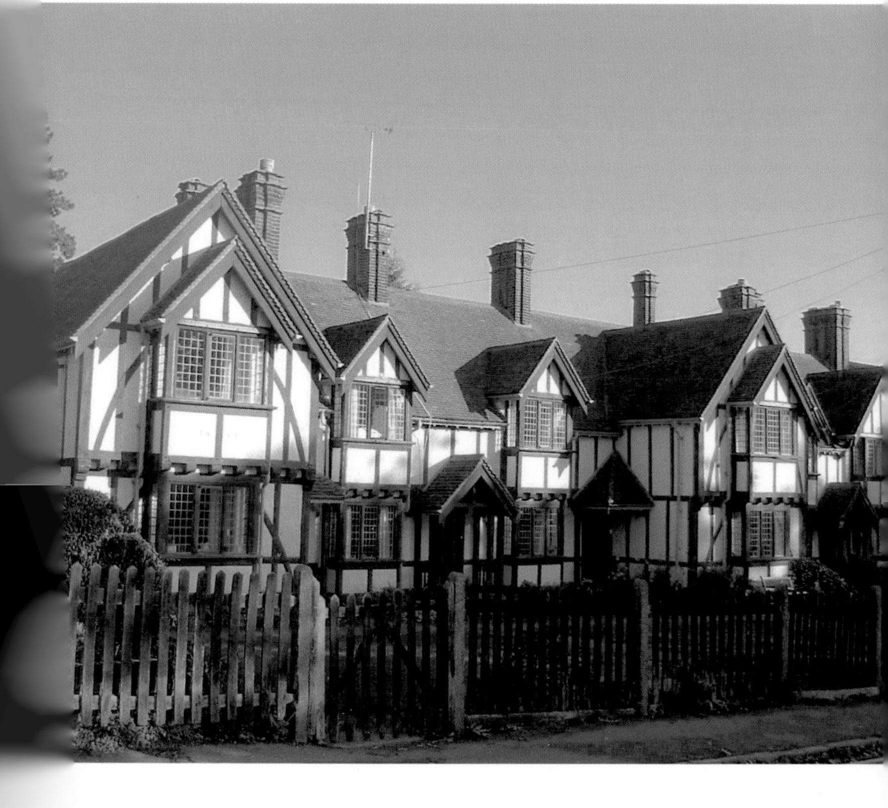

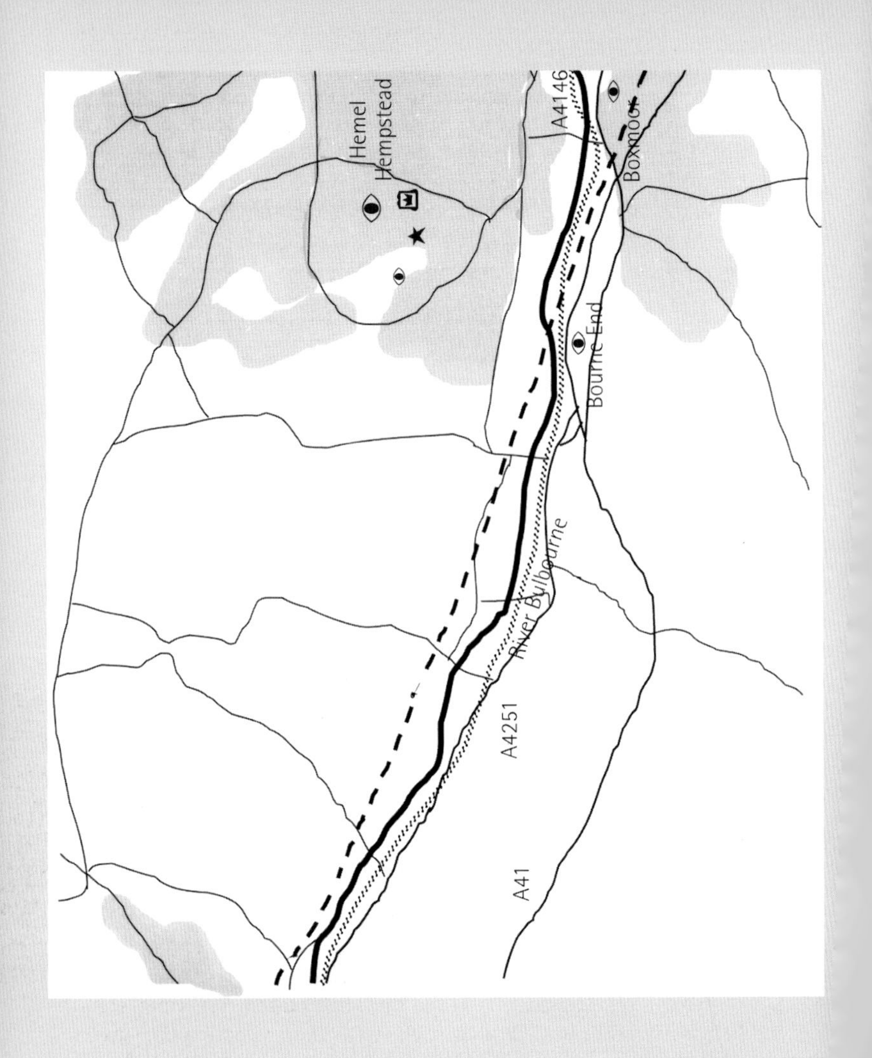
Hemel Hempstead
A4146
Boxmoor
Bourne End
River Bulbourne
A4251
A41

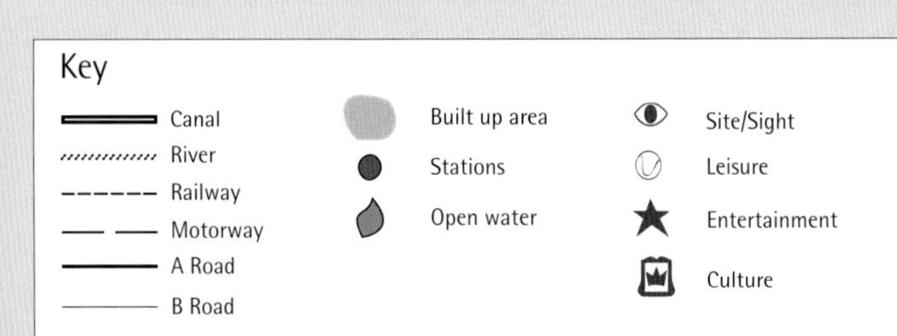
Key
Canal
River
Railway
Motorway
A Road
B Road
Built up area
Stations
Open water
Site/Sight
Leisure
Entertainment
Culture

There's a dovecot and weathervane in the grounds of Galleon Cottage in Aldbury. It is worth pausing here to take in the pond with its stocks and whipping post. Inside Aldbury's church of St John the Baptist lies the imposing Pendley Chapel, home to the late medieval effigy of Sir Robert Whittingham, whose feet lie on a 'wild man'. Aldbury acts as a gateway for Ashridge Park, now home to a Management College. Although the grounds and gardens are private, the latter are open to the public on summer weekends.

The half-timbered New Villas near Tring Station are worth pausing to look at, as is the blue and white old Toll House the other side of the bridge, where boatmen used to have to stop and run up the bank to pay their tolls.

Anyone with an interest in the canals is almost obliged to make a pilgrimage to see the Doric column that is the Bridgewater Monument within Ashridge Park (see Sampling). The monument was erected in 1832 and commemorates the Third Duke who, along with his engineer James Brindley, pioneered the technology of cutting canals on his other estate at Worsley outside Manchester.

The canal that now carries his name was the country's first, and defied the accepted wisdom of the time to show that such an achievement was possible. If the canal was to be his most lasting tangible memorial, this monument is also fitting. The monument can be climbed and from the top it is just about possible to make out the Grand Union, and although neither Bridgewater nor Brindley had a hand in this canal, it is appropriate that some kind of canal should be visible.

Berkhamsted was the birthplace of the novelist Graham Greene, and each year a festival is held in his honour, at the school which he attended and where his father was headmaster.

Berkhamsted Town Council produces a useful (and free) Heritage Walk pamphlet, available from the library and civic offices, while the Graham Greene Birthplace Trust produces another called The Graham Greene Trail (available from the same places). Particular highlights from the eastern end of the town include The Dower House, a lime-green early nineteenth-century house with a porch and doorcase, and The Polars, a row of middle-class houses from the same era, one of which was the birthplace of the actor Sir Michael Hordern.

Towards the centre there is the town hall, which was designed by the eccentric Victorian architect, Edward Buckton Lamb, in the gothic style, and was rescued from dereliction in 1992. There is also the Court House, an Elizabethan hall where the town corporation used to meet, and 179 High Street, a building that dates back only to the 1920s but has some fine art-nouveau wood carvings.

Out by the western end of town it is worth looking out for the Sayer Alsmhouses, John Sayer having been cook to King Charles II. These were instituted in 1684 to provide shelter for poor widows, and continue to do so to this day. Also nearby is The Monk's House (now Café Rouge), a sixteenth-century building, and the Bourne School (now the Britannia Building Society), which was the first school to be opened in the town for 200 years when it was founded in 1737.

Castle Street, which also houses Berkhamsted School, is worth walking down just to take in some of the interesting architectural features of the houses that line its sides. This street used to be the second most important in the town as, unsurprisingly, given its name, it linked the castle with the High Street. The Boote beyond the school is dated 1605, and was once one of six pubs along this road.

Above: *Bedmond church looks like it might be more at home in the Wild West.*

Opposite above: *This glorious lychgate protects the entrance to Abbot's Langley church.*
Opposite below: *The Crow Bridge outside Watford, and evidence that the canals are about more than just narrowboats.*

An unexpected, but genuine, totem pole just outside Berkhamsted.

Another was the Gardener's Arms, one of a pair of mid-nineteenth-century ale houses.

Berkhamsted School was founded in 1541 and its old school hall has early Tudor brickwork and gothic windows. These can be best appreciated from the churchyard. There is also an impressive gate guarding the entrance to the school. The school was extended considerably in the nineteenth and twentieth centuries, and in 1994 took the radical step of admitting girls.

> Clementine Hozier, later the wife of Sir Winston Churchill, was born in Berkhamsted, and was educated in the building originally established as Bourne School, by then Berkhamsted School for Girls.

The church of St Peter, on the corner of Castle Street, has a particularly ornate war memorial, and is one of the largest churches in Hertfordshire. Look out for the large yew tree on the corner, so old no one can date it.

> The church of St Peter was used to house prisoners during the Civil War, and at one point also acted as the town's fire station.

Berkhamsted Castle, to the north of the town just behind the railway station, can be accessed either from Brownlow Road or Castle Street. Parking is limited near the castle, so it may be best to use one of the many town car parks.

The castle is free to visit and a surprising amount of it remains. It is easy to make out (and climb) the castle's Motte or main mound, as well as the line of the moat. The Bailey, the area within the bounds of the walls, is also visible, and there are some signs indicating the uses different areas were put to.

North of the castle lies Berkhamsted Common, a particular favourite of Graham Greene, who chose the spot to play the now infamous game of Russian Roulette, which, thankfully, he survived. It was also here that he ran to when fleeing his school, and the spot featured subsequently in his writing.

On leaving the town by the canal, you may also make out a totem pole on the right by some modern housing. This is the genuine article and was given to the owner of the local timber yard that originally stood on this site. It has four faces on it and there is even a separate publication detailing the symbolism of the different carvings.

Bridge 143 is known locally as 'Battles Bridge', a nod to the time when navvies would gather and tempers would boil over.

Finally, in Berkhamsted, you may notice a sign welcoming you to the Port of Berkhamsted. This is the section of water between Ravens Lane and Castle Street, once a bustling hive of industry occupied by a number of boatyards, as well as supporting industry such as coal merchants and timber yards.

This industrial theme once continued into Bourne End, whose mill, once known as the Domesday Mill, is today a hotel. The village is bisected by the A41 and was once famous for its watercress beds, fed by the village's chalk stream that now flows into and alongside the canal. A little further down, Winkwell is set off from the busy main road and is worth visiting for its Three Horseshoes pub.

The Boxmoor Trust Centre outside Bourne End (01442 253300) manages 450 acres of amenity land, woodland and agricultural holdings within Hemel Hempstead and Bovingdon, some of which dominates the scenery on the approach into the modern town of Hemel Hempstead. Comprising mainly water meadows, the land was originally granted by Elizabeth I to her favourite, the Earl of Leicester, in 1574, and is today in the care of twelve trustees publicly elected for life.

Hemel Hempstead Old Town is worth strolling through both to provide contrast with the bleak 1960s and 1970s modernity of the new town, and for its own sake. It is the sort of place in which it is worth training your eyes to glance upwards, away from the shop windows and towards the nineteenth-century rooflines of the various properties that still dominate the High Street.

The façade of the Old Bell has two inscriptions, one of which offers the plea, 'God have mercy on the sinner, who must write with no dinner'.

Although it may look like it has Victorian origins, the Old Town dates back to Saxon times. However, the High Street itself, originally known as Market Street, probably dates to the seventeenth century, and inscriptions in the leaden heads of drainpipes suggest a period of expansion early in the following century. The Old Bell, in the centre of the High Street, is dated 1603. A bad fire in 1749 caused a re-think, and it is from this date that the foundations of the current High Street were laid.

The Old Market Place in the centre was built by the Town Improvement Committee in 1888, and sits just above St Mary's church, which in turn seems to nestle in a hollow to the west. At the northern end there is a more half-timbered influence, and also the charming multi-coloured cottages that sit in the area known as 'below railings', for reasons that are self-evident.

At the far northern end of the street there is a lamp-post erected by public subscription in 1848, which bears a relief of the classic Holbein representation of an aged Henry VIII. This is a homage to the king who presented the town with its charter of incorporation in 1539; it is said in gratitude to his auditor,

SECTION D HEMEL HEMPSTEAD TO BATCHWORTH

Top left: *The Boys Home pub depicts the relief many must have felt when the troops finally returned in 1918.*
Top right: *Only joking – or are they?*
Above: *Metal masks in Watford's centre celebrate the town's various 'twins'.*

Opposite above: *This Chipperfield pub comes complete with its own double-decker for hire!*
Opposite below: *Common Moor Lock, overlooking the River Gade near Croxley Green.*

John Waterhouse, who had entertained him to a fitting standard at the nearby Manor House, 'The Bury'.

While in this area, Gadebridge Park is worth a visit. This large park runs from the Old Town centre along the Gade Valley on both sides of the Leighton Buzzard Road. Within it are, not only St Mary's church, but the remains of the old Charter Tower, and the site of a Roman Villa, excavated in the early 1960s and re-excavated in 2000.

Finally, at this end of Hemel, there is a curiosity outside the Cas Amigos restaurant in St Johns Road, opposite the cricket ground that acts as a green space on the northern approach to the town by canal. This is another commemorative lamp-post-cum-drinking fountain, erected 'for the public benefit' in 1835 to mark the third centenary of the printing of the English Bible. An inscription quotes from John IV in the Good Book: 'Whosoever drinketh of this water shall thirst again. But whosoever drinketh of the water that I shall give him shall never thirst but the water I shall give him shall be within him a well of water springing up into everlasting life'.

CULTURE AND ENTERTAINMENT

There is a good variety of cultural attractions along this stretch, and a visit to the local tourist-information centres in Tring (on Akeman Street 01442 823347), Berkhamsted (in the Civic Centre on the High Street 01442 228882) or Hemel Hempstead (in the pedestrianised area of the Marlowes shopping centre 01442 867827) can unearth surprises.

The Kodak Tower in Hemel epitomises the town's 1960s expansion.

The Court Theatre at Pendley in Tring (01442 824673) is set in a Victorian building adjacent to the Pendley Manor Hotel, and is a few minutes south of Bridge 135. The theatre has a regular programme of touring and local artists, ranging from tribute pop and rock bands through to comedy, musicals and cabaret.

Berkhamsted Civic Centre (01442 228918) is home to the Berkhamsted Jazz Society and Film Society, and also hosts regular performances by local voluntary drama societies and music ranging from folk to rock. Berkhamsted Jazz, in the Civic Centre, is one of the most popular jazz venues in the South East, embracing all styles, and its concerts are often sell-outs. On the subject of music, Berkhamsted School is a regular venue for the local Dacorum Symphony Orchestra, which also operates the Dacorum Sinfonietta Chamber Orchestra.

The Old Town Hall in Old Hemel (01442 228091) is another arts venue, offering a varied programme of drama, talks, dance, comedy and music, and is convenient for those cruising the canal. In addition to these venues, various pubs also host regular music evenings, a particular hotspot being The Goat in Berkhamsted (01442 866936).

Children may be interested in the amenities at Gadebridge Park off Hemel Old Town, which include a large playground, a paddling pool and crazy golf, as well as giant chess and draughts, or at Long Chaulden, close to the canal on the approach into Hemel (access from Bridge 148). The latter has an adventure playground and indoor activities.

If it's night clubs you're after then this is not a fruitful stretch, although there are plenty in Section D. There is no shortage of sports and leisure centres though, including Tring Sports Centre (01442 228957), which has a swimming pool and a full-sized artificial pitch, as well as other sporting facilities. Used by the local school during term time, it is open to the public in the evenings and during school holidays.

> The Berkhamsted Bowmen claims to be the oldest archery club in England.

Berkhamstead Sports Centre (01442 228123) is a larger centre, also with a pool, as well as a fitness centre and outdoor floodlit sports facilities. There are also plenty of opportunities for football, tennis and squash in the Canal Fields area of Berkhamsted. Hemel Hempstead also has a variety of sporting facilities, covered in more detail in Section D. Berkhamsted also has a Kidszone (01442 878441), offering indoor fun for children.

Finally, in this section, Dacroum Sports Centre on Park Road in Hemel Hempstead (01442 228188) is a sports complex with a 25m competition pool, and a similar sized outdoor pool (open mid-April to mid-October), as well as a fitness centre.

No Vehicular Access
except for residents and
British Waterways vehicles.

SECTION E BATCHWORTH TO BRENTFORD

Opposite above: *The River Colne and canal flow side by side at Copper Mill Lock.*
Opposite below: *One of the many long stretches of canal outside Iver and towards Uxbridge.*

Above: *The Glaxo Building outside Brentford is a landmark visible for miles around.*

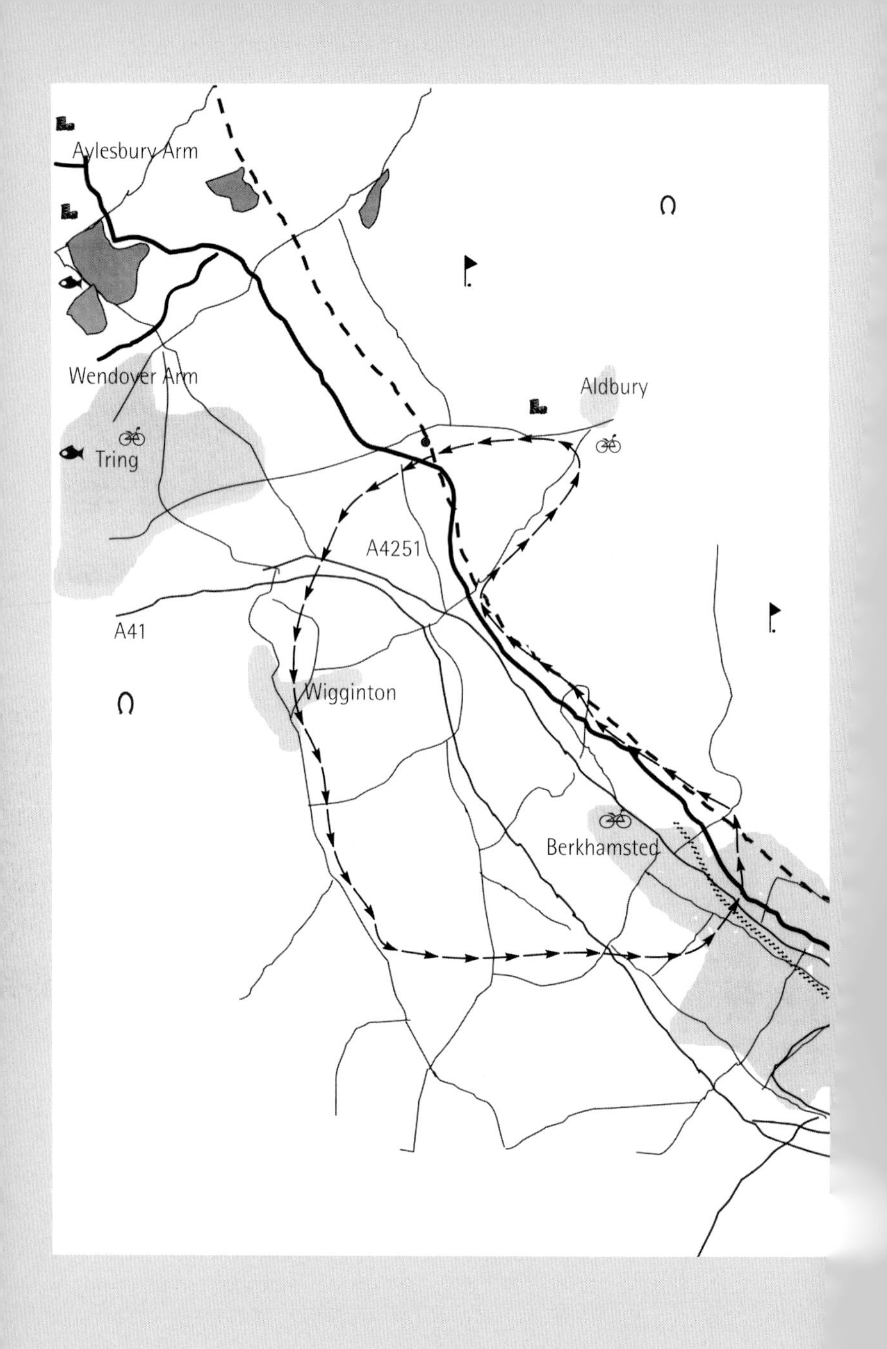
Aylesbury Arm
Wendover Arm
Tring
Aldbury
A4251
A41
Wigginton
Berkhamsted

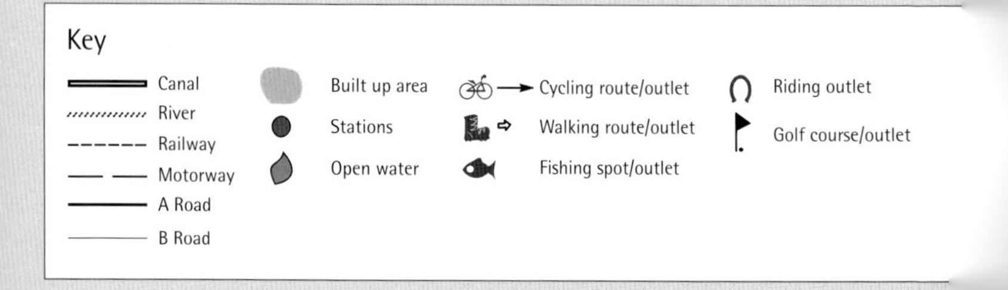
Key
Canal
River
Railway
Motorway
A Road
B Road
Built up area
Stations
Open water
Cycling route/outlet
Walking route/outlet
Fishing spot/outlet
Riding outlet
Golf course/outlet

SAMPLING

INTRODUCTION

Teetering on the edge of London, this section has much to recommend it in the variety of options it offers for sampling. Walking routes in particular are many and varied, although the steep hills either side of the canal can make for tough going. Those looking to linger here are recommended to visit the Chilterns Area of Natural Beauty website (see Learn More and Links) for downloads of recommended walks and cycle and horse-riding routes along this section.

WALKING

Other than the towpath, the main designated walking route through this section is the Ridgeway, which cuts across the north-western corner of the map, passing between Wigginton and Tring. A section of Grim's Ditch lies to the west of Aldbury, where there is a patchwork of public footpaths, many of which link up with paths through the woodland encompassed by the Ashridge Estate and Berhamsted Common, to the east of that same village.

A similar network exists on the slopes to the north of Berkhamsted, although the hills to the north between here and Hemel Hempstead are less walker-friendly. Tring Reservoirs also provide a good walking spot, with flat and firm surfaces especially suitable for those less able to meet the gradients that feature elsewhere in this section. The reservoirs have car parks, although these carry a small charge.

Duckie's Piece in Aldbury covers 2 acres on a hillside divided by the Ridgeway path. This area is a haven for flora and fauna, including common milkwort, clustered bellflower and lady's bedstraw, as well as redwings and various different types of finches, along with dozens of variety of butterfly. Aldbury also has its own way-marked Millennium Walk.

To the north of Aldbury the Ashridge Estate, now owned by the National Trust, covers 4,000 acres, and has a 16-mile boundary walk as well as six self-guided walks. There is a car park and visitor centre near to the Bridgewater Monument, and two short trails for those with restricted mobility. Call 01442 851227 for more details, or visit the National Trust website (see Learn More and Links).

The towpath of the old Wendover Arm offers a delightful walk. The nearby Halton House was once owned by Lionel de Rothschild, and the blue Rothschild Bridge halfway along the route, which carries his coat-of-arms, looks magnificent reflected in the water on a sunny day.

The waterway is in the process of being restored and this may be the best time to walk it, with many stretches still holding water and the wildlife settled and undisturbed by passing boats. Look out for the section of 'Wides' near the source of the spring, whose supply of water was a major plus-point for the original backers of the canal. Walk C takes advantage of some of the paths to the south of the towpath near Winkwell, to allow the walker to enjoy the pleasures of walking between the canal and the 'gamine' River Bulbourne, which dips and darts along the southern part of this stretch. It then strikes south up the side of the valley to offer a series of spectacular views.

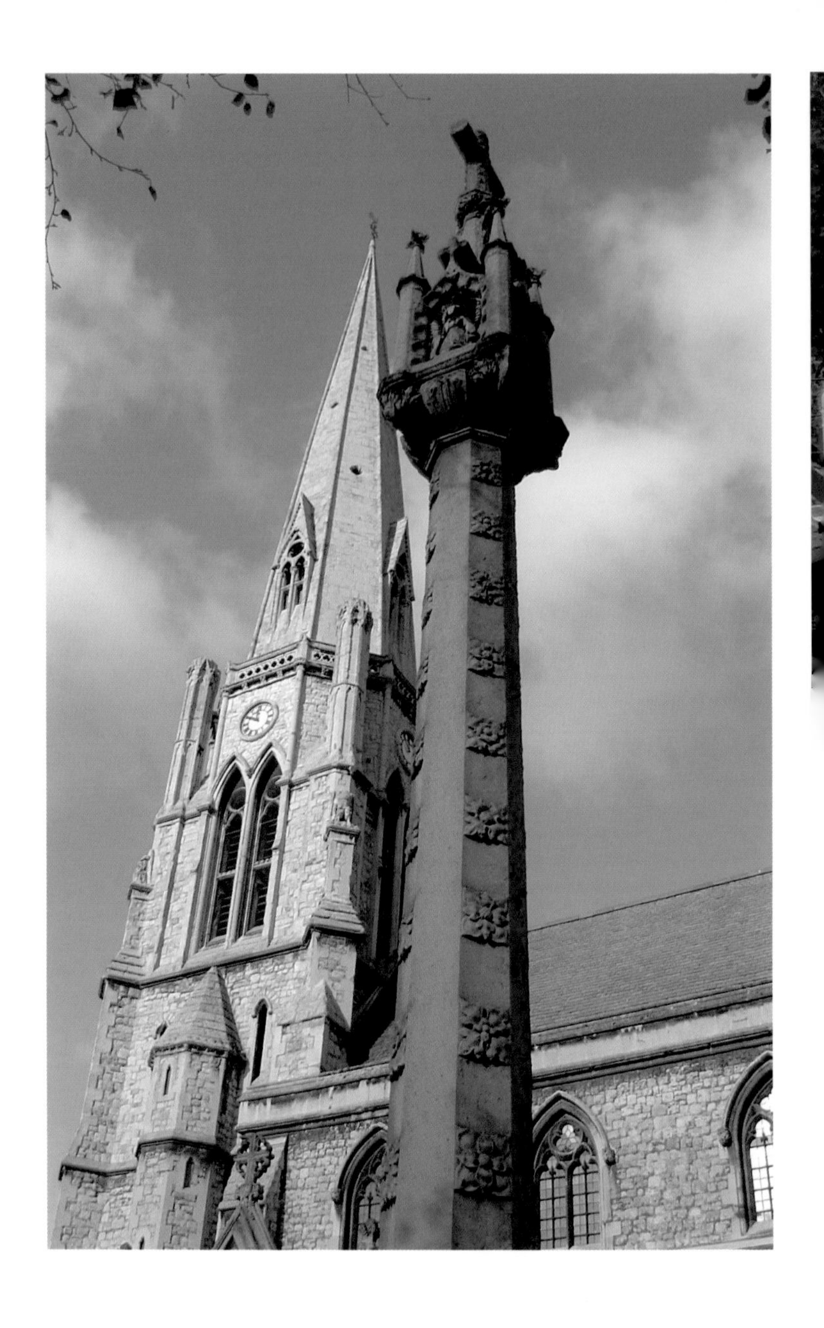

SECTION E BATCHWORTH TO BRENTFORD

Above: *Ealing's Church of Christ the Saviour and adjacent war memorial provide a contrast to the modern shopping centres nearby.*

Opposite above: *At over 11ft, Denham Deep Lock is well named.*
Opposite below: *Denham Village is an oasis of gentility hidden behind a maze of busy main roads.*

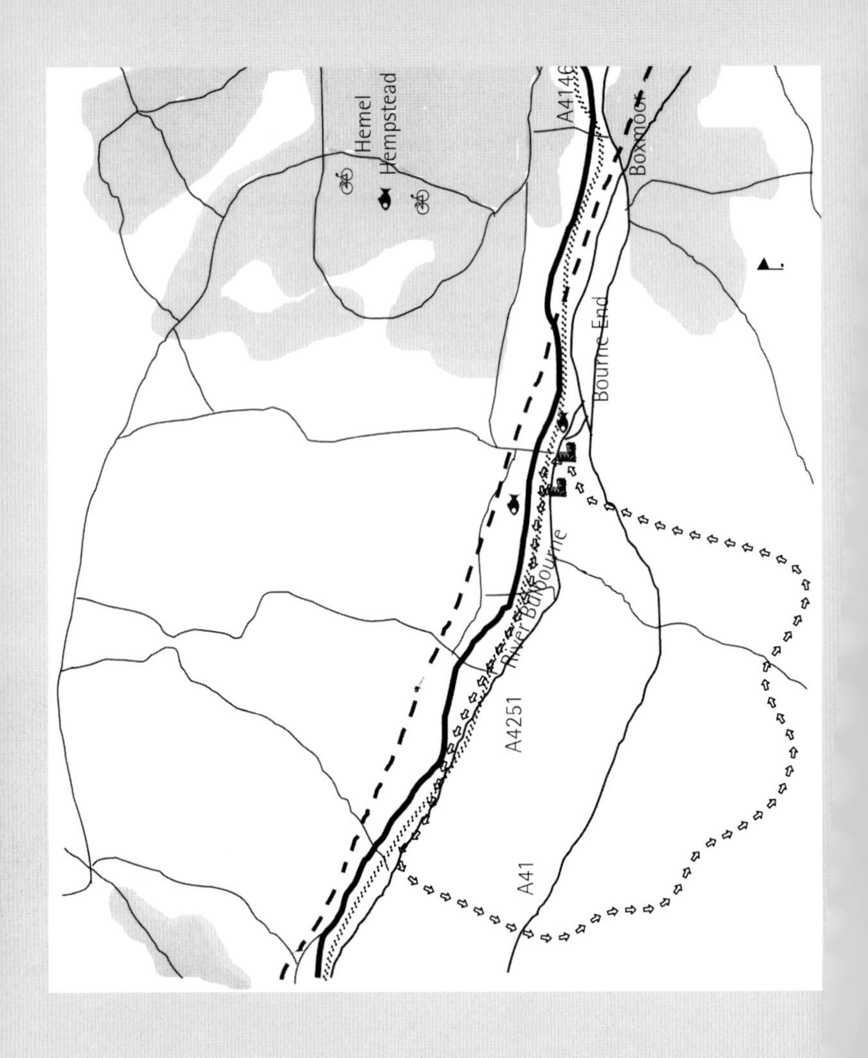
Hemel Hempstead
A4146
Boxmoor
Bourne End
River Bulbourne
A4251
A41

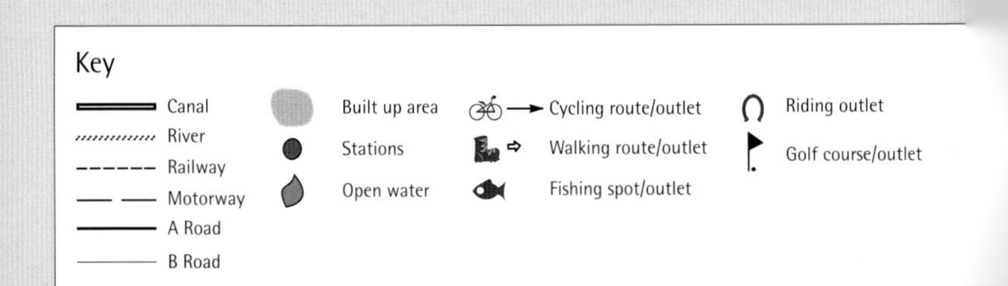
Key
Canal
River
Railway
Motorway
A Road
B Road
Built up area
Stations
Open water
Cycling route/outlet
Walking route/outlet
Fishing spot/outlet
Riding outlet
Golf course/outlet

SECTION C WALK

Winkwell and the Bulbourne Valley

Description:	*A steep climb up the valley side using field paths, returning via a golf course*
Distance:	*6 miles*
Duration:	*2.75 hours*
Starting point:	*Grid Reference 027064, OS Explorer 182*
Nearest Refreshment:	*The Three Horseshoes pub in Winkwell.*

Park in the Three Horseshoes car park. The pub is easy to miss, being down a single-track road by a petrol station off the A4251, just off the A41 on the Hemel Hempstead side of Bourne End. Head north on the towpath with the pub behind you and the river to your left, past a series of locks, until you reach Bridge 144, where you turn left to cross another bridge over the river, forking left at the junction to reach the main road.

Turn left and, after about 50 yards, pick up Gardenfield Lane on the opposite side of the road. The path becomes a tree-covered track and you must go left at each of the next two forks until you reach an underpass under the very busy A41. Cross the stile the other side and continue downhill past a copse, until you reach a T-junction, where you turn left.

Follow this round to the right and pass through a metal gate onto a minor road. Follow the road to a bend where you pick up a path by the side of a field, heading uphill. Follow this until you come out onto a road where you turn left and then right after 100 yards, following a path that traces the edge of a golf course. Follow this round to another road where you turn left, and then after a short while left again, into Gorsefield Wood. Keep to the left, passing the Golf Course Clubhouse, and follow the well-marked path over the course to a footbridge. This takes you over the A41, and then down to a road where you turn right until you rejoin the track down to the pub.

Walking equipment outlets along this section include:

- The Complete Outdoors Camping Shop, Bourne End (01442 873133) – *a good range of walking kit.*

CYCLING

The towpath and the surrounding network of roads and bridleways make this a good area for planning cycle routes, although this is not an area for the faint-hearted when it comes to hills.

A good route for sampling this section by bike, taking in roads, canal towpath and even a short section of the Ridgeway, starts at Aldbury, where you pick up Newground Road, the main road heading south out of the village, and follow it until you reach Bridge 136 on the canal. Turn left, heading south-east, and keep with the towpath all the way into Berkhamsted, a total of around 3.5 miles, during which the towpath switches sides a couple of times.

THE SWAN
CHILL-OUT ON OUR PATIO+GARDEN!

SECTION E BATCHWORTH TO BRENTFORD

Opposite above: *The Slough Arm, a long straight stretch of canal built to carry bricks.*
Opposite below: *The Swan at Iver, a good starting point for a walk.*

Above: *Harefield's millennium sculpture commemorates different elements of the village's history.*

Halfway through the locks, at the un-numbered bridge just after Lock 52, leave the canal by turning right. On reaching the High Street, turn right and then take the first left, heading uphill in a south-westerly direction. At the crossroads by a water tower, turn right, and then, after 250 yards, pick up the bridleway on your left. This leads you under the A41 via an underpass, and heads to the right of Marlin Chapel Farm.

Shortly after the farm, pick up the minor road and turn left at the junction, then proceed until you reach a road, where you turn right. The route still climbs, but more gradually now, and takes you into Wigginton via Wigginton Bottom, and the Greyhound pub, if you feel like you've earned a rest.

Things now start going downhill. Follow the road towards Tring, but be careful with the brakes as, on reaching The Ridgeway part-way down the road known locally as The Twist, you need to turn right. Keep with this road, passing over the A41 this time, and over the A4251, until you reach a minor road, where you need to turn left, and then right shortly afterwards onto Station Road. This now takes you past Tring's out-of-town station and the Pendley Court Hotel, then back into Aldbury – a total of around 12, quite hard but ultimately exhilarating, miles.

Cycle outlets along this section include:

- Mountain Mania, Tring (01442 822458)
- Bike Knight Mobile Repairs, Berkhamsted (01442 842405)
- Leisure Wheels, Hemel Old Town (01422 213401)
- Hemel Hempstead Bicycle Centre, Hemel Old Town (01422 242410)

RIDING

There is a network of bridleways to the south-west of Tring and west of Wigginton, along with a number of paths through the Ashridge Estate east of Aldbury. These, along with the small section of the Ridgeway, make for plenty of riding opportunities along this section.

Elsewhere, riding is confined largely to the south of the A41, with a short stretch of bridleway linking Boxmoor with Bovingdon, just off the map, which itself links up with another route heading north-west towards the southern outskirts of Berkhamsted. Those who decide to explore the Wendover Arm will also find the Wendover Woods a popular riding spot.

Horse-riding establishments and outlets along this section include:

- Hastoe Hill Stables, south of Tring (01442 828909) – *riding school and livery yard with riding lessons for beginners to advanced, as well as good countryside hacking*
- White Lion Equine, Berkhamsted (07976 816519) – *livery*

FISHING

Fishing opportunities abound in this section. As well as the Tring and Marsworth Reservoirs, there are a number of pools and canalside fishing. The two main angling societies are the Boxmoor and District (01442 398022), which controls some of the local pools, and the Berkhamsted and District

The mock-Elizabethan Rose and Crown in Tring.

Angling Society (01442 875106), which operates two ponds at Cublington and near Cheddington – both of which are off the map. In addition, there is also the Tring Anglers, which provides access to waters owned by other societies.

The Boxmoor and District Angling Society operates Westbrook Mere and Snooks Pool, west of Bridge 147, which are best accessed via the car park at the Three Horseshoes in Winkwell. The former is owned by the club, and contains carp (up to 10lb), roach, tench and perch, with these and bream available at Snooks Pool. Pixies Mere is a lake at Winkwell owned by the Boxmoor Trust (07860 426690), with carp running up to 25lb, and tench up to 10lb.

The canal provides good fishing for carp, roach, perch and gudgeon, with tench, chub and bream occasionally present. It is possible to fish sections of the Wendover Arm and the Aylesbury Arm, where there are perch, roach and bream. The latter's waters are particularly prized by local anglers, with gudgeon, roach, rudd, bream, perch and carp all present, along with tench and chub in some pounds.

The canal is best accessed at Marsworth, Bulbourne and Tring, Bridges 134 and 135, with the deep cutting at the latter providing good shelter in windy conditions, while the two arms can be both accessed from Marsworth and from their bridges.

The London Anglers Association (0208 5207477, see Learn More and Links) controls a total of 14 miles of canal between the south of Hunton Bridge in Section D and Tring, including three sections pertinent to this section, all of which can be fished on a day-ticket basis.

The canal varies from pound to pound along here because of the influence of the Bulbourne, and is traditionally associated with roach, some up to 2lb. In recent years, bream has become more prominent, along with the odd large carp, with plenty of gudgeon along the way. Crayfish, however, can be a problem.

Stretches controlled by the association are:

- Tring (Bridge 135) to Dudswell Lane
- Bullbeggars Lane (Bridge 144) to Dudswell
- Hemel Hempstead to Bullbeggars Lane

Outlets selling fishing supplies along this stretch include:

- Chiltern Tackle, Western Road, Tring (01442 825257)
- Old Town Angling Centre, Hemel Old Town (01422 252373)

OTHER

There are plenty of opportunities to sample this section by walking along one of the area's many golf courses, listed below:

- Ashridge Golf Club (01442 842379) – *18 holes, 6,547 yards, with a practice-area putting green*
- Berkhamsted Golf Club (01442 865832) – *heathland wooded grass bunkers. 18 holes, 6605 yards, with two practice grounds*

Boxmoor Golf Club (01442 242434) – *moorland course, 9 holes, 4,112 yards*

- Little Hay Golf Complex, Bovingdon, south of Boxmoor (01442 833798) – *an 18-hole, 6,678-yard, pay-and-play club in parkland, run by Dacorum Council, with pitch-and-putt and a coffee shop, as well as a practice area and driving range*
- Stocks Hotel Golf and Country Club (01442 851341) – *an 18-hole, 7,016-yard, parkland course with a feature lake, practice range and chipping green*

SECTION D

HEMEL HEMPSTEAD TO BATCHWORTH

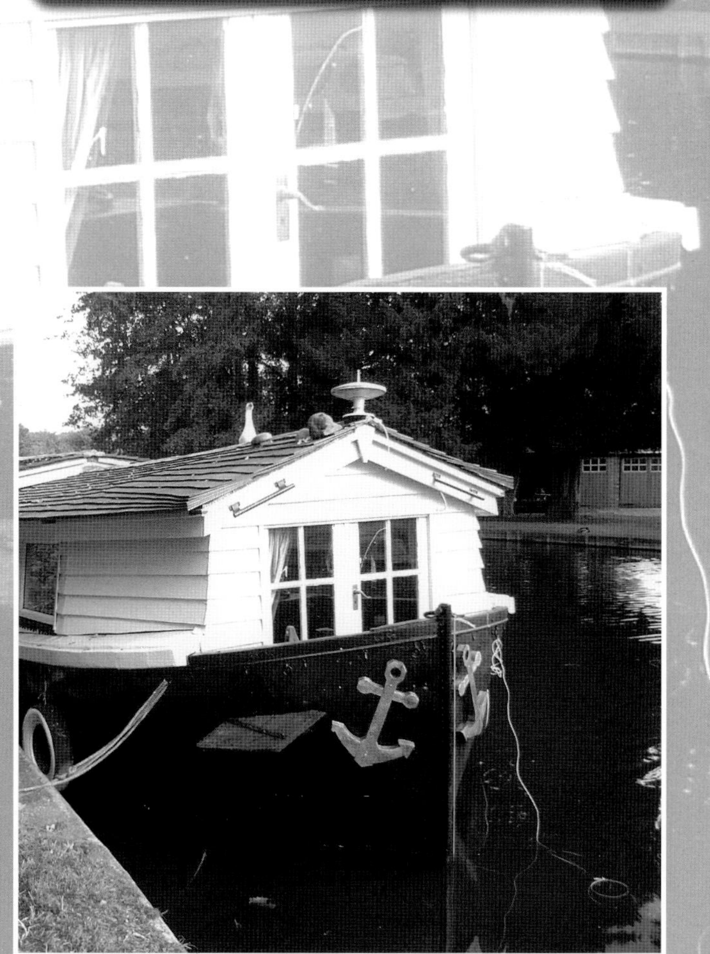

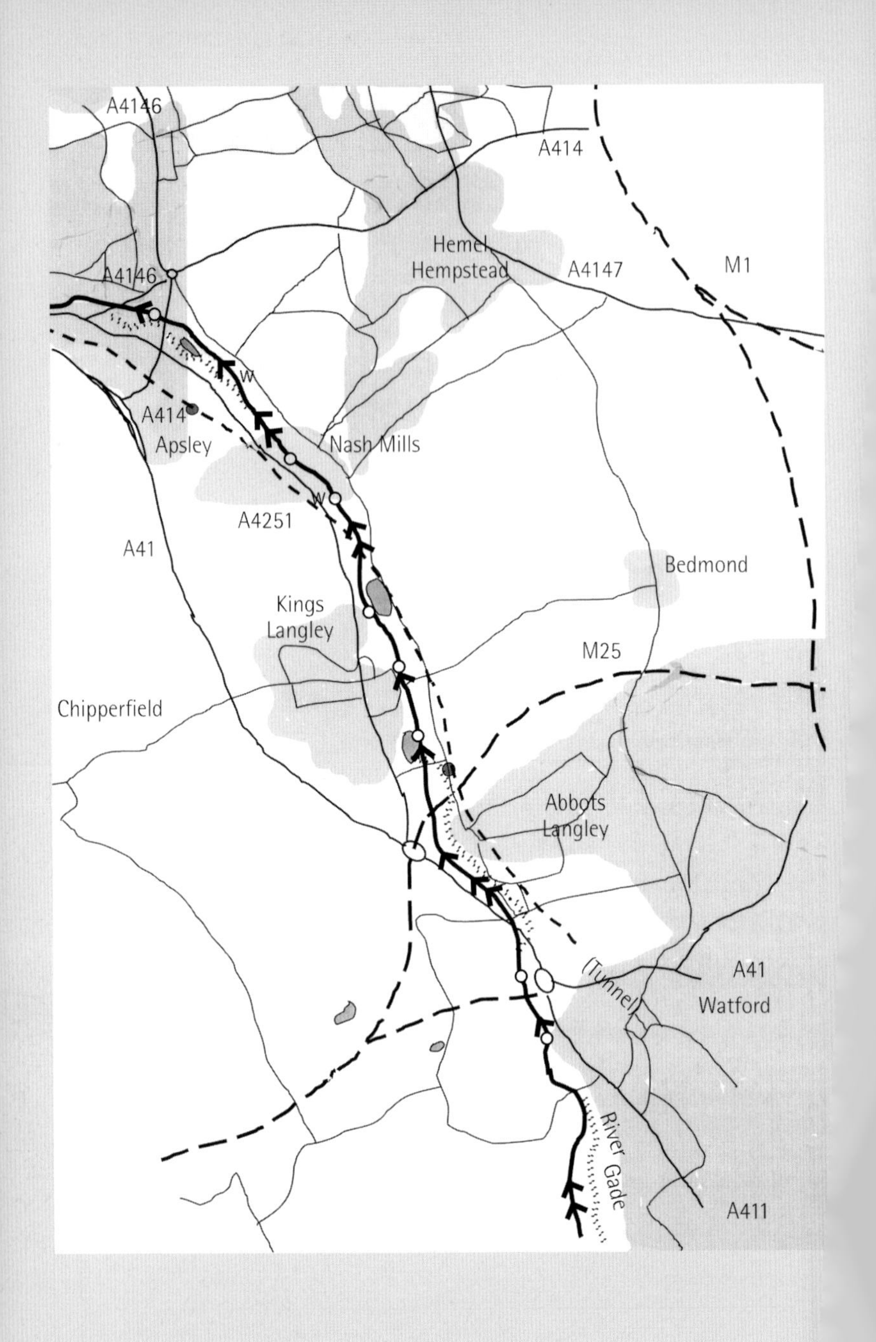
A4146
A414
Hemel Hempstead
A4147
M1
A4146
w
A414
Apsley
Nash Mills
w
A4251
A41
Bedmond
Kings Langley
M25
Chipperfield
Abbots Langley
A41
(Tunnel)
Watford
River Gade
A411

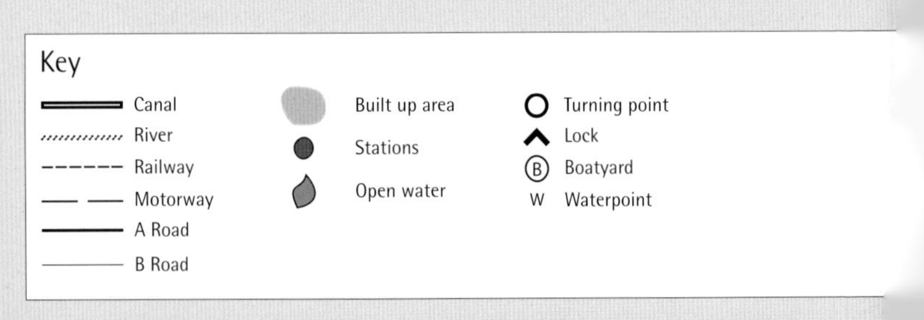
Key
Canal
River
Railway
Motorway
A Road
B Road
Built up area
Stations
Open water
Turning point
Lock
Boatyard
Waterpoint

SHAPERS

THE CANAL ON THIS STRETCH

KEY FACTS

LENGTH: 2.5 miles

BOATYARDS: 1
Bridgewater Basin

WATER POINTS: Three
Apsley Locks
Nash Mills Locks
Cassio Bridge

TURNING POINTS: 13
Boxmoor Lock
Apsley Marina
Nash Mills
Leewood Farm
Kings Langley
Home Park
Clarenden Park Farm
Lady Capel's Lock
Iron Bridge
Cassio Bridge
Common Moor
Lot Mead Lock
Batchworth

LOCKS: 20
Boxmoor Lock (7ft 1in)
Apsley Locks (3) (16ft)
Nash Mills Locks (2) (12ft 2in)
Kings Langley Lock (8ft 9in)
Home Park Lock (5ft 2in)
Lock 71 (6ft 11in)
Hunton Bridge Locks (2) (11ft 2in)
Lady Capel's Lock (5ft 4in)
Cassiobury Park Locks (2) (10ft)
Iron Bridge Lock (9ft 4in)
Cassio Bridge Lock (9ft)
Common Moor Lock (9ft 5in)
Lot Mead Lock (6ft 3in)
Batchworth Lock (6ft 8in)
Stocker's Lock (5ft 2in)

Although the canal crosses the M25 early on in this section the mood remains relaxed, with the towpath doing its best to avoid large built-up areas on its way to the large reservoirs south of Rickmansworth. Passing through woods and parkland, there is a distinctly rural feel at times, although the environs of Watford give a taste of the more built-up areas to come.

Just after the Fishery Inn beyond Boxmoor there is the first glimpse of the iconic Kodak Tower ahead and to the left, as well as some more open space and cricket greens on the non-towpath side. The tower marks the western approach to Hemel, although the route is determinedly not through the

SECTION D

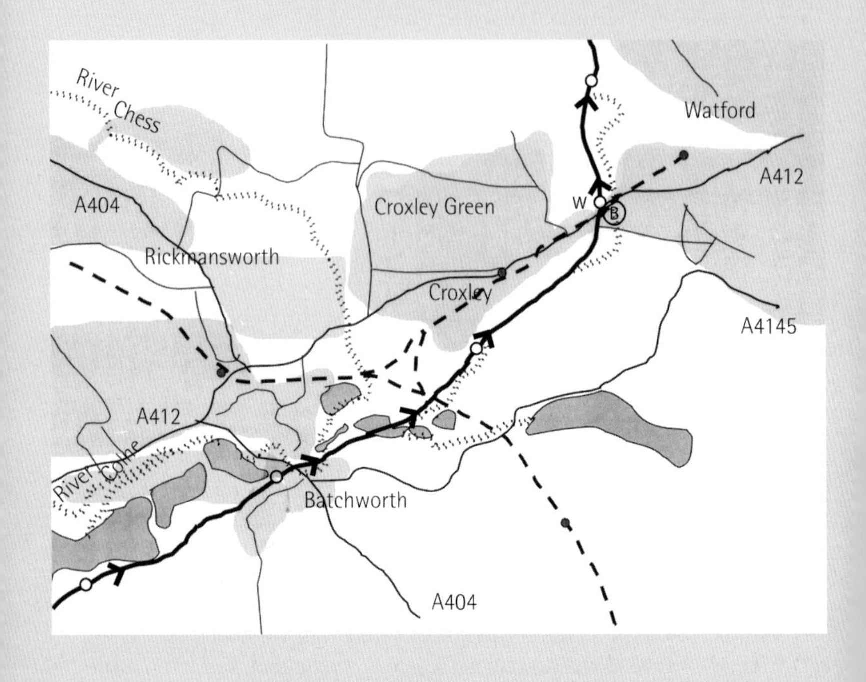
River Chess
Watford
A412
A404
Croxley Green
W
B
Rickmansworth
Croxley
A4145
A412
River Colne
Batchworth
A404

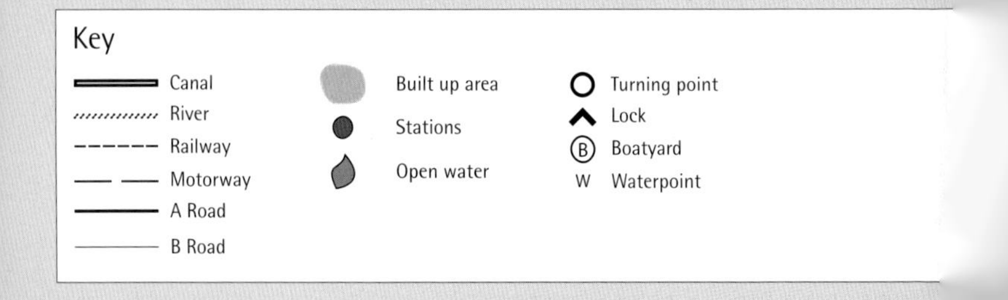
Key
Canal
River
Railway
Motorway
A Road
B Road
Built up area
Stations
Open water
Turning point
Lock
Boatyard
W Waterpoint

centre, with the water preferring to contribute to the open feel south of the town.

> In late 2004, it was announced that Kodak would be vacating their office block, throwing its future into doubt.

It is possible to moor either side of Bridge 151 for access to the town, although it is a short trek in. There are some shops near a petrol station further down from the large B&Q which dominates the view here. Around here, almost unnoticed, the river rejoins the canal and diverts away towards the town centre.

Boxmoor Lock, just before the bridge, is the second of a run of seven. This stretch is popular with both anglers and locals, offering as it does a quiet walk around the edge of the town, with the large children's play area to the right of Bridge 152 no doubt contributing to its popularity.

It is only now that the backs of some town houses begin to appear. These have well-tended gardens and seem to revel in exploiting their location. There is a pretty white stone bridge (No.153) decorated with colourful murals just before the first of the three Apsley Locks.

The local landscape is now more light-commercial than housing, although some flats start to emerge, culminating in the modern Apsley Mills Marina development, which is guarded by a wooden-lift bridge. This is approached under an impressive white steel bridge, and ends with another, more traditional, stone bridge, also painted white, where the towpath crosses over once again.

Another long straight precedes Nash Mills Lock (No.68), followed shortly afterwards by the Red Lion Lock, with the pub from which it derives its name sitting in a massive garden on the right. Continuing the uncertain theme, the towpath crosses over once more at this point, and the river (now the Gade) flows into the canal again, under a wooden-slatted bridge.

The sense of order being restored is complete when the railway crosses back over to the left over a grandiose concrete-arched bridge, after which there is a long stretch of good (if somewhat noisy), reinforced steel moorings. This is a pleasant, if unremarkable, part of the canal, with the road high up to the right and some council depots and industry to the left, followed by a lake hidden behind a high hedge.

The water splits before Kings Langley Lock and Bridge 157 (shortly before which there is a turning point), creating an island with housing on it, after which the towpath decides to switch sides again. Bridge 159 is a modern

psley Marina, outside Hemel, has its own lift bridge.

concrete affair but is followed immediately by a charming brick-and-stone footbridge, just before the relatively modest Lock 70.

The River Gade makes one of its sojourns over to the left here, forming a meadow along the long straight that leads up to the less elegant, but still impressive, bridge, carrying the M25. The towpath is solid enough but by the standards of this canal this stretch makes for uninspiring walking. Look out though for the large modern wind turbine over to the left.

Lock 71, along with its cottage, sits on the brow of a long curve, with the Gade rejoining the canal on the other side. There are plenty of moorings along here, and the quality of the towpath picks up. The attractive dark-grey bricks of Hunton Bridge appear after a curve, as trees comes in and stifle the view, which is probably just as well as it consists mainly of the busy main road to the right. There is access to nearby Abbots Langley at Bridge 162, and a couple of canalside pubs.

The two Hunton Bridge locks follow, and the scenery picks up a little, although it has a dash of the suburban about it. There is a straight section with moorings, after which the canal bears sharp right and then left again, under the A41. The towpath drifts to the right briefly and rejoins the canal just before it passes underneath the M25 again.

There is pleasant open ground including a golf course and the Gade, once again, to the right, with Lady Capel's lock appearing suddenly after a sharp bend to the right. This is a relaxing quiet stretch which twists and turns, carrying the towpath to the other side via an elegant turnover bridge (No.163). The equally bright, but much more impressive, Grove Bridge follows, with its separate archway for the towpath. Shortly after, Grove Park Mill appears on the right, complete with weir.

The towpath crosses back over to the right at Bridge 166, just before the two Cassiobury Park locks, the second of which has a very elegant lock-keeper's cottage. There are some good views from the bridge and it is worth lingering a second here. Just after, there are some good quiet moorings in what is effectively the heart of the park, and boaters seeking to avoid the more built-up ambience of Croxley Green and Rickmansworth may consider stopping here, or to turn just before the next lock.

After the pretty Iron Bridge and lock, it is a case of more of the same, with a long straight preceding a footbridge and Cassio Bridge Lock and another turning point, where there is also a boatyard and a water point, preceded by visitor moorings. There is definitely a more built-up fell here, with more detritus and less order.

> It was at Cassiobury Park, in 1881, that Watford Rovers first played. These days, the side is known simply as Watford FC, and plays at Vicarage Road in the heart of that town.

> At Iron Bridge there is a tree planted by the (contemporary) Duke of Marlborough to commemorate 200 years of the Grand Union Canal.

It is possible to access Croxley Green from Bridge 169 and, although the Green itself would be a bit of a trek, there are some basic shops available at the base of the hill, the other side of the roundabout to the west (right from off the towpath). After the bridge the canal curves gently to the right before straightening out and diverting to the left.

This becomes one of the periodic rural stretches along the canal with willows overhanging a well-made-up towpath and adjacent gardens set well back. The River Gade makes an occasional appearance on the left and there is some modern housing before a long straight stretch of wide water in the lead-up to Common Moor Lock.

A boat leaves Cassiobury Locks, outside Watford.

Open views to the left become more apparent after the lock, where there is a line of permanently moored boats on the non-towpath side, and further evidence of the river. The towpath deteriorates somewhat here, but is still well made up, although cyclists may need to keep an eye out for the odd rogue rock.

It is possible for boaters to turn at this spot, and mooring may be a tempting proposition along this pleasant stretch, although behind the next bend there is a bridge carrying the Metropolitan Line railway. Lot Mead Lock is accompanied by a couple of white painted cottages, and after these there is another (unofficial) turning point where the river rejoins the canal.

Some formal visitors' moorings follow, and there are some permanently moored houseboats on the opposite bank, which look out onto meadows and woods. A small bridge carries the towpath over a stream, feeding Batchworth Lake to the right, while another long line of permanently moored boats offers a miscellany of styles on the opposite bank.

As these recede, to be replaced by some rather more exclusive moorings belonging to the houses backing onto the canal, another line starts up along the towpath side. The water now splits either side of a small island, with the main channel passing to the right, as the towpath reaches Batchworth Lock and the Batchworth Canal Centre, run by the Rickmansworth Canal Trust. Batchworth is something of a waterways junction, with the Rivers Gade and Chess coming together with the canal, and it is worth pausing to study the plan on the side of the centre explaining the various waterways.

> Batchworth itself has a side lock, built in 1805 by Samuel Salter to allow him to take beer barrels from his brewery down to Uxbridge

> There is a collection of aged canal artefacts outside the old lock-keepers cottage at Stokers Lock.

After the bridge, with its silhouette of a horse-drawn boat inside, the towpath resumes its previous excellent state, with good formal visitors' moorings. A long straight follows with house gardens backing onto the water on the opposite bank. Trees hide open land to the right. After the houses, the hills rise up and the canal continues its somnolent way. For those who are self-sufficient, this is an excellent place to stop, and there is a long run of visitors' moorings on the approach to Stokers Lock.

The hills now sweep down from the left, causing the canal to divert to the right, where there is yet another run of permanent moorings. Halfway along here there is a small stone obelisk marking the Hertfordshire and Middlesex border, with a smaller sign acknowledging the beginning of the Hillingdon Canal Walk.

PRINCIPAL TOWNS AND VILLAGES ALONG THIS STRETCH

ABBOTS LANGLEY:

So-called because it was once owned by the Abbot of St Albans, these days Abbots Langley is dominated by large post-war estates, spreading out east from the railway line. The centre of the village sits on a hill near to the church, and a little way down lies Kitters Green, which has a remnant of a village green.

> Abbots Langley was the home of Elizabeth Greenhill, who holds the record for being the mother of the most children growing to adulthood – a total of thirty-nine!

APSLEY:

These days an offshoot of Hemel Hempstead, Apsley has a place in history as being the site of the world's first mechanised paper mill, paper having been a staple of industry in this area for 150 years from the beginning of the nineteenth century. Apsley lies just off the canal and can be reached via its fancy new bridge near the modern private marina.

BATCHWORTH:

It is difficult to draw a line defining where Batchworth starts and Rickmansworth ends. Even the local church, St Mary's, declares itself to be in Batchworth on one side, and Rickmansworth on the other. Generally, however, it may be regarded as the houses clustered around Tesco on the south side of the canal.

BEDMOND:

Existing in splendid isolation between Hemel Hempstead and Watford, Bedmond's heart has an old side and a new side, divided by the road that runs through it. The old side consists mainly of ivy-clad terraced houses, while the new side is mostly post-war.

CHIPPERFIELD:

Chipperfield is a well-to-do village with a small newsagent and a large 4x4 dealership. The village centre is neat and tidy with a number of large houses set back from the road, and a fair proportion of fields given over to horses. The common to the south of the village extends to over 100 acres, and is surrounded by wood and heathland.

CROXLEY:

An archetypal suburb sandwiched between Watford and Rickmansworth, consisting mainly of semi-detached houses, a parade of shops and a station on the Metropolitan Underground Line.

CROXLEY GREEN:

On first sight an extension of Croxley, with more semi-detached housing and flats. A trek up the hill from the roundabout, however, reveals a massive village green with a large ivy-covered wall surrounding Croxley House at one end and a pub at the other.

HEMEL HEMPSTEAD NEW TOWN:

The 'Magic Roundabout' that greets the motorist is perhaps Hemel's most iconic feature. The centre is dominated by Marlowes Shopping Centre, a windswept but comprehensive mall, with an attempt to make a feature of the point where the Rivers Gade and Bulbourne meet just below it, in bad need of a revamp.

HUNTON BRIDGE:

On the edge of Abbots Langley, Hunton Bridge sits next to the A41, which bypasses the village and has removed much of its identity. In the past, its function was as a staging post between Hemel Hempstead and Watford. Brewing malt, drawing on the water of the nearby River Gade, was another of the village's occupations.

KINGS LANGLEY:

The canal neatly divides Kings Langley, with the eastern side dominated by industrial units, including the old Ovaltine factory, while the west side has the feel of a small town or large village. The village was once the site of a royal palace, hence its name, founded by Edward I, although it fell into decline during Tudor times. Kings Langley Common, to the west, remains a reminder of more regal times, and is surrounded by modern housing and a school.

NASH MILLS:

Just about distinct from Hemel Hempstead, Nash Mills dates back to medieval times, with the mills in its name being originally used to mill corn, and then converted to paper making. Nash Mills is now the home of the Croxley paper range. Like its counterpart, Apsley, Nash Mills is easily accessible from the canal.

> The paper maker, John Dickinson, built his country house at Nash Mills. It is now a private school called Abbot's Hill. This provides a certain symmetry, as Dickinson also founded the village's first school, 'for the benefit of apprentices and the very young people of the village'.

RICKMANSWORTH:

The town's centre lies to its extreme south, and consists of a long High Street with a theatre and museum, all nestling in a small flat area with most of the housing spreading north up the hill. The area around the shops has been subject to much recent building of exclusive developments of flats. Growth to the east has been limited by the presence of the River Chess.

WATFORD:

Much revamped in recent years, Watford's planners have made a real attempt to inject some life into the town, with some modern sculptures and a spruced-up centre. However, the ring road surrounding it can have the effect of making you feel as if you're caught up in a spiral of shopping hell, and the small parades of shops and terraced housing that seem to have spun off it do little to add to the appeal.

HISTORY

The phrase 'north of Watford' is used disparagingly by some to mark the boundary of civilisation. One theory behind the saying is that Watford was the first place that horses were changed on the north-west route out of London. However, it is equally likely that the Watford in question was the much smaller Northamptonshire Watford, better known by Watford Gap service station, which was a junction between the old east-west and north-south coaching routes.

Whatever the origin (and verisimilitude!) of the phrase, Watford does seem to represent a psychological point dividing the outskirts of the capital with the Home Counties. Parked on the south-western edge of one of those counties, Hertfordshire, on leaving Watford's near neighbour Rickmansworth, the canal plunges south into Middlesex, a county that these days really only exists in name, being more accurately described as 'West London'.

Although there is evidence of flint mines dating back 12,000 years in Watford, the area was little more than the ford in its title, and the hamlet gets only a cursory mention in the Domesday Book. Prior to this time, Roman settlement had been focused towards Verulaminum 10 miles to the north-east, although there is speculation that the Romans enhanced the ford to provide access to the nearby Akeman and Watling Streets.

At the time of the Norman invasion, both Rickmansworth and Abbots Langley were more significant settlements. Both were owned by the Abbey in St Albans by Offa, and Abbots Langley, the Manor of Rickmansworth having been granted to the Abbey by Offa in the eighth century, and Abbots Langley a couple of centuries later just before the invasion, by the Saxon, Ethelwine the Black.

> Abbots Langley was the birthplace of Nicholas Breakspear, who, as Adrian IV, became the only English pope in 1154. He is alleged to have choked to death on a fly.

Croxley Green also gets a mention in the Domesday Book, and Richard of Croxley, a knight from St Albans, is the village's first recorded inhabitant. St Albans in fact has a dominating influence on the early history of this area, first in its role as a Roman centre, and secondly through its Abbey. The one settlement to achieve any real distinction in its own right was Kings Langley. The royal prefix flows from King Edward I's granting of the manor to his wife Eleanor, and the establishment of a hunting park followed by the building of a palace on the hill above the church and existing village.

> Edmund of Langley became the Duke of York and the founder of the House of York, whose line subsequently occupied the throne.

Originally called Langley Regina (Queen's Langley), the village gained its current name when it became a favourite of Edward II, who founded a large friary on the site, and celebrated the birth of his son Edmund of Langley here in 1341. Along with other local villages, Kings Langley suffered badly from the Black Death around this time, and the growing economic power of those that survived was reflected in rioting around the time of the Peasant's Revolt in 1381, although again the focus of revolt was St Albans.

The Abbots resident in St Albans continued to exercise considerable power over the area until they met their nemesis in Henry VIII. From Tudor times onwards, the local villages were forced to exist independently of St Albans. The manor of Abbots Langley was sold to the military engineer Sir Richard Lee by Henry, and the friary at Kings Langley fell into ruin. After the Dissolution, the Manor of Rickmansworth passed through various hands, at different times being held by the Bishop of London and the Prince of Wales.

Even Kings Langley had to find an alternative way to survive as it lost royal favour and patronage. Such was the state of the friary that Queen Elizabeth ordered the transfer of Edmund of Langley's tomb to the local parish church for safekeeping. Perhaps the most significant legacy of this period is the large open expanse of Chipperfield Common, the site of the original hunting grounds, and near to the fish ponds that belonged to the friary (see 'Sampling').

Chipperfield Common passed out of royal ownership in 1630, when Charles I sold it to the City of London to help pay his debts. It was finally gifted to the local authority in 1936.

Hertfordshire sided with Parliament during the Civil War and, as a result, suffered badly from starvation. Following the restoration of the monarchy, a period of relative calm descended, with local lords of the manor controlling large estates and the area becoming quite fashionable for those who wished to be close enough to London to participate in its social scene – a trend that continues to this day.

It was the canal, with the stretch from Brentford to Tring from 1793, that precipitated the next major shift in local circumstances. Suddenly, the raw materials for industry became available. The impact of the canal was both physical and symbolic, cutting as it did through the estates of both the Earl of Essex and Lord Clarendon.

Paper making became a favoured industry, with the name of Croxley still associated with that product today, and a gas works was established in Watford. The sleepy hamlet, which had grown slowly to become a small market town specialising in wool and leather, was about to wake up.

Less than fifty years later it was the turn of the railway, although the landed gentry had learned their lesson by now and made sure the route was diverted away from their land, necessitating the building of cuttings and embankments as well as a mile-long tunnel.

With its proximity to London and access to the railway line, Watford grew steadily as an industrial centre, and printing was a staple of the local economy for decades. These attributes also meant that the town suffered considerably from stray bombs and damaged planes during the Second World War. In recent times, Watford has also become known as a retail centre, appropriately perhaps, as it was in Watford that the national chain Mothercare was 'born'.

The post-war era was also a significant one for Hemel Hempstead, which was designated a 'New Town' in 1949, in order to take overspill population from London. The town grew rapidly, with the planners dividing it into several residential neighbourhoods, with each supposedly having its own 'village centre'.

With hindsight, their vision of a few major feeder roads with a cobweb of cul-de-sacs and crescents may have been well-intended, but the power of the car has won through, and today, as with so many similar towns of the period, Hemel seems to be struggling to re-assert its structure and identity from the straight-jacket imposed by this vision. Today, Hemel Hempstead provides an interesting counterpoint to Milton Keynes, the other, more recently conceived, New Town in this Guide.

THE NATURAL LANDSCAPE

The steep-sided Gade Valley continues to dominate the landscape in the northern part of this section, although this tends to plateau out around Chipperfield, to the west and north of Abbots Langley to the east. The scenery changes quite dramatically at Chipperfield, with a large open common criss-crossed by paths.

Mature woods are a feature, offering a reminder of what this area might have looked like many centuries ago. Whippendell Wood occupies the area west of Watford and north of Croxley Green, while there is a sprinkling of woods to the north of Rickmansworth. For periods, the canal runs through these, largely protecting the visitor from the steady encroachment of the built-up area, especially in the area immediately south of the M25. In fact, the areas between the various settlements along this stretch are remarkably open, with land continuing to be cultivated, although this shortly becomes an increasingly rare sight.

The River Gade, which comes alongside the canal at Hemel Hempstead, becomes a constant companion to the canal along this stretch, with the two waterways combining, parting only at locks. Water becomes an even more defining feature to the south of the section, with the River Chess joining the party at Rickmansworth, which marks the beginning of a series of large lakes.

ACCESS AND TRANSPORT

ROADS

It is on this section that motorways, until now largely absent, begin to make their mark. The M1 swoops in from the north and links up with the more symbolic M25 just south of Kings Langley. From here on, the canal is within the M25 'belt', and enters Greater London.

Elsewhere, the A41 forms an efficient link between Hemel Hempstead and Watford, although the A4251 offers a useful 'back road' between the former and Junction 19 of the M25. Watford and its satellite towns and districts fill the south-east corner bounded by the M25 and the canal, with the A411 and A412 providing channels into the heart of the town with a network of local, mainly residential, roads making getting about by car an easy affair.

South of Watford, the canal swings to the west, and the built-up areas of Croxley Green and Rickmansworth sit to the north, linked by the A412, which eventually connects to Junction 17 of the M25, west of Rickmansworth. There is a second link with the motorway north of the town, with the A404 joining Junction 18 at the eastern edge of Rickmansworth, and eventually passing to the south via Batchworth. It is here that another 'A' road, the A4145, echoes the path of the A412, but south of the canal and the River Gade.

RAIL

Although there is no main-line station on the map Hemel Hempstead Station lies just to the north-west (See Section C), and Watford Junction Station lies slightly to the east. The main train operator serving the local area remains Silverlink (01923 207298), while Virgin Trains (08457 222333) run the main London to Birmingham route.

If the appearance of the M25 is one talisman of the capital, another arrives in the form of the underground railway, although the line itself is all above ground here. There are four underground stations, all on the outer edges of the Metropolitan Line. These are Moor Park, Rickmansworth, Croxley and Watford. Chorleywood Station, one stop on from Rickmansworth, is also convenient for those accessing the area from the west.

National Train Enquiries can be reached on 08457 484950. The telephone contact for London Travel Information is 020 7222 1234.

BUSES

The following list sets out the main buses servicing this stretch, although it is advisable to check before using them as some buses only run on certain days and others may have been withdrawn since publication of this Guide. It is also worth checking for more local services, in particular those linking districts of both Hemel Hempstead and Watford.

- 4/5 – *Abbots Langley to Rickmansworth via Watford and Croxley Green (Sullivans and Arriva)*
- 6 – *Rickmansworth to Hemel Hempstead Rail Station via Croxley Green and Watford (Arriva)*
- 41 – *Watford, Rickmansworth, Croxley Circular (Arriva)*
- 322 – *Watford to Northchurch via Kings Langley, Hemel Hempstead and Berkhamsted (Arriva)*
- 352 – *Watford to Hemel Hempstead (Arriva)*
- 500 – *Aylesbury to Watford via Tring, Berkhamsted, Hemel Hempstead and Kings Langley (Arriva)*
- 815 – *Watford to Kings Langley via Abbots Langley (Mullany's)*
- H19/H20 – *Abbots Langley to Hemel Hempstead via Kings Langley (Arriva)*
- R8 – *Abbots Langley to Watford (Red Rose)*
- R9 – *Chipperfield to Watford Asda via Kings Langley and Abbots Langley (Red Rose)*
- R19 – *Chipperfield to Garston via Kings Langley and Abbots Langley (Red Rose)*
- W4 – *Abbots Langley to Maple Cross via Watford Junction, Croxley Green and Rickmansworth (Sullivans)*
- W6 – *Maple Cross to Hemel Hempstead Rail Station via Rickmansworth, Croxley Green and Watford (Arriva)*

Contact details for bus operators in this area are listed below, although Traveline (www.traveline.org.uk) on 0870 6082608, can give details of specific services between 7 a.m. and 10 p.m.:

- Arriva (01923 682262)
- Mullany's (01923 225412) – *Mullany's services operate in school terms only*
- Red Rose (01296 399500)
- Sullivans (01707 646803)

TAXIS

The following list gives a selection of the taxi operators in this section:

- AA United Taxis, Watford Junction (01923 252525)
- Abbots Village Cars, Abbots Langley (01923 670707)
- Ace Watford Taxis (01923 212121)
- Allied Taxi Service, Watford (01923 250502)
- Area Cars, Rickmansworth (01923 711588)
- Baz Taxis, Boxmoor, Hemel Hempstead (01442 266000)
- Boughtons Taxis, Rickmansworth Station (01923 896060)
- Cab Cars, Abbots Langley (01923 260700)
- Crown Taxis, Hemel Hempstead (01442 230032)
- Eagle Car Hire (01923 771111) – *next to Croxley Underground Station*
- Hemel Cars, Hemel Hempstead (01442 232353)
- Kings Cabs, Kings Langley (01923 262266)
- Lucketts, Watford (01923 333777)
- United Kab Co, Marlowes, Hemel Hempstead (01442 255558)
- Watford Cars, Watford (01923 232312)

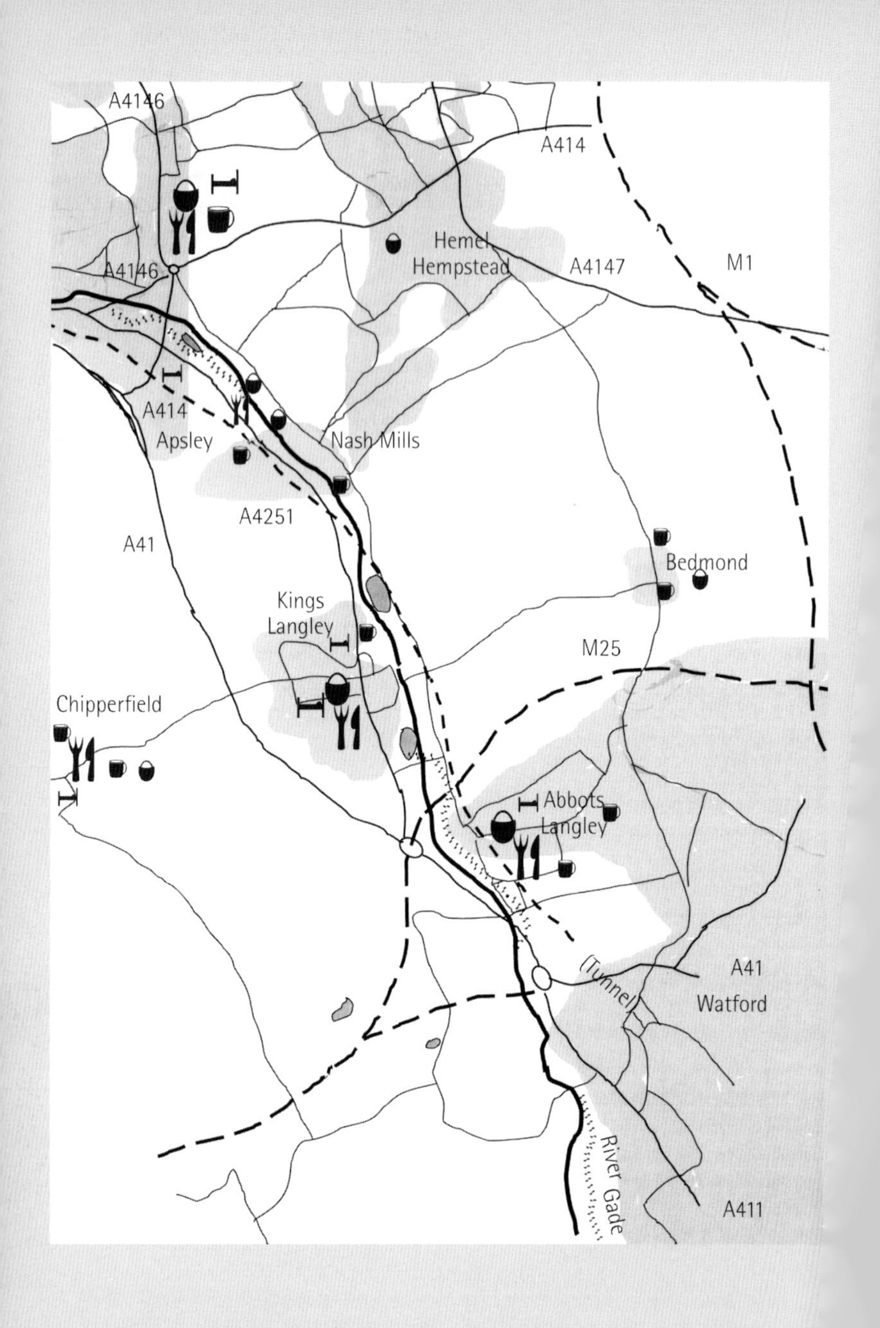
A4146
A414
Hemel
Hempstead
A4147
M1
A4146
A414
Apsley
Nash Mills
A4251
A41
Bedmond
Kings
Langley
M25
Chipperfield
Abbots
Langley
(Tunnel)
A41
Watford
River Gade
A411

Key
Canal
River
Railway
Motorway
A Road
B Road
Built up area
Stations
Open water
Shops
Accomodation
Campsite
Pub
Restaurant

BASICS

INTRODUCTION

The presence of both Hemel Hempstead New Town and Watford, as well as a number of smaller towns and villages, means it is easy to access the necessities of life along this section. Both the two major towns are a little way off the towpath, and while this makes for a more peaceful passage, it also means it is best to plan a major shopping expedition.

Rickmansworth, towards the southern end of the section, is a short ten-minute walk away from the canal, and easier to get into and out of again than Hemel Hempstead if you are travelling by car. The rail station is also quite central, something which can't really be said of either Hemel or Watford.

If your needs are quite basic, then one of the smaller towns such as Kings Langley and Croxley may fit the bill, as they are both close to the towpath. While Chipperfield and Abbots Langley may be light on services, they do offer pleasant places to visit or stay when passing through.

Both Hemel Hempstead and Watford have major hospitals, although non-emergency health concerns can be addressed by calling NHS Direct on 0845 4647:

- Hemel Hempstead Hospital, Hillfield Road, Hemel Hempstead (01442 213141)
- Watford Hospital, Vicarage Road, Watford (01923 244366)

SHOPPING

The Marlowes Shopping Centre in Hemel Hempstead, a pedestrianised precinct with an attached mall, is comprehensive and fine if your needs are predictable. It is here that the major banks, coffee bars, High Street clothing chains and fast-food restaurants can all be found, while there is a run of restaurants west of the mall towards the grandly named Water Gardens. There is also a Tesco superstore on the St Albans Road at the Jarman Park complex.

The Old Town (covered in Section C) is better if you are looking for surprises, while Marlowes Street, in the middle of these, predictably falls between the two extremes. This is mainly populated with various takeaway food restaurants and a café bar, while the open-air market sells mostly basic goods.

Outside Hemel, there is a large Sainsbury's at Apsley, as well as a parade of local shops, which is very similar to those at Nash Mills. None of these are terribly inviting unless you need basic supplies, to get your hair cut or are in a desperate need to place a bet.

The centre of Kings Langley, which has a long linear High Street, has a Spar supermarket, an off-licence and other local services such as a butchers, a launderette and a health-food shop among others. Abbots Langley has a parade of shops including a Budgens supermarket, banks, a newsagent, an off-licence and a selection of restaurants. While Chipperfield can only claim to have a small newsagent and post office, it can boast two garden centres, while Bedmond also has the Bedmond Stores and a post office.

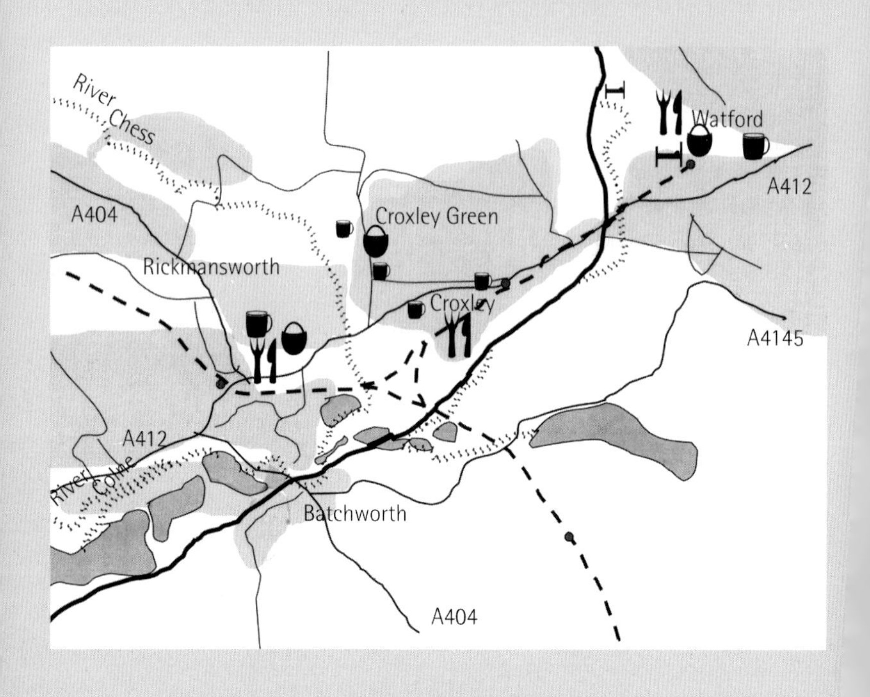
River Chess
A404
Rickmansworth
Croxley Green
Watford
A412
Croxley
A4145
A412
River Colne
Batchworth
A404

Key
Canal
River
Railway
Motorway
A Road
B Road
Built up area
Stations
Open water
Shops
Accomodation
Campsite
Pub
Restaurant

Watford is a major regional shopping centre. Its long High Street is defined by a glass pyramid at one end, which houses a sofa shop, and an almost Guggenheim-ish green building, also built out of glass, at the other. By way of contrast, this houses an extension to the Peace Hospice.

The heart of Watford shopping is its Harlequin Centre, which houses over 140 stores and has all the big-brand names. Next to the Harlequin is Charter Place, an earlier shopping centre that now houses the indoor market. This is the place to head if you're looking for fruit and vegetables, clothes or jewellery.

There is a large Sainsbury's in the heart of Watford, and a parade of shops along the northern end of the High Street, parallel with the A412, and there are more along the roads striking out off the High Street towards the ring road, some of which can be worth checking out for specialist ethnic goods. Finally, there is a run of shops with a preponderance of fast-food outlets and newsagents near to the football stadium and hospital on Vicarage Road.

Croxley Green has a parade of shops, clustered around its underground station, catering for local needs, including a newsagent and some convenience stores, and another further up the hill towards the Green. The former includes a large Spar and a newsagent, while the latter also has a newsagent and convenience store, as well as a fish and chip shop.

Rickmansworth has a long, traffic-controlled, High Street, with an Iceland supermarket and some scaled-down representatives of major chains such as Boots, WH Smith and a Marks and Spencer food-only outlet. Otherwise, it is worth looking out for local specialists such as the Brown Sugar delicatessen and health-food shop which specialises in coffee, local butchers, bakers and a large wine importers opposite the theatre.

Finally, there is a small newsagent between the canal and Rickmansworth High Street near to the church, as well as some restaurants and a large Tesco at Batchworth, the rear of which backs onto the canal, although it is a small trek to reach the entrance from the towpath.

EATING AND DRINKING

PUBS

The following list covers many of the pubs in this section but cannot claim to be totally comprehensive. Many of those featured offer food, although serving times and menus will, naturally, vary:

- The Full House, Hemel Hempstead (01422 265512) – *large city-centre pub*
- Harrys, Market Square, Hemel Hempstead (01442 213092)
- Hogshead, The Marlowes, Hemel Hempstead (01442 255746)
- The Society, Marlowes, Hemel Hempstead (01442 240095)
- The Wishing Well, The Marlowes, Hemel Hempstead (01442 216777)
- The Spotted Bull, Apsley (01442 268912)
- The Three Tuns, Nash Mills (01422 255978) – *by the side of the canal*
- The Bell, Bedmond (01923 262910)
- White Hart Inn, Bedmond (01923 262779)
- Dog and Partridge, Kings Langley (01923 441116) – *near the canal*
- The Rose and Crown, High Street, Kings Langley (01923 290129)
- The Saracens Head, Kings Langley (01923 400144)
- The Unicorn, Kings Langley (01923 262287)

- The Boot, Chipperfield (01442 833155) – *has a large red double-decker bus available for hire*
- The Royal Oak, Chipperfield (01923 265163)
- Boys Home, Abbots Langley (01923 262554)
- Kings Head, Abbots Langley (01923 261811) – *close to the canal*
- Royal Oak, Kitters Green, Abbots Langley (01923 265163) – *hidden away on the green to the north of the village*
- Lloyds Bar, High Street, Watford (01923 811540)
- Moon Under Water, High Street, Watford (01923 223559)
- The One Bell Pub, Watford – *opposite BHS in the High Street (01923 224198) – by the face sculptures*
- The One Crown, High Street, Watford (01923 222626)
- Walkabout Australian Bar, High Street, Watford (01923 240688)
- The Red House, Watford Road, Croxley (01923 772107)
- The Duke, Watford Road, Croxley (01923 772538)
- The Coach and Horses, Croxley Green (01923 774457) – *on the green itself*
- The Artichoke, Croxley Green (01923 772565)
- The Coach and Horses, High Street, Rickmansworth (01923 772433)
- The Hogshead, High Street, Rickmansworth (01923 774369)
- The Jenny Wren, Rickmansworth Road, Rickmansworth (01923 282053)
- The Pennysylvanian, High Street, Rickmansworth (01923 720348)
- Scotsbridge Mill, Park Road, Rickmansworth (01923 778377)
- The White Bear, Batchworth (01923 772381) – *right on the canal just above the Batchworth Canal Centre*

Cafés and fast-food outlets along the route and in surrounding areas include the following:

- Apsley Fish and Chips (01422 263888) – *fish and chips*
- The Snack Shack, Apsley (01422 245800)
- China Garden, Nash Mills (01422 264956) – *Chinese takeaway*
- The Langley Fish Bar, Kings Langley (01923 262445) – *fish and chips*
- The Lunch Box, Kings Langley (01923 262302) – *café*
- Bloomers Coffee Shop, Chipperfield (01442 834845) – *in Chipperfield Garden Centre*
- Dolphin Fish Bar, Abbots Langley (01923 262567)
- Lee Garden, Abbots Langley (01923 268783) – *Chinese takeaway*
- Aromas Café and Restaurant, High Street, Watford (01923 250066)
- Café Giardino, Watford (01923 213568) – *in the Harlequin Centre*
- Steve's Diner, Charter Place, Watford (01923 253586)
- Taylors Café Bar, High Street, Watford (01923 238897)
- Seaworld Fish and Chips, Watford Road, Croxley (01923 779300) – *fish and chips*
- The Charcoal Grill and Fish Bar High Street, Rickmansworth (01923 772525) – *fish and chips and more*
- The Upper Crust Café and Takeaway Bar High Street, Rickmansworth (01923 897710) – *café*

SECTION D

There is no shortage of places to stop and eat along this section. The road alongside the Water Gardens in Hemel Hempstead has a run of restaurants, as does the High Street in Rickmansworth, but you do not need to confine yourself to the larger centres, with plenty of options in some of the smaller towns and villages many of which are only a short walk away from the towpath. The Marlowes

Centre and the centre of Watford also offer a selection of the large pizza- and fast-food outlets.

The following list offers a selection of places to try:

- The Bengal Spice, near the Water Gardens, Hemel Hempstead (01422 242937) – *Indian restaurant*
- Casanova, near the Water Gardens, Hemel Hempstead (01422 247482) – *Italian restaurant*
- K2 Balti Centre, Two Waters Road Hemel Hempstead (01422 239993) – *just off the canal*
- The Kings Lodge, Kings Langley (01923 441141) – *Indian restaurant and bar*
- La Casetta, Kings Langley (01923 263823) – *Mediterranean restaurant*
- The Taste of India, Kings Langley (01923 270668) – *Indian restaurant*
- The Two Brewers, Chipperfield (01422 265266) – *sixteenth-century pub and restaurant*
- The Forest of India, Abbots Langley (01923 270077) – *Indian restaurant*
- The Viceroy Brasserie, Abbots Langley (01923 262163)
- Alibaba Tandoori, Kings Street, Watford (01923 229793) – *Indian restaurant*
- Hanako, The Parade, Watford (01923 255222) – *Japanese restaurant*
- Mezza Luna, Queens Road, Watford (01923 246966) – *Italian restaurant*
- Pancho's Villa, The Parade, High Street, Watford (01923 252225) – *Mexican café/bar and restuarant*
- Mangiamo, Abbots Langley (01923 261010) – *Italian restaurant*
- Harvester Restaurant, Watford Road, Croxley (01923 236784) – *family dining*
- Standard Tandoori, Watford Road, Croxley (01923 240031) – *Indian restaurant*
- Croxley Tandoori, Watford Road, Croxley (01923 223547) – *Indian restaurant*
- La Perla Café Bar and Pizzeria, High Street, Rickmansworth (01923 779492) – *Italian restaurant*
- Maharaja Tandoori Restaurant, High Street, Rickmansworth (01923 770107) - *Indian restaurant*
- Maurizio's Restaurant, Church Street, Rickmansworth (01923 775701) – *Italian restaurant*
- Rasal Brasserie High Street, Rickmansworth (01923 778722) – *Indian restaurant*
- Za Zas, Church Street, Rickmansworth (01923 772287) – *Italian restaurant*

SLEEPING

Hotels and guest houses are in plentiful supply along this section, although, once again, campers miss out.

HOTELS

- Hemel Hempstead Travelodge (0870 1911536)
- Midland Hotel, Midland Road, Hemel Hempstead (01442 253218) – *small family-run hotel*
- Southville Hotel, Charles Street, Hemel Hempstead (01442 251387) – *nineteen rooms*
- Kings Head Hotel, Abbots Langley (01923 261811) – *seven rooms*
- Grove Hotel, Hempstead Road, Watford (01923 221503) – *a superior hotel (winner of the AA Hotel of the Year for 2004-05), this establishment actually has the canal running through its grounds. The hotel's golf course will host the World*

Golf Championships in 2006

- Hunton Park Hotel, Hunton Bridge, Watford (01923 261511) – *Queen Anne house in own grounds, sixty rooms*
- Travel Inn, Water Lane, Watford (0870 990 6620)
- Watford Moat House, St Albans Road, Watford (01923 429988) – *ninety rooms*
- Wellington Arms Hotel, Woodford Road, Watford (01923 220739) – *fourteen rooms*
- White House Hotel, Watford (01923 237316) *eighty-four rooms*
- The Two Brewers, Chipperfield (01422 265266) – *twenty rooms*
- Ramada Jarvis, Watford (020 8901 0000) – *modern conference-style hotel with leisure facilities and 135 rooms*
- Long Island Hotel, Rickmansworth (01923 779466) – *fifty rooms*

BED AND BREAKFASTS/GUEST HOUSES

- Bayview Guest House, Hemel Hempstead (01442 392828) – *seventeenth-century building that once housed Hemel's first bank*
- Hemel Guest House, St Albans Hill, Hemel Hempstead (01442 398366)
- Brinns Rockview Guest House, London Road, Apsley (01442 247210)
- 67 Hempstead Road, Kings Langley (01923 400453) – *overlooking the Gade Valley*
- Woodcote House, Kings Langley (01923 262077) – *large timber-frame house within an acre of grounds offering one double, one twin and two single rooms*
- Finch House, St Albans Road, Watford (01923 01923221858) – *guest house with twelve rooms*
- Midmar Guest House, Watford (01923 242015) – *four rooms*
- Redford Lodge, Upton Road, Watford (01923 223785)

Rickmansworth's past is evident along its skyline.

- Ricky Road Guest House, Rickmansworth Road, Watford (01923 465910) – *en suite and family rooms with self-catering suites*
- The Millwards, Hazelwood Road, Croxley Green (01923 226666)
- Eversley Bed and Breakfast, Rickmansworth (01923 334922) – *two rooms*
- Old Ale Guest House, Rickmansworth (01923 775824) – *three rooms*
- Tall Trees Guest House, Rickmansworth (01923 720069) – *four rooms*

CAMPING

This is not a section rich with camping opportunities. The Breakspear Way Caravan Club (01442 268286), set in parkland on the edge of Hemel Hempstead, just to the north of the map, is the exception.

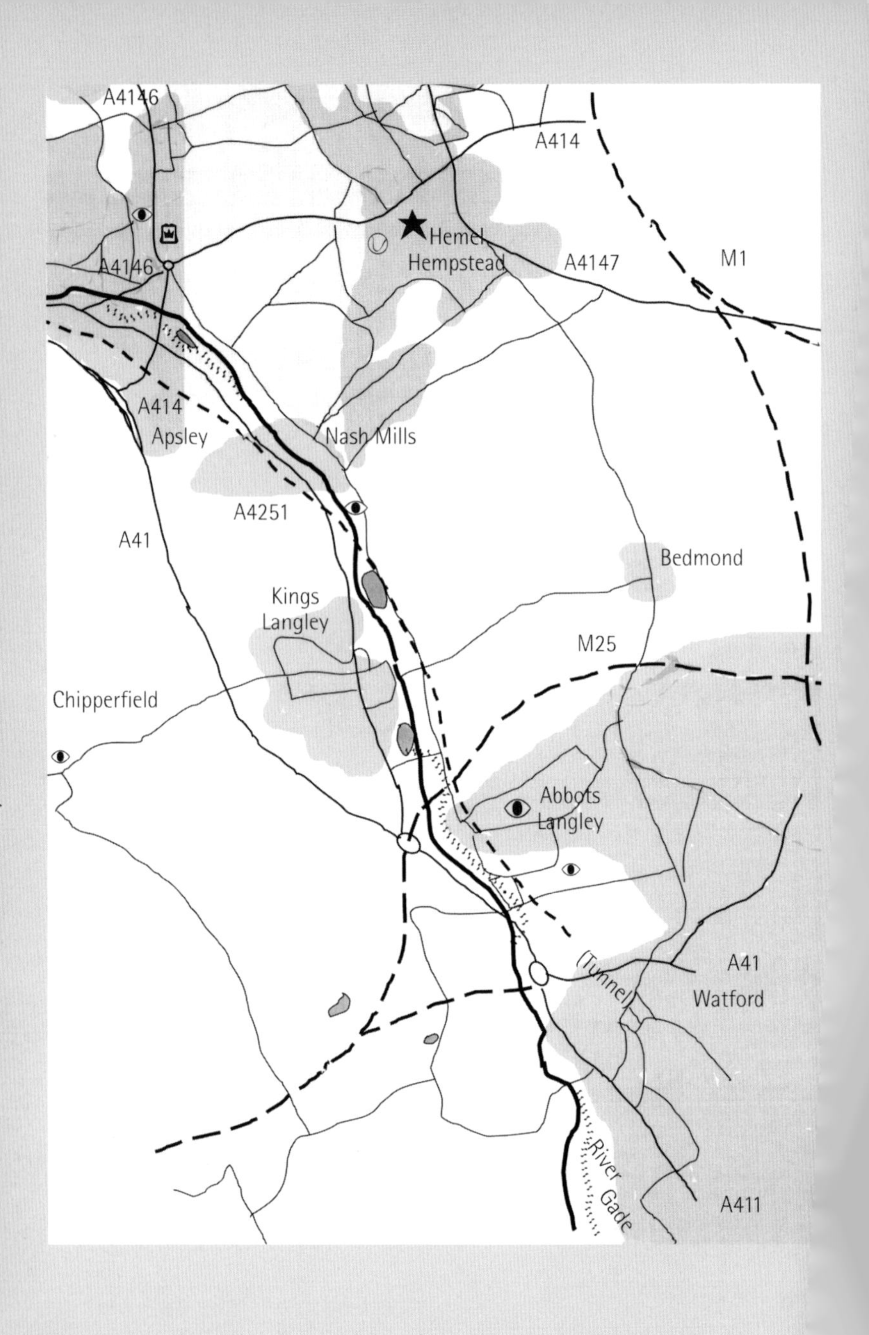
A4146
A414
Hemel Hempstead
A4147
M1
A4146
A414
Apsley
Nash Mills
A4251
A41
Bedmond
Kings Langley
M25
Chipperfield
Abbots Langley
A41
(Tunnel)
Watford
River Gade
A411

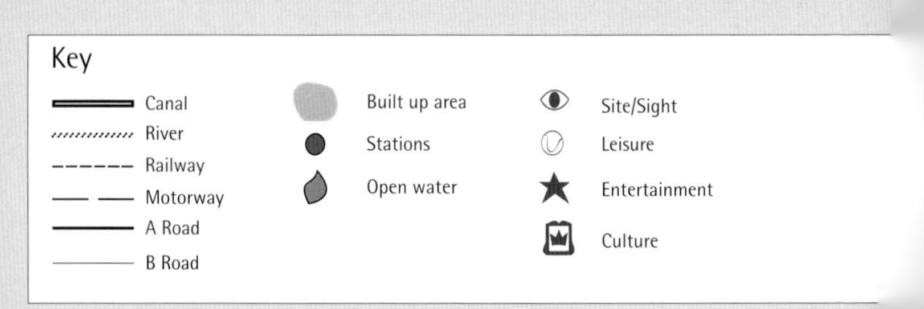
Key
Canal
River
Railway
Motorway
A Road
B Road
Built up area
Stations
Open water
Site/Sight
Leisure
Entertainment
Culture

SEEING AND DOING

INTRODUCTION

Hemel Hempstead in the north, and Watford and Rickmansworth to the south, dominate this section of the towpath, but there is plenty to see and do both between, as well as in, these towns. Chipperfield and Croxley Green both offer a surprising expanse of common among the increasingly built-up landscape, while there are some gems hidden among places such as Abbots Langley and Bedmond that reward those straying away from the canal.

Watford is a more natural focus for arts and entertainment, with Rickmansworth offering some solid alternatives while, with the exception of its large out-of-town complex, Hemel Hempstead has some catching up to do on this front. There are Tourist Information Centres in both Hemel (in the pedestrianised section of the Marlowes Shopping Centre 01442 234222) and Rickmansworth (01923 776611), as well as the Batchworth Lock Canal Centre (at Bridge 173 01923 778382).

SIGHTS

Hemel's status as a New Town restricts its attractions as a tourist destination. Time has had an impact upon the ideals of the town's planners, and what little there is to see here looks a little tired and unloved. A good example is the Water Gardens to the west of the Marlowes Shopping Centre.

The idea of the gardens was to use the river valleys as linear parks and to conceal the housing behind tree belts while harnessing one of the town's greatest assets, its water. The gardens contain a number of statues but also a car park, and it is the influence of the latter that tends to dominate, the result being that the area is probably not the most salubrious in Hemel.

Heading out of Hemel, the old Ovaltine factory on the eastern edge of Kings Langley, not far off the canal at Bridge 159, is currently in the process of being refurbished. It retains its art-nouveau appearance and aficionados of this style may wish to catch a glimpse of it. The famous Ovaltine drink was produced here from 1913 to 2002, with the site also at one point encompassing both an egg farm and a dairy, with milk and eggs both key ingredients of the drink – there is even a road in Kings Langley called Egg Farm Lane. There are plans to create an Ovaltine Heritage Centre there.

> The Ovaltine company also had its own fleet of narrowboats, which used the Grand Union to fetch coal from Birmingham, a journey that typically took ten to fourteen days. There were seven pairs of Ovaltine boats, with the lead boat being motorised, towing a non-motorised 'butty' behind it. Each pair were given names, with the last pair, *Albert* and *Georgette*, making their final journey in April 1959.

The Green that gives Croxley Green its name is worth visiting, if for no other reason than to take in its sheer scale. This is a surprising oasis in an area of otherwise unrelieved uninspiring housing, made all the better by the efforts of the local inhabitants to keep it so. There is even a conservation

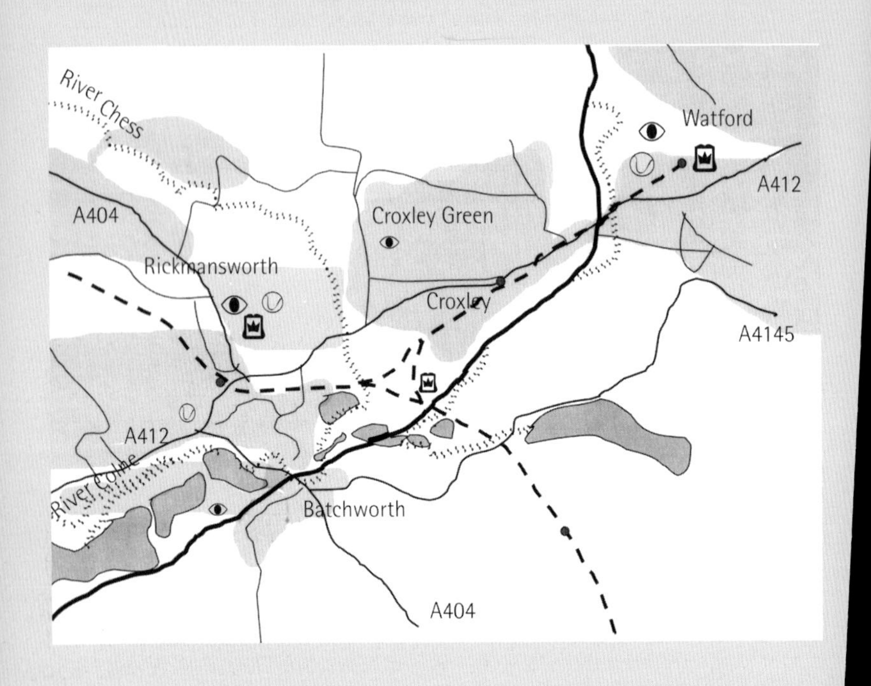
River Chess
Watford
A412
A404
Croxley Green
Rickmansworth
Croxley
A4145
A412
River Colne
Batchworth
A404

Key
Canal
River
Railway
Motorway
A Road
B Road
Built up area
Stations
Open water
Site/Sight
Leisure
Entertainment
Culture

area by a seat carved out of a fallen log where rare wild flowers are grasses are encouraged to prosper.

The area to the south of Abbots Langley is popular with film and TV location managers, due in part to the proximity of Leavesden Country Park and the Leavesden Studios. Films shot here include *Harry Potter, Braveheart* and *Mission Impossible.*

The centre of Abbots Langley village comes as something of a surprise after the relentless housing estates that precede it. The church of St Lawrence has a wooden lychgate, and probably sits on the site of a Saxon church. A Norman nave and aisles were added in the mid-twelfth century, with the tower following shortly afterwards. In 1969 the church suffered from a serious fire which destroyed the organ, choir and much of the roof, but thankfully the bulk of the church survived. There is also a rather splendid Catholic Church of St Saviours in the village with a glorious steel relief over its front doors.

The white corrugated iron-clad Church of the Ascension in Bedmond is worth a detour, with its almost American pioneer-like appearance.

Chipperfield has a wide green with a cricket pitch, and is worth seeing if you wish to see a quintessential English village. A route through Chipperfield Common leads to a 400-year-old Spanish chestnut tree, some prehistoric burial mounds, a dew pond and the Apostles Pond, so-called because it is surrounded by twelve lime trees, first planted in 1714. One of the tress failed to thrive and inevitably became known as the Judas Tree.

> In the seventeenth century, Chipperfield Common was a training ground for prize fighters.

Cassiobury Park, in Watford, is easily accessed from the northern side of town (although cycling is discouraged) and provides an excellent haven away from the busy High Street. A public footpath follows a line of horse-chestnut trees all the way to Whippendell Wood, where there is some parking, and also a permanent orienteering course. Whippendell Wood is an ancient semi-natural wood designated a Site of Special Scientific Interest. It is possible to access the trail from the towpath near Cassiobury Park Locks.

> Cassiobury House was once the home of Queen Adelaide, widow of William IV, and more recently gained a reputation for its sumptuous parties attended by luminaries such as Winston Churchill.

To the south of Watford lies the Cheslyn Gardens (01923 235946), a small 'secret garden' near Watford Junction Station, a mile east of Iron Bridge Lock. Contained within less than 4 acres is a range of garden styles, from formal bedding and manicured lawns to woodland. While in this neck of the town, it is worth looking out for the green-glass construction at the northern end of the High Street belonging to the Peace Hospice.

Watford's town centre seems to have attracted street sculpture in recent years, with examples including the delicate-looking hornet outside McDonalds at the southern end of the High Street, the older war memorial outside the college to the north; and the Friendship Faces outside the One Bell pub, which represent the various fiestas held by the different towns across the world which Watford has a twinning arrangement with.

The Bury in Rickmansworth is a small woodland area, and a path round the back of St Mary's church and some almshouses acts as a route into the Colne Valley Park. The Bury itself is a house built in the sixteenth century for the crown, and occupies what were once the grounds of the Manor House of Rickmansworth. There is a delightful wooden bridge over a stream with

The pedestrianised High Street in Watford makes for easy shopping.

inscriptions carved into its banisters, describing some of the history of the area. The stream itself is lovely and clear, and well it may be as it was once a watercress bed.

Batchworth Lakes, outside Rickmansworth (follow signs to the aquadrome for parking), is a designated nature reserve with a series of lakes for various uses such as watersports and fishing. This resource on the western edge of London is particularly prized by birdwatchers, and includes a heronry. It is possible to weave your way through the lakes and alongside the River Colne all the way from here to Denham, following the route of the canal.

> The hornet represents a nod towards the nickname of the local football team, whose kit used to be predominately yellow and black. They still wear these colours, although in recent years a good dash of red seems to have crept in.

CULTURE AND ENTERTAINMENT

Understandably perhaps, Hemel Hempstead and Watford act as the twin foci for arts and entertainment in this section, although Rickmansworth is also very active and plays host to the aquadrome on the edge of the West London lakes.

The Campus Hall of West Herts College in Marlowes, Hemel Hempstead (01442 228091), regularly stages shows and concerts ranging from performances of the Dacorum Symphony Orchestra to pantomime. Watford has its Palace Theatre (01923 225671), which has recently completed a detailed refurbishment and represents the epitome of local theatre. As well as the now-normal fare of tribute bands, the theatre offers a wide range of dance, new plays, opera and its famous Christmas pantomime.

Also in Watford is The Pump House (01923 225671), a theatre and arts centre on the Lower High Street, hidden away in the town's one-way system. As well as playing host to regular jazz and folk nights, the theatre has its own company and children's theatre group.

The Watford Museum (01923 232297) is a collection of permanent and temporary exhibitions detailing Watford's past, with an emphasis on the publishing and brewing industries that once underpinned the local economy. These days, the focus is as much on the local football club, in which the museum invests much pride.

Rickmansworth has the Watersmeet Theatre (01923 771542) in the centre of the town, which offers a mixture of arts and entertainment centred around cinema, opera, theatre, comedy, music and children's shows. Also in Rickmansworth is the Three Rivers Museum (01923 710365), which includes a collection of artefacts collected from old buildings in the local area. This eclectic collection ranges from archaeological remains to Victorian and wartime memorabilia, and includes a large collection of photographs.

The Batchworth Lock Canal Centre (01923 778382) explores the past of this section of the Grand Union Canal, and is home to both 'Roger' and 'Albert', two narrowboats which offer a connection with the old Ovaltine factory in Kings Langley. Although the centre is free to enter, it is best to check first for opening times. The annual Batchworth Canal festival is also based here. Lasting for a week, this is held every May.

Hemel's entertainment centre is undoubtedly the out-of-town Jarman Park complex, which, as well as having a Tesco superstore, has the following:

- Silver Blades Ice Skating (01442 292202)
- Aquasplash indoor tropical water park (01442 292203) – *has a variety of rides and flumes*
- Hotshots Tenpin Bowling (01442 292208) – *twenty lanes*
- Indoor bowls 901442 292207)
- Odeon Cinema (0870 5050007) – *an eight-screen complex*
- Toddler World Play Zone (01442 212901)

Children may also enjoy local adventure playgrounds situated at Rant Meadow in the Bennetts End district of Hemel Hempstead (01442 242301), and Turners Hill in Adeyfield (01442 242852). There is also a Quasar-laser gun centre in the Marlowes Centre (01442 213200), and a 200-yard dry-ski slope at the Hemel Ski Centre on St Albans Hill (01442 241321).

The Longdean Sports Centre in Bennetts End (01442 407535, open evening only) has a sports hall and aerobics studio, as well as an all-weather pitch. Finally, in this town the Dacorum Athletics Track on Jarman Park has a floodlit eight-lane track to international specifications.

The YMCA Woodlands in Abbots Langley (01923 662222) is run by the YMCA as a leisure facility with a gym, fitness and dance studios.

Within Watford, there is a paddling pool complex and children's putting golf course at Cassiobury Park, and children's adventure playgrounds at Harebreaks in Leggatts Way and Harwoods in Vicarage Road, as well as numerous local parks.

The YMCA Woodlands was originally a Physiotherapy Development Unit, but was acquired from the NHS by the local council, and is leased to the YMCA.

The Watford Leisure Centre (01923 670644) on Horseshoe Lane, towards Abbots Langley, has a state-of-the-art fitness suite, a nine-court sports hall, squash courts, a softplay area, an astro-pitch, and an eight-lane athletic track at the nearby Woodside Stadium.

Watford also has its own out-of-town Woodside Leisure Park. This is a combination of American-diner style eating places as well as a Hollywood Bowl (01923 682929) tenpin-bowling alley and a Warner Village Cinema complex (01923 682886), alongside a Playdome children's play area for the under-fives.

On the road to Rickmansworth there is a Skate Park at Croxley Green (01923 779392), with state-of-the-art concrete ramps suitable for all abilities.

Rickmansworth itself is well provided for with sport facilities, including the William Penn Leisure Centre (01923 771050) in Mill End, which has an indoor swimming pool and a sports hall, as well as squash courts, a dance studio, a gym and The Palms health suite. Rickmansworth also has The Centre (0208 428 4954), a fitness facility with a children's play area.

Perhaps the most significant leisure feature in Rickmansworth, however, is the aquadrome. Spread over 100 acres of water, grassland and woods, this consists of the three Batchworth lakes. Batchworth Lake itself is used for fishing and water skiing, Bury Lake for sailing, windsurfing and canoeing, and Stockers Lake is a bird and wildlife sanctuary owned by Three Valleys Water. There is also the added attraction of a children's play area adjacent to Batchworth Lake.

> The three Batchworth lakes were the result of gravel extraction connected with the construction of the original Wembley complex.

Hemel is a little light on nightlife, although Watford offers four clubs clustered around The Parade area:

- Area, The Parade, Watford (01923 281100)
- Colosseum, Rickmansworth Road, Watford (01923 445000)
- Destiny, The Parade, Watford (01923 239848)
- Jongleurs Comedy Club, The Parade, Watford (01923 240688)
- Jumpin Jaks, Jarman Park, Hemel Hempstead (01442 292209)
- Visage and Ethos, Jarman Park, Hemel Hempstead (01442 292201)

The Litten Tree pub (01442 253212) and Jumpin Jaks in Hemel Hempstead both offer live music, as does The Horns in Watford (01923 225020).

This statue of a hornet in Watford is a homage to Watford FC – 'The Hornets'.

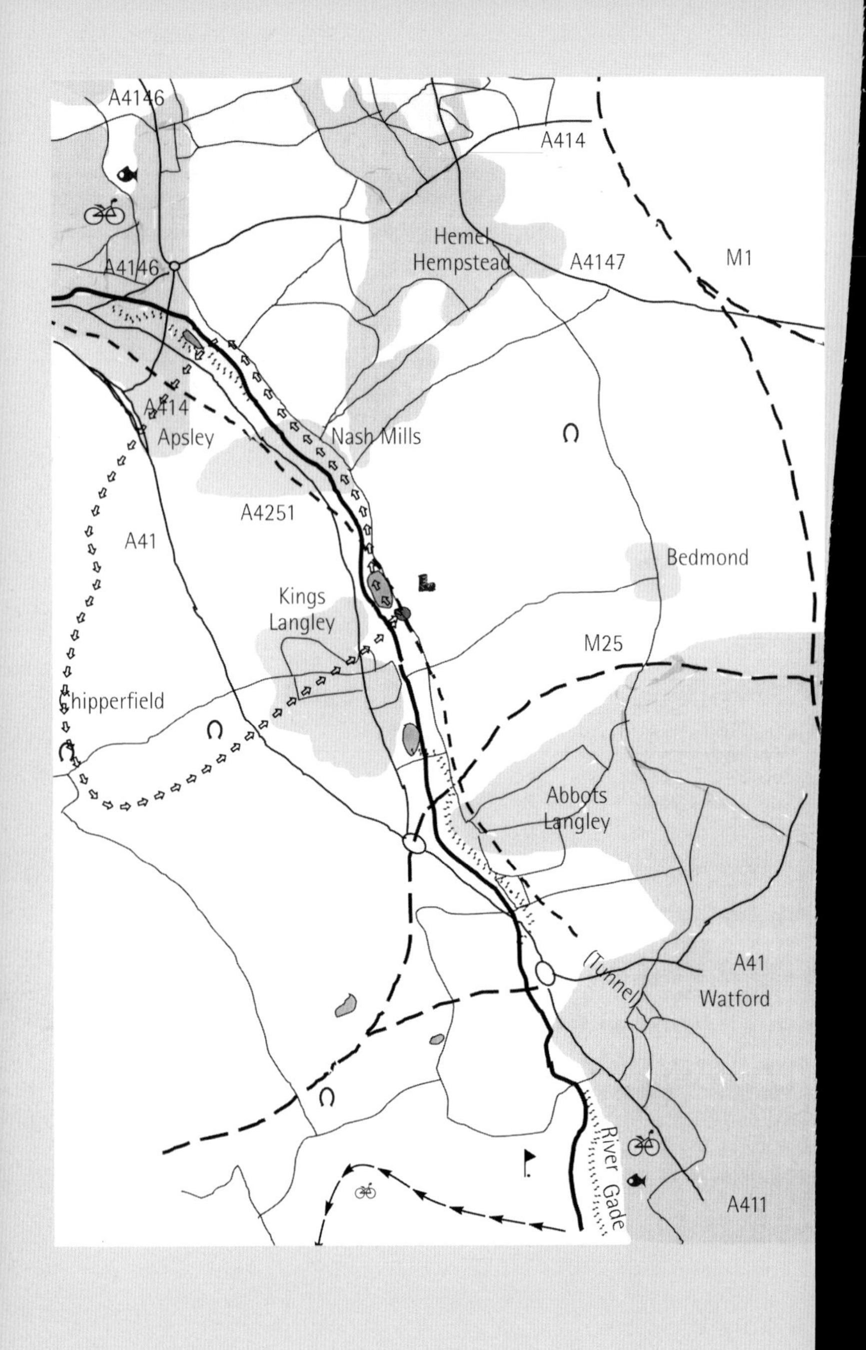
A4146
A414
Hemel Hempstead
A4147
M1
A4146
A414
Apsley
Nash Mills
A4251
A41
Bedmond
Kings Langley
M25
Chipperfield
Abbots Langley
(Tunnel)
A41
Watford
River Gade
A411

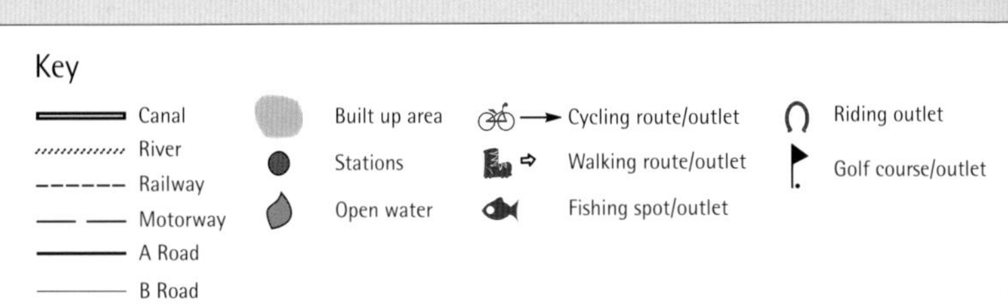
Key
Canal
River
Railway
Motorway
A Road
B Road
Built up area
Stations
Open water
Cycling route/outlet
Walking route/outlet
Fishing spot/outlet
Riding outlet
Golf course/outlet

SAMPLING

INTRODUCTION

Whatever your preferred modus operandi, there are plenty of opportunities for sampling the delights of this section, characterised to the north by its steep-sided valleys, and to the south by its expansive lakes.

Walkers are particularly favoured in this section, although the steep gradients in some parts can make for 'challenging' routes, with this applying to cyclists also. Riders are less fortunate, although there is no shortage of stables, while golfers can be forgiven for thinking they've died and gone to heaven, and the profusion of rivers and lakes to complement the canal is good news for anglers also.

The Three Rivers Council has produced a number of leaflets detailing traffic-free routes through the southern part of this section. Details on these are given below, and they can be obtained direct by calling 01923 776611 or online (see Learn More and Links).

WALKING

Generally, walkers are spoiled for choice along this section, with an intricate network of paths linking up either side of the towpath, with most following field edges, although there are also plenty of other paths through woodland to offer some variety. In addition, the valleys of the Rivers Gade, Chess and Colne all provide natural routes, around which both linear and circular walks can be constructed. A number of leaflets have been produced detailing more formal walks, and Learn More and Links gives details on how to download information on these.

One such route heading north out of the section into the heart of Herts is The Nicky line, which starts at the Midland Hotel in Hemel Hempstead, and is well way-marked. Suitable for walkers and cyclists alike, this 8.75-mile path follows the route of an old steam railway line, a branch of the London North Western Railway.

There are a number of formal walks through the Colne Valley Park, some of which are exclusive to this section, while others stray into Section E. As its name suggests, the Chess Valley Walk follows the route of the River Chess from Rickmansworth back to its source at Chesham, with a section known as the Lower Chess Valley particularly pertinent to this section. South of Rickmansworth, the Old Shire Lane Circular Walk follows a course south of Batchworth to Denham in Section E, and then back again.

Other formal walks include those developed by the Three Rivers Council around Croxley Common and Croxley Green, along with one that allows the walker to explore Abbots Langley. The Three Rivers Council has also produced leaflets on the Alder Nature Trail, a mile-long walk that starts at the Aquadrome.

Walk D starts at Apsley on the outskirts of Hemel Hempstead, and cuts across the one-time royal hunting ground at Chipperfield Common.

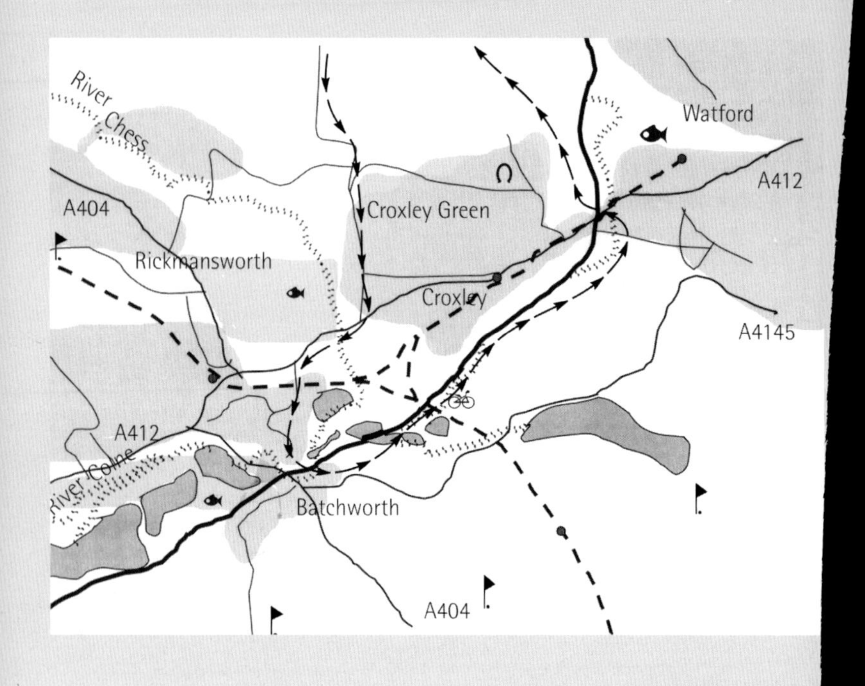
River Chess
Watford
A412
A404
Croxley Green
Rickmansworth
Croxley
A4145
A412
River Colne
Batchworth
A404

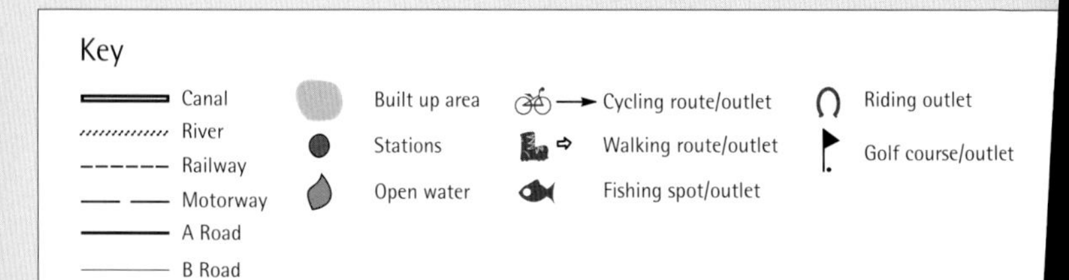
Key
Canal
River
Railway
Motorway
A Road
B Road
Built up area
Stations
Open water
Cycling route/outlet
Walking route/outlet
Fishing spot/outlet
Riding outlet
Golf course/outlet

SECTION D WALK

Kings Langley, Apsley and Chipperfield

Description:	*A challenging combination of roadside and field walking with a steady climb in the middle.*
Distance:	*10.5 miles*
Duration:	*4.5 hours*
Starting point:	*Grid Reference 080020, OS Explorer 182*
Nearest Refreshment:	*Any of the pubs along Kings Langley High Street*

Park in or near the railway station car park in Kings Langley, just off the High Street. Pick up the towpath down a short footpath behind the Ovaltine factory that leads to Bridge 159. Turn right, heading north, and keep with the towpath until Bridge 152 at Frogmore End. Turn left, to join Featherbed Lane, and stick with this, passing over the A41. Where the lane bends to the right, pick up the footpath straight in front of you.

You now cross some fields, heading towards Great Wood and Phasels Wood, a scout-camping ground. This will emerge onto Rucklers Lane, where you turn right. Barnes Lane will follow shortly on your left, and you need to go down this, passing Badgerdell Wood on your right. After about half a mile, pick up the path on your right, which takes you through Scatterdells Wood and emerges onto Scattersdells Lane. At a junction of paths, turn left towards Chipperfield. Turn right on reaching the road and take the first road on the left.

At the crossroads, turn left and follow the edge of Chipperfield Common, past the Manor House, until you reach a footpath on the left towards Topcommon. Take this and descend through fields for 1.5 miles, passing under the A41, just after which you pick up a path to your left. This leads you past the site of the old Royal Palace and Priory, and on reaching a road you need to turn right. Follow this downhill until you reach Kings Langley High Street where you turn right and then left at the roundabout, which brings you back to the canal and thence to your starting point.

Walking equipment outlets along this section include:

- Culverhouse, The Parade, Watford (01923 244100)
- Fra Angelico, Watford (01923 297890)
- Millets, The Harlequin Centre, Watford (01923 212427)
- Venturesport, High Street, Watford (01923 244100)

CYCLING

The Ebury Way passes all three of the main rivers in this section, as well as the canal, and is a valid route for walkers, cyclists and horse-riders, although the latter are restricted to the section between Moor Lane crossing and Rickmansworth. The route covers a total of 3.5 miles and starts at Batchworth, passes south of Croxley Green Moor, and ends in West Watford. Once again, a leaflet on the route is available from the Three Rivers Council.

The Hemel Hempstead Cycling Club (01442 256506) meets every Monday evening at the Nash Mills Recreation Centre, and is open to anyone aged twelve and above, catering for all aspects of cycling, including touring and racing. In Watford, the Westerley Cycling Club (0208 4285946) organises rides into the nearby Chiltern lanes, as well as longer tours and competitive racing.

Another good way to sample this section on two wheels is to follow the Ebury Way to its end and pick up the Riverside Road, turning left, and then left again into Wiggenhall Road (the A4178). Turn left at Vicarage Road, going past the football stadium, and then right along Hagden Lane for 200 yards before crossing straight over into Queens Avenue. After another 100 yards turn left into Whippendell Road.

> On the last sharp turn right on the Ebury Way, there is an RBS Millennium Cycleway marker and, shortly afterwards, the Riverside community park, complete with skateboarding facilities.

At the roundabout turn right, and then left at the next, and continue until you cross the canal. Pick up the towpath (Bridge 169) and turn right, following the towpath to the next bridge (168), where you turn left onto Rousebarn Lane. Follow this past the golf course, to Chandlers Cross, where the road becomes Redhall Lane. On reaching a T-junction, turn left (Sarratt Road), turning right at Thurwood House shortly after a sharp turn to the left.

> The route here takes you past two of Watford's cycle shops, just before Vicarage Road.

Go straight on over the crossroads and turn right at the next junction into The Green, through Croxley Green. On reaching the main road turn right, and follow this through Rickmansworth and back to Batchworth, a total of a little over 13 miles.

Cycle outlets along this section include:

- Cycleopedia, Watford (01923 221901)
- Dee's Cycles, Watford (01923 243707)
- Neale and Sons, Watford (01923 223916)
- Pedal Power, Leavesden Road, Watford (01923 247462)
- Sports and Leisure, Marlowes, Hemel Hempstead (01442 231411)
- Thirteens Cycles, Chalk Hill, Watford (01923 234221)

RIDING

Many of the routes highlighted elsewhere in this section are also suitable for riders, otherwise formal bridleways tend to be thin on the ground. Where they do exist, for example around Pimlico south-east of Hemel Hempstead and Chipperfield, these tend to coincide with stables and liveries, with the following a list of some of the horse-riding establishments along this section:

- Coltspring School of Riding, Chandlers Cross, between Hunton Bridge and Croxley Green (01923 774964) – *riding school*
- Greinan Farm Livery and Tuition, Chipperfield (01442 832134) – *stables*
- High Herts Riding School, Pimlico, Hemel Hempstead (01442 269265)
- Kings Langley Riding Schhol, Chipperfield Road, Kings Langley (01923 270719)
- Puddingstone Stables, Hemel Hempstead (01442 241971)
- Rucklers Lane Livery Yard, Kings Langley (0411 494914)
- Watford Riding School, Watford (01923 212670)

Not a mirage but a mural, showing how things used to be at Batchworth.

FISHING

Once again, as in Section C, the London Anglers Association (0208 6207477) has day-ticket rights along two portions of the canal along this stretch, namely the short run between Apsley End (accessed via Red Lion Lane) and Hemel Hempstead, taking in Nash Mills, and the stretch from Hunton Bridge to Apsley End.

Also featured in Section C, the Boxmoor and District Angling Society (01442 230925), has non-canal fisheries on this section, namely Durrants Hill just to the east of the A414 and north of Apsley, and a short stretch of the River Colne near Watford.

The first of these is broken into two lakes, only one of which is a day-ticket water. Bream feature once again here, but there is also a good head of crucian carp, rudd and perch. The second stretch of Boxmoor water is a very short distance between the A41 and the M1 in Otterspool. Fish here include chub, perch, roach and pike.

Uxbridge Rovers Angling Society (see Learn More and Links) control the fishing on Batchworth Lake, which is known locally as being good for carp, as well as bream and tench. A feature of this lake is that night-fishing is allowed.

Fishing is also possible on the three rivers that run through this section: River Chess at Rickmansworth, a short stretch of almost canal-like river with a weir pool at the far end which is controlled by the West Hampstead Angling Society; the River Colne at Rickmansworth Aquadrome, which is controlled by Uxbridge Rovers Angling Society and includes half a mile of river with two weirs, rapids and some deep slow water where barbell up to 10lb, chub up to 5lb and bream up to 7lb can be caught, along with other species; the River Gade at Cassiobury Park (contact 01442 401154), where carp up to 30lb and chub up to 5lb can be caught.

Murals brighten up the scene at Bridge 153.

Outlets selling fishing supplies along this stretch include:

- Oxhey Angling Centre, Pinner Road, Watford (01923 252373)
- Queensway Angling, Hemel Hempstead (01442 254723)
- The Tackle Carrier, Watford (01923 232393)

OTHER

This is an area rich in golf courses, ranging from the municipal to the highly exclusive, with most taking advantage of the steep-sided valleys that are such a distinguishing characteristic of the local landscape. The following represents a list of the main clubs in the area:

- Batchworth Park Golf Club, London Road, Rickmansworth (01923 711400) – *18 holes, 6,723 yards, practice green and chipping area*
- Moor Park, Rickmansworth (01923 773146) – *two courses in parkland: the High Course is 18 holes 6,713 yards, and the West Course is 18 holes 5,815 yards, and also has a practice ground.*
- Rickmansworth Public Golf Course (01923 773163) – *an undulating parkland course of 18 holes 4,557 yards*
- Shendish Manor Golf Club, between Kings Langley and Hemel Hempstead (01442 251806) – *mature parkland course with a 18 holes, 5,660 yards, and a 9-hole pitch-and-putt course*
- West Herts Golf Club, Cassiobury Park, Croxley Green (01923 224264) – *18 holes 6,488 yards*

SECTION E
BATCHWORTH TO BRENTFORD

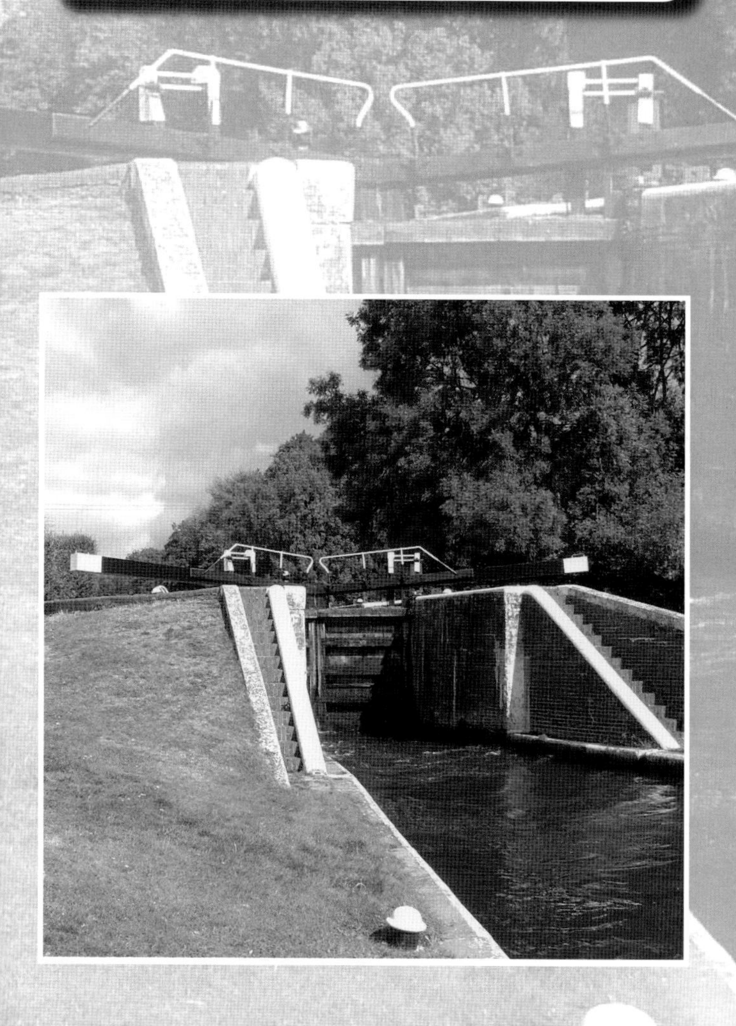

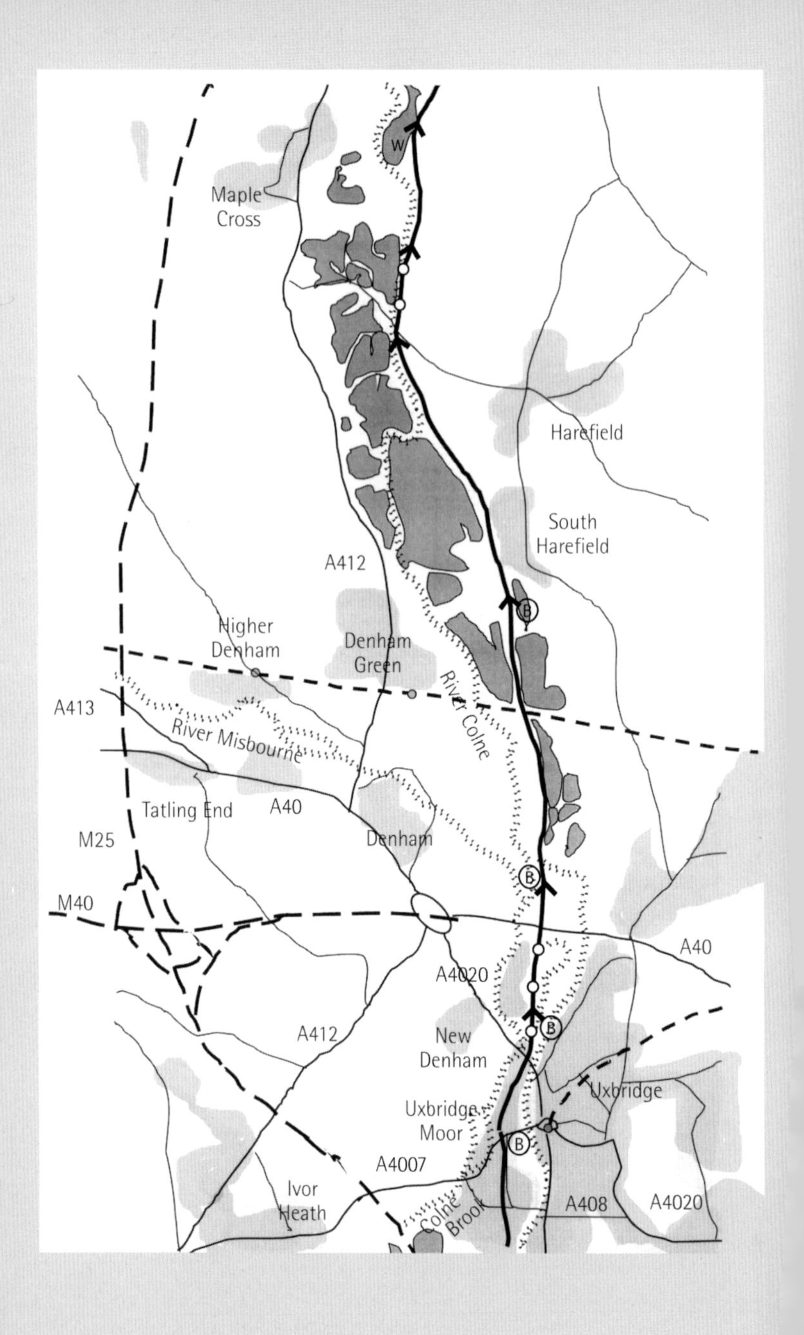

Maple Cross
Harefield
South Harefield
A412
Higher Denham
Denham Green
River Colne
A413
River Misbourne
Tatling End
A40
M25
Denham
M40
A40
A4020
A412
New Denham
Uxbridge
Uxbridge Moor
A4007
Ivor Heath
Colne Brook
A408
A4020
W
B

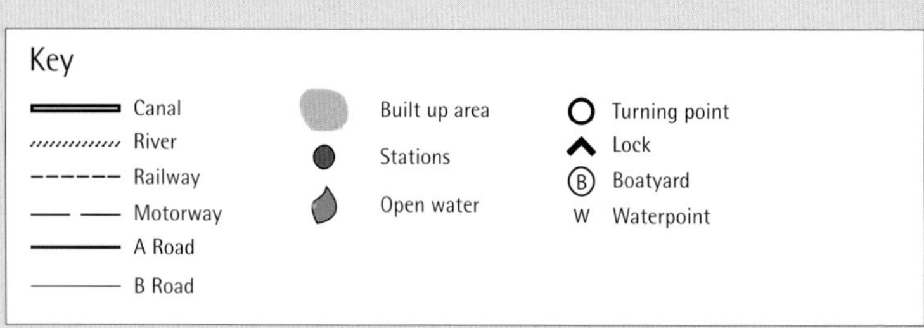

Key
Canal
River
Railway
Motorway
A Road
B Road
Built up area
Stations
Open water
Turning point
Lock
Boatyard
Waterpoint

SHAPERS

THE CANAL ON THIS STRETCH

KEY FACTS

LENGTH: 16.5 miles

BOATYARDS: 8
- Harefield Marina
- Denham Marina
- Uxbridge Boat Centre
- Highline Yachting
- Adelaide Marine
- SPL Marine
- Brentford Marine Services

WATER POINTS: 5
- Copper Mill Lock
- Iver Lane
- Bulls Bridge
- Norwood Top Lock
- Brentford Gauging Locks

TURNING POINTS: 12
- Troy Cut
- South Harefield
- Below Bridge 183
- Above Uxbridge Lock
- Below Uxbridge Lock
- Below Cowley Lock
- Bridge 190
- Bridge 191
- Hayes
- Bridge 202
- Between Norwood & Hanwell Locks
- Three Bridges

LOCKS: 19
- Springwell Lock (7ft 11in)
- Copper Mill Lock (5ft 10in)
- Black Jack's Lock (3ft 8in)
- Widewater Lock (8ft)
- Denham Deep Lock (11ft 1in)
- Uxbridge Lock (4ft 7in)
- Cowley Lock (6ft 6in)
- Norwood Locks (2) (15ft 9in)
- Hanwell Locks (6) (53ft 2in)
- Osterley Lock (5ft 7in)
- Clitheroe's Lock (7ft 7in)
- Brentford Guaging Locks (5ft 6in)
- Thames Locks

West London's lakes dominate the beginning of this section, with the Thames offering a fitting conclusion. In between, the scenery becomes increasingly urbanised, but never overwhelmingly so, with both Osterley and Syon Parks offering wide expanses of greenery, and the Hanwell Locks an unexpected and pleasant respite from a more industrial landscape.

Batchworth, Stockers and Springwell Lakes occupy the low-lying land to the right of the towpath, although all are hidden by trees. There is a car park just after Springwell Lock, which offers easy access, as well as access to the wider Colne Valley Walk.

Feeders in and out of the lakes occur regularly along this stretch, where there is also the Springwell Reed Bed Nature Reserve. Taking aside the rather obvious sewage works that follow, this is a pretty stretch of the canal, wide and almost

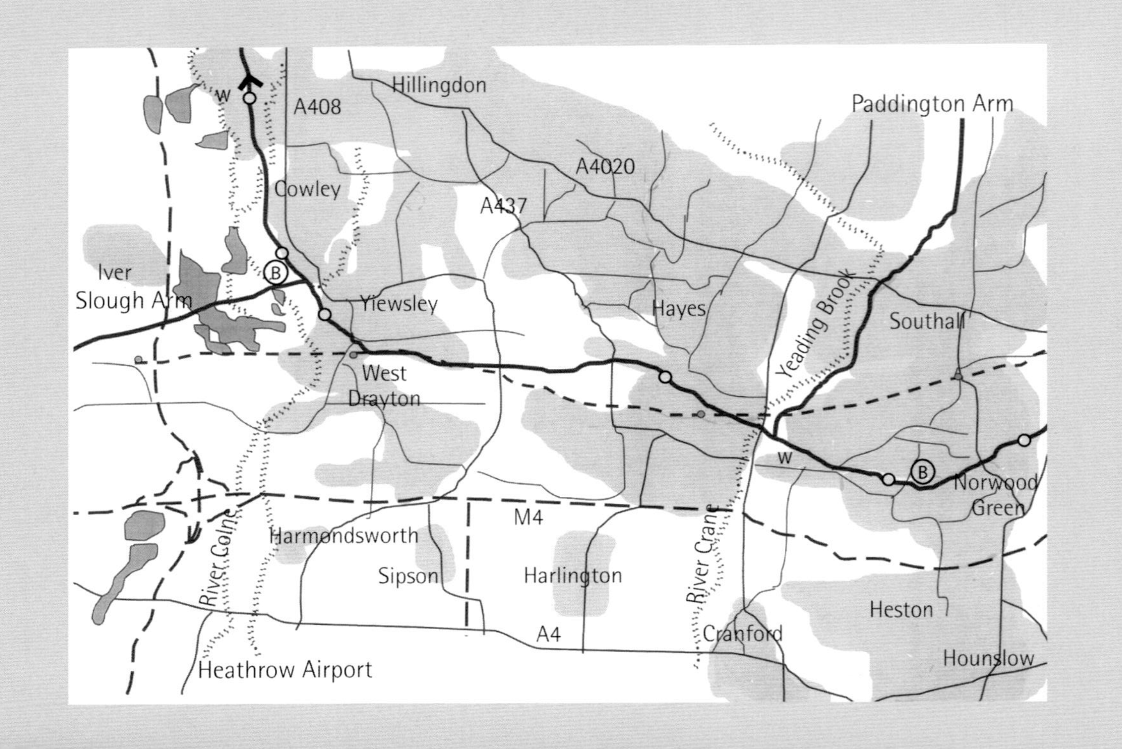

Hillingdon
A408
W
Paddington Arm
A4020
Cowley
A437
Iver
Slough Arm
B
Yiewsley
Hayes
Yeading Brook
Southall
West
Drayton
W
B
Norwood
Green
M4
Harmondsworth
River Colne
Sipson
Harlington
River Crane
Heston
A4
Cranford
Hounslow
Heathrow Airport

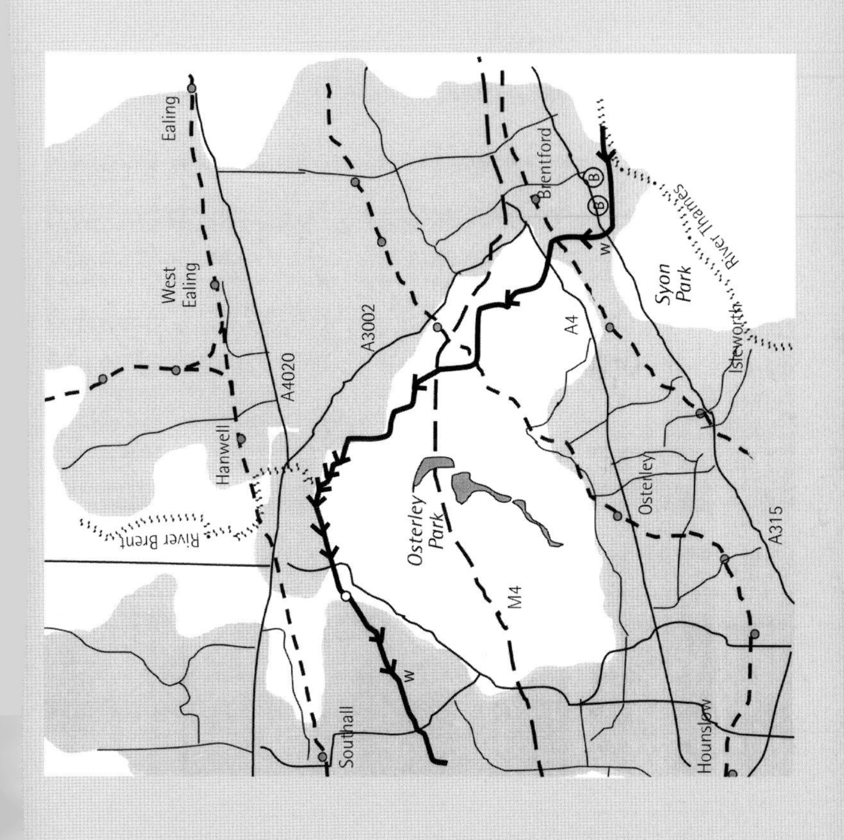
Ealing
West Ealing
Hanwell
River Brent
A4020
A3002
Brentford
River Thames
Syon Park
Isleworth
A4
Osterley Park
M4
Osterley
A315
Hounslow
Southall
B
B
W
W

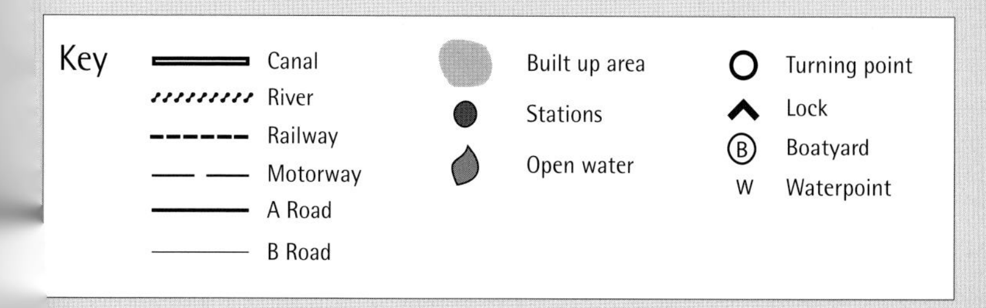
Key
Canal
River
Railway
Motorway
A Road
B Road
Built up area
Stations
Open water
Turning point
Lock
B Boatyard
W Waterpoint

river-like, with good scenery. Weeds can be a problem for boaters though, and the towpath does not quite meet the standards reached elsewhere on this canal, being a bit rutted.

A row of cottages to the right, and converted wharf buildings to the left, precede Copper Mill Lock, where the river also comes alongside. On the opposite side there is the old mill weir, used these days by canoeists. After the lock, the towpath becomes more solid, leading up to some traffic lights just before the Coy Carp pub. It is possible to moor here.

A run of sympathetic modern canalside houses follow, complete with private moorings. Some views of the lakes at last emerge to the right, including one with a magnificent C-shaped weir, and another just before Black Jack's Lock, home of Black Jack's Restaurant.

A long straight follows, after which walkers may again spy the lakes to their right. Long straights seem to be vogue here, no doubt encouraged by the local topography, and there is another just after a redundant footbridge, and yet another in the run-up to Widewater Lock, with Harefield Marina and access to South Harefield at Bridge 180. In fact, this particular straight is almost 2 miles long, and ends at Denham Deep Lock, where there is another boatyard and a small café.

It is here that a new river joins the journey, the Colne, which until now has been wending its way through the lakes after approaching from the west. The elegant whitewashed Bridge 183 follows, and marks a confluence of footpaths, one of which is the South Bucks Way, the beginning of the end of a very pleasant rural stretch.

Just after the bridge, there is a run of three pipe bridges and some measure of respite before the landscape becomes more built up in the form of meadows to the left, used mainly by horses. Boaters can turn where the River Colne makes a grander entrance onto the canal.

Bungalows with private moorings gather up opposite, while horse chestnuts line the towpath side. After a bend in the route, a run of long-term moorings starts, continuing all the way up to Uxbridge Lock, and Bridge 184, a turnover bridge which takes the towpath to the right. This is the home of Denham Marina, although technically it lies on the outskirts of Uxbridge, whose presence becomes increasingly insistent from hereon. The clearest evidence of this is large concrete and glass office buildings, many of which seem to be unoccupied.

> In the early 1900s, this was a favoured spot for cyclists, with the Swan and Bottle a favoured lunch stop for Londoners on a Sunday.

The historic Swan and Bottle pub lies just before Bridge 155, sitting on an island between the canal and the Colne, and it can be worth pulling off the towpath to explore this area more deeply, especially its history of milling, including an Old Mill House, dated 1696.

Another long run of moorings follows, a combination of long-term and visitor, as the canal curves to the left and past the comprehensive, but not always easy to get to, Uxbridge Boat Centre. A long straight follows, with mainly visitor moorings, and the landscape becomes decidedly more built up, although never overpowering.

Trees hide most of the surrounding buildings, and it is surprisingly quiet around here. There is even a glimpse of fields to the left at the designated Uxbridge Visitors' Moorings just before Cowley Lock and Iver Lane Bridge (No.188), where the towpath crosses back over to the left, and again after the bridge, where there is a pub and a tearoom. A large open space with a children's play area tucked away in the corner follows on the towpath side, and Bridge 189 is a startling white affair.

Just after the bridge there is a series of houseboats and larger river craft, including both Dutch and Thames Barges in various states of repair. After a slight kink to the left, the modern-looking Packet Boat Lane Marina appears just after the Turning Point pub.

Cowley Peachey Junction soons follows, with the Slough Arm of the canal heading off to the right, following an almost straight line due west into Slough, and the entrance to the marina actually lies just off the Slough Arm. It is around there that the first of a series of metal kissing-gates appear, which can be an encumbrance to cyclists.

An unexpected open space appears on the non-towpath side, the result of the clearance of some industrial units, which allows views of the planes taking off from Heathrow to the south. The sight (and sound!) of these becomes a growing presence from hereon in.

Elsewhere, industrial development remains the hallmark of the towpath along this stretch, although there seems to be a growing trend to convert old warehousing into flats. Boats can turn along this stretch and there is access to the pubs and shops at West Drayton from Bridge 192, with the railway running along the offside for a mile or so along this long straight section of the canal, and the stone Bridge 193 sitting in the middle of it.

Soon after this, the landscape opens up to the left, with the advent of Stockley Park and the industrial units on the non-towpath side beginning to fade away. The more traditional Bridge 195 looks incongruous alongside its modern (unnumbered) neighbour, which carries the A408. The local tradition of brick-making is echoed shortly afterwards by a large cement works to the right. Although mooring is possible along this section, it hardly qualifies as a picturesque spot.

Parkland is the dominant feature by the towpath, although a high hedge prevents full enjoyment of it, with yet more industrial units on the opposite bank.

Bulls Bridge, where the Paddington Arm swings away to the north.

SECTION E

The land hereabouts is probably best described as 'having potential', and there are plans to build a marina in the vicinity.

A noticeboard by the towpath describes Stockley Park as the 'realisation of a vision, a transformation of derelict land into a successful business park and an outstanding community leisure facility'. Two features stand out: a golf course and a large Glaxo office building.

Another of the long straights so characteristic of this stretch follows Bridge 198, as the canal runs through the heart of Hayes Town. Again, mooring is possible here, but not particularly desirable given the immediate surroundings. A sign just before Bulls Bridge Junction declares, 'you are now entering the London Borough of Ealing'.

Bulls Bridge itself is a white affair where the canal splits, with the Paddington Arm heading northwards. There is a Tesco and retail park here with convenient mooring. Coal, brought all the way from Wales, used to be loaded onto boats for transport to Brentford at Bulls Bridge until Brunel built his railway in 1859. There is a small development of houseboats here, some of which run to two stories, although many do not resemble boats at all, and are more like Portakabins dropped in the water.

From the 1920s, Bulls Bridge was a repair and maintenance yard for the newly created Grand Union Canal Carrying Co., and in the Second World War the area was a training base for women recruited to run the canals.

More conventional housing running right up to the towpath follows, with a turning point just before Bridge 202, where there is also a park with children's play equipment. A further long straight stretch follows, leading up to the start of the final flight of locks on the canal. Those looking to moor can to do so here, with houses now occupying both sides of the canal. Many of these are pre-war, and it is possible to imagine what the canal would have looked like during that period, with even an old-style gasometer on the skyline to the left.

Look out for the Braille reliefs along this stretch, depicting canalside scenes.

The towpath, which has been fairly solid from Cowley Peachey, begins to become slightly more rutted around here, with housing rather than industry dominating both banks, and the Adelaide Dock on the left. This was taken over by British Waterways in 2004, with the previous owners falling victim to the foot-and-mouth restrictions of 2001, when there was no pleasure traffic at all along this stretch of the canal.

The short arm to the left before the locks is Maypole Dock, a half-mile run built in 1912 to serve the Monstead margarine factory.

The locks are preceded by Norwood Yard long-term moorings. An easily missed feature after the first two (Norwood) locks is Three Bridges at Bridge 205. This is an intersection of three transport routes – the canal, road and railway – intersecting at different angles and on three levels. Particularly striking are the high brick arches Brunel chose to employ to carry his railway. This spot, now scheduled as an ancient monument, is best viewed from the road-bridge above the canal.

Three Bridges is also home to three species of fern: the Black Spleen Wort, Wall Rue and Harts Tongue.

St Bernards Hospital, or Hanwell Asylum (see Seeing and Doing), sits in the middle of the Hanwell Locks, on a bend in the canal. The towpath cheers up along the locks, of which there are six. With open space both sides, the area to the south, the non-towpath side, being the grounds of Osterley Park, this run is something of an oasis in an otherwise uninspiring section of the canal. Halfway through the locks, the River Brent comes alongside, signalling the beginning of the end of the canal itself.

> Look out for the bricked-in arch in the asylum wall. Coal used to be brought in by boat to feed the hospital's boilers, and any surplus from its vegetable gardens brought out; the hospital was self-sufficient in providing both vegetables and meat from its own herds.

The towpath loses its hard standing after the locks, and before long the by-now familiar sight of industrial activity returns. The canal begins to wiggle around a bit more, following the course of the Brent, with scrub being the main towpath theme. A large, and potentially quite dangerous, weir appears on the left, made all the more so by the fact that Osterley Lock follows soon after, where there is a small picnic area.

The towpath passes under the M4 at Bridge 206, as the ever-present planes start to get larger and noisier. An open railway bridge follows, with the iron-roving Gallows Bridge taking the towpath over to the right. A second weir appears on the left, this one less obvious and therefore even more dangerous, with Clitheroe's Lock shortly after it.

> Look out also for the bricks laid into the ground at Osterley Lock, depicting various canalside scenes, made by children from a local school.

The defining feature of a second Glaxo SmithKline office building rises up on the left, with its large yellow sculpture and other metal *objets d'ârte* in the shape of knots lying less obviously on the side of the water. In the same way the Kodak Tower defines Hemel Hempstead, this building stands out on the Brentford skyline, with its glass panels reflecting images of the planes flying in and out of Heathrow.

Having passed under the A4, the towpath approaches an old BW shed and the canal becomes much wider, with visitors' moorings and a vast complex of flats being built in an area known as The Island, around the approach to the Brentford Gauging Locks, a pair of locks with one for traffic going upstream, and the other for traffic going downstream.

The towpath leaves the canal at the next bridge, Brentford High Street, and although it is possible to pick it up on the other side, this is only for a couple of hundred yards alongside permanent residential moorings. After this, you need to head left and thread a path through the garages servicing London taxi cabs, and follow signs for the Thames Path. This brings you back to the final stretch of the canal, which ends at the Thames Locks (No.101), another double, where there is a powerful weir to the left.

THE SLOUGH ARM

The Slough Arm heads off in a westerly direction in an almost straight line from Cowley Peachey. One of the country's most recent canals, it was opened in 1882 to link the brickworks in Slough to its main markets. The arm is not used much by boaters, and offers a not-terribly-inspiring 5-mile (but lock-free) route into the town so famously derided by John Betjeman, although there is some good flora along the route.

The area to the north of the canal is largely open, while Langley sits to the south. Slough is a large and busy place, with all main services and facilities in its centre.

THE PADDINGTON ARM

There are a further 14 miles of canal out to the north and west, leading to the picturesque Little Venice and beyond, with the water threading a path across north and east London via the Regent's Canal. Paddington Basin itself is currently the subject of a major redevelopment, along the lines of that also taking place in Brentford, although on a much larger scale. The route is largely urban, and although golf courses line parts of the canal, railway lines to the north and south are defining features.

PRINCIPAL TOWNS AND VILLAGES ALONG THIS STRETCH

The towns and villages along this section can be seen as falling into three broad 'zones':

The first includes those to the north, just either side of the M25, which sit in either Buckinghamshire, or the outer fringes of Middlesex. Of these, Uxbridge is by far the largest, although not the most distinctive, with villages such as Denham, Harefield and Iver perhaps vying for this crown.

The second incorporates the long strip of development linking Uxbridge and Ealing along the A4020, and includes places such as Hillingdon, Southall and Hanwell, as well as other communities north of the M4 such as Hayes. Although each of these is distinct in its own right, it is often difficult to distinguish where one begins and other ends – the line between Yiewsley and West Drayton being a classic example of this.

Finally, there are those towns south of the M4 where the Thames has had as much influence as the airport in defining local communities. Although these too can often be hard to separate, towns such as Osterley and Isleworth, along with Hounslow and Brentford, seem to offer clearer identities and strive harder to maintain these.

BRENTFORD:

A canal and riverside town, often mistakenly thought to be the county town of Middlesex. Brentford is currently in the process of a major regeneration to exploit its waterside connections, and is set to become a location of choice for the urban flat dweller.

COWLEY:

A largely built-up area lacking a clear focus. There is a large recreation area bordering the canal, which does something to break up the rows of semi-detached and terraced housing. The idea of Cowley as a village, as some signs would have you believe, was probably long since passed.

CRANFORD:

A small village sandwiched by the outskirts of Hounslow and the boundaries of Heathrow airport to the east and west, and Cranford Country Park to the north.

DENHAM:

Very much a village of two contrasts. The main shopping area sits just off the A40 and is surrounded predominately by flats. The much older Denham village, which runs round the back, is a gem. It has a stream running through it and, along with a couple of pubs and restaurants, has a number of historic and ivy-clad buildings

The village is sandwiched between Denham Court and Denham Place, with the latter having a long brick wall protecting its privacy, while the former sits on the banks of the Colne.

On its signs, Denham proudly declares itself to be twinned with Denham Shark Bay, Western Australia.

DENHAM GREEN:

The most built up of the different places carrying Denham in their name, Denham Green has the distinction of having the main station. There is a 'garden village' to the north-west of the village, currently being redeveloped as homes for those of retirement age.

The name 'Denham' derives from the words 'denu' and 'ham', which together mean 'valley homestead' – a description as true today as when it was first coined.

EALING:

A focal point for West London on the end of the Central Underground Line, largely defined by its shopping centres and its spacious common. Housing is spread across a series of distinct districts, broken up by park-land and the intersection of different transport routes.

Denham Garden Village also plays host to a Licensed Victuallers' nursing home, for those who once ran their own pubs.

HANWELL:

A tale of two settlements, Hanwell has both its main street and its more village-like core. A cemetery belonging to the Royal Borough of Kensington and Chelsea sits on the eastern fringe, and its old asylum is near the heart, while the Hanwell Locks pass to the south.

HAREFIELD:

Situated on top of a hill, Harefield commands some of the last views out towards London before the metropolis takes over. The village is probably best known for its pioneering heart hospital, but it has a vibrant High Street and a village green.

HARLINGTON:

Squashed between Hayes and Heathrow, this is small town with some shops and a distinctive local church.

Harlington's church of St Peter and St Paul holds annual bell-ringing events.

HARMONDSWORTH:

A village south of the A4, with a mix of Georgian and Victorian architecture, and now home to British Airway's Waterside headquarters.

HAYES:

A centre consisting of shops on one side, and a heath on the other, dominates Hayes, with streets of 1930s terraced and semi-detatched housing radiating off the main road, with the occasional tower block adding to the mix. The Church Road conservation area preserves some of the original village.

HESTON:

Probably best known for its motorway service station, the village of Heston lies just south of the motorway and to the west of Osterley Park. These days, much of its attention is turned to the provision of cargo-handling services.

HIGHER DENHAM:

A well-laid-out pre- and post-war development consisting mainly of bungalows and detached houses, with good views overlooking the Misbourne valley. The village has a small centre but does have the distinction of having its own railway station, Denham Golf Club.

The botanist, Samuel Reynardson, lived at Cedar House in Hillingdon, and planted the first Cedar of Lebanon here, a direct descendant of which still survives.

HILLINGDON:

Clinging onto an almost village-like atmosphere, Hillingdon sits on the side of a hill and has a line of trees down the middle of its main road. The church and cemetery occupy a central position, as does Hillingdon Heath, with a long parade of shops occupying the space opposite.

HOUNSLOW:

Sandwiched between Osterley Park to the north, and Hounslow Heath to the south-west, Hounslow has no less than three tube stations and a busy centre. It sits at the confluence of a number of roads and, although it has been a popular stopping point for travellers since the thirteenth century, more recently it is Heathrow which has driven its rapid expansion.

ISLEWORTH:

Sitting on the edge of Syon Park, as well as on the Thames, Isleworth still regards itself as a town in its own right, although the reality of this may be fading. The centre is dominated by the brooding presence of the large St Bridget's Catholic church, and the war memorial, known locally as the Clock Tower.

IVER:

Sometimes called Iver Village in order to distinguish itself from Iver Heath to the south, although this has the ring of an estate agents' ploy, its centre is clustered around a run of shops and a church whose tower includes bricks from Roman times. The village can date itself to the Domesday Book, and represents a haven of calm before the M25 to its east, with a mix of old and new housing, with an accent on the old.

Iver Heath is an expanse of heathland criss-crossed by tracks and bridleways. King Edward III spent three weeks hunting here in 1347, and in the eighteenth century it was the haunt of highwaymen, including Dick Turpin.

IVER HEATH:

A village of two halves, with the southern side being fairly select, and populated with large houses, while the north has a small run of shops and much more modern housing estates.

MAPLE CROSS:

A small village presided over by a medium-sized commercial park, housing the likes of Cadbury Schweppes.

NEW DENHAM:

Built as a model housing estate by a local squire in the 1870s, these days New Denham is basically a run of shops beside the A4020, with the original housing to the north-west near the canal.

NORWOOD GREEN:

A suburban residential area clustered around a triangular green, now largely absorbed into its surroundings, sandwiched as it is between Southall and the A4.

> Osterley's outskirts are dominated by a large industrial estate, which includes the headquarters of Sky television, as well as a retail park.

OSTERLEY:

Osterley is divided in two by the A4, on which its tube station sits. On one side is Osterley Park and a small parade of shops surrounded by housing, while the other is a warren of residential streets. These days, Osterley is almost a suburb of the Heathrow 'village', with many of its inhabitants working there.

SIPSON:

Overshadowed by Heathrow airport, this village nevertheless has a number of pubs.

SOUTHALL:

A corner of Asia in West London, Southall's main street is a cacophony of sights, sounds, smells and colour. There is a rich sense of culture and dynamism here, and more than a hint of wealth. Although the housing in the side streets reflects that seen elsewhere in this part of London, the skyline is marked by the domes of a number of mosques, including one with a gilded roof.

SOUTH HAREFIELD:

A collection of mainly semi-detached houses with a handful of shops, on the edge of a large open area in the lee of the hill where Harefield itself stands. South Harefield is perched on the edge of the lakes that separate Buckinghamshire from Middlesex.

TATLING END:

A small linear development between Gerrards Cross and Denham on the A40, dominated by office buildings and garages.

> RAF Uxbridge was originally a training base, and T.E. Lawrence, Lawrence of Arabia, passed through here as Aircraftsman Ross.

UXBRIDGE:

A sweeping ring-road runs round the edge of Uxbridge, through an area dominated by modern office developments, not all of which are occupied, and parking for the central shopping malls. Just outside Uxbridge, on the Hillingdon Road, is RAF Uxbridge.

UXBRIDGE MOOR:

The moor in the name refers to the area of open land to the west of Uxbridge, although these days the area comprises, almost exclusively, commercial and industrial estates, with the canal being one of the area's few redeeming features.

WEST DRAYTON:

Although first impressions may suggest that West Drayton is simply a continuation of Yiewsley High Street, evidence of a more gentile past is hidden off the High Street. A wide green with some interesting housing leads the way to St George's Meadow, a large area of open ground bordered to the west by the River Colne, and to the south by the M4.

WEST EALING:

A distinct, but increasingly less so, outpost of Ealing, with its own High Street and railway station, as well as local identity. West Ealing is delicately poised between Southall to the west, and its namesake to the east.

YIEWSLEY:

An aggregation of housing, with much evidence of new and recent building, with flats catering for the modern town dweller. Yiewsley and West Drayton pretty much merge into one another, with the canal and accompanying railway acting as useful demarcation points.

HISTORY

The historical roots of the towns and villages in this section can probably best be explored following the three broad demarcations outlined above.

Those to the north of the section lying either side of the M25 can often trace their modern antecedents back to the Domesday Book and beyond, with evidence of settlement back to Neolithic times in some cases. The beginnings of these settlements can be traced to the scattered manors and monasteries, as well as the occasional convent, that existed after the Norman Conquest. Although some of these offered a convenient bolthole a good day's ride out from the capital, others existed as traditional landed estates.

It was in medieval times that most of the names we recognise today really began to establish themselves, and the Dissolution of the Monasteries led to the influx of fresh money and landlords, although these often proved to be more transient than the more established families. In the centuries that followed, places such as Iver, and to a lesser extent Denham, have managed to retain a discrete independence from the influence of what has become Greater London, while others such as Maple Cross have become little more than a combination of housing and industrial estates.

Harefield offers a particularly good example of a settlement that has retained much of its original shape. Perhaps it is its imperious position on top of a hill that has allowed it to resist many of the distorting influences of modern development, but Harefield still retains a village atmosphere. It remains a microcosm of historical trends in this area, having earned its living, at different times, from the growing and milling of corn and paper, through to using the nearby canal to support quarrying and brickfields. These days it is the world-renowned hospital on its edge that most people associate with the village.

> Uxbridge Mill was acquired in the nineteenth century by a man called King, who named it Kingsmill, a name which survived as a brand when it was bought by Allied Mills.

> George Orwell was a teacher at Fray's School in Uxbridge, and based his novel, *A Clergyman's Daughter*, on his experiences during this time.

Although not featured in the Domesday Book, there is evidence of settlement at Uxbridge going back to the Bronze Age, although more modern civilisation is best dated from the thirteenth century when St Margaret's church was built.

The town grew as a market centre and, by Tudor times, was sufficiently large to be the centre of religious dissent, and around forty prominent Catholics, known collectively as The Douai Martyrs, died during this turbulent period of history. The tradition of rebellion survived through to the Gunpowder Plot, with one of the conspirators, Robert Catesby, being a local man.

East of the M25 lie the outskirts of the ancient county of Middlesex, which exists today only as a postal destination and cricket team, with Uxbridge probably its most famous location. For centuries, Middlesex acted as a buffer between London and the Home Counties and beyond, bearing more of a resemblance to the latter than the former, with its wide open fields and dispersed populations.

Here, too, there were scattered manors, with that at Hayes at one time belonging to the Archbishops of Canturbury, with Cranmer making his home there. Others, such as Syon House, and Osterley Manor to the south, also stand out.

Settlement on any scale here also started after the Norman Conquest, with the establishment of churches beginning in the thirteenth and fourteenth centuries, although the villages surrounding them remained small and grew slowly. A survey at the end of the sixteenth century by the local Lord of the Manor identified only nineteen dwellings in Southall, none of which was anything as grand as a cottage.

Although parishes such as Hayes and Harlington have a history that reaches back over 1,000 years, throughout this time they existed as sleepy, largely agricultural communities. Even Heathrow was once an obscure little hamlet surrounded by grazing cattle.

Further to the east, Ealing can trace its history to prehistoric times, but it was only from the twelfth century that it began to become settled. Around this time, it was part of the huge forest that still carpeted much of what we regard today as west London, and it was only in comparatively modern times that Ealing and its adjoining villages, such as Hanwell, really took off.

Some towns benefited by being on trading routes, and linear development along major roads, a feature which remains apparent today, became common. For many of these places, however, it took the arrival of the canal to really establish them, and set them on their way to become the industrial and distribution centres we know them as today.

Specialisms grew, with West Drayton and Yiewsley both expanding rapidly during the second half of the nineteenth century on the back of brickworks, which supplied the demand for new building elsewhere in London. This industry exploited the London Clay that underpinned the area, and the canal was ideal for transporting the finished product, as well as bringing rubbish back out of the capital, which filled the holes left by excavation. During this time the view along the towpath would have been of lines of kilns and stack upon stack of drying bricks, as well as docks for loading, with Paddington and Brentford offering a choice of destination.

Today's Hayes is a relatively modern creation, being developed in the nineteenth and twentieth centuries as an industrial centre, with housing added as more companies chose the town as a base. Proximity to both the M4 and the airport have perpetuated this functional status, with the town largely lacking a retail or cultural centre, forcing residents to look north-west to Uxbridge or south-east to Hounslow for sustenance.

In more modern times, Heathrow has sustained the need for distribution centres, with the airport also proving a magnet for businesses with international interests. Places such as Hayes, Harlington, Harmondsworth and Hounslow – Professor Higgins would have approved of this part of the world – all owe much of their present prosperity to the airport.

After the canal, the railway provided a link between the capital and the suburbs, with Brentford in particular geographically well placed to act as a bridge between the two. This did not go unnoticed by Brunel, who ran his Great Western Railway along the southern limit of this section, and built a massive freight terminal by Brentford Dock.

This opened in 1859, and brought together traffic borne by the canal, the river and the railway. Subsequent spurs off both the railway and the canal helped to add to the sum of activity, and it took a new transport artery, the M4, to displace the dock, which finally closed in 1964.

Long before the canal and railway, however, it was the Thames that provided Brentford with its *raison d'etre*, a distinction it shared with Isleworth. Brentford's debt to its riverside location is reflected in its name, with the town known as Bregentforda at the time of the Council of Brentford in 781.

Brentford's history pre-dates Roman times, and one of its greatest claims to fame is being the point where Julius Caesar crossed the Thames during his invasion of Britain. Although some historians question this claim, we know that the town was the scene of battles between Canute and Edmund Ironside in 1016, and again during the English Civil War.

Although Brentford enjoyed considerable prosperity during both Elizabethan and Jacobean times, it did not become a town in its own right until the 1870s, when new and old Brentford became one. The Butts in the heart of Brentford still has a number of red brick houses dating to the 1680s, and bears testament to the town's role as a coaching stop in the pre-industrial era.

The abundance of water made brewing a popular choice of industry in the period that followed, with tanning also prevalent, as was soap manufacture, with the town's Thames Soap Works acquired by Lever Brothers in 1916. In time, the town also became renowned for its gas works.

The earliest form of Isleworth's name is Gislhaesuuyrth, meaning Gilhere's settlement, and the town was well established by the time of the Norman Conquest, with the Romans having a castle here. Later on, the presence of the nearby Syon House, originally a monastery and later a convent under Mary, dictated much of Isleworth's history up until the Dissolution. It was a favourite of King Henry VIII's first wife Catherine of Aragon, and as such suffered badly when the Queen fell from favour. Subsequently, it exploited its surrounding area by establishing a series of market gardens providing fresh fruit and vegetables for the capital.

All Saints Church in Isleworth has occupied its riverside site from the thirteenth century, although it was rebuilt in 1705, and more recently in 1970. The Lower Square in Isleworth is still distinguished by buildings that date to the eighteenth and early nineteenth centuries, although more recent development threatens to overshadow them.

This remains a theme across the towns in this section. While it has been relatively easy for villages such as Iver and Harefield in the north to retain their distinct character, many of the villages to the south and east have been completely absorbed by the encroaching metropolis. Local identity has been further threatened by the dispersal of communities employed in local industries.

Although this is a common story, all is not lost, with many of the towns covered in this section fighting back. Brentford for one is in the process of a major re-development that will regenerate its heart, and hopefully reinforce its historically strong sense of community. Elsewhere, places such as Hanwell and Isleworth have a deep well of history upon which to draw, and local residents have recognised the value of community in developing and sustaining a good quality of life.

Places such as Ealing and Uxbridge have established themselves in more recent years as mini-regional centres, building large shopping centres to reinforce their status as administrative foci, a trick Hounslow is aiming to replicate. Southall exists like a part of Asia in West London, a colourful combination of tastes, sounds and cultures that epitomises the rich diversity available in this section for the visitor prepared to explore.

THE NATURAL LANDSCAPE

Water dominates the northern part of this section, with the West London lakes and the River Colne defining a route for the canal. The valley is steepest to the east, with Harefield in particular enjoying some spectacular views to the south. Further south, Uxbridge and Cowley sit lower down, with the latter fronting yet more lakes in the shape of the Little Britain complex.

Moving east, the different districts of London which the canal passes through continue to lie relatively low as the route moves on towards the tidal Thames. The River Brent picks up the cudgels left by the Colne towards the end of the section, with a few other smaller streams adding to the mix such as the River Crane flows south from Bulls Bridge and through Cranford Countryside Park. The countryside is unexpectedly open, with parkland a recurring feature, although, as might be expected this close to London, this tends to be grassland rather than woods, with much of it used as golf courses.

ACCESS AND TRANSPORT

ROADS

This section is interlaced with an intricate road network, although this should not be taken to mean that getting around by road is easy. The proximity of Heathrow airport in the south-west corner means that the roads are almost always busy, while routes heading east into the heart of west London pass through heavily built-up areas. When the roads are flowing, progress can be made (albeit not always quickly), but it does not take much to destroy the fragile equilibrium.

The M25 acts as a boundary for the western limit of this section, while the M4 does a similar job towards the south. The A4020 behaves as an arterial cutting east–west through Uxbridge, Southall, Hanwell and Ealing, while the A4 offers an alternative east–west thoroughfare further to the south.

Further north, the A40 picks up where the M40 leaves off at Junction 1, where there is a busy roundabout offering a choice of routes north-west to Denham, south-west to Iver and south-east to Uxbridge via various different A-roads. The A40 soon passes to the north of the section, however, and is not a main route through it.

The A408 heads south out of Uxbridge, and passes through Cowley before diverting around Yiewsley and to the east of West Drayton, while the A437 branches off the A4020 south of Uxbridge, and heads south-east to Hayes and the A4, while the A3002 links Brentford and Hanwell. Elsewhere, there are more minor roads and 'rat runs' available through residential areas for those prepared to gamble!

RAIL

Rail and tube lines offer a tempting alternative to the roads, with this section being blessed with a good network of lines.

Denham and Denham Golf Club, to the north of the section, are both on the Chiltern line operated by Chiltern Railways, although only the former is a regular stop, with the Golf Club halt more restricted to commuting times.

Iver, West Drayton, Hayes and Harlington, Hanwell, West Ealing and Ealing Broadway are all on the main Paddington line to the west and south-west of the country, with local trains operated by First Great Western Link. Brentford, Syon Lane, Isleworth and Hounslow meanwhile sit on lines operated by South Western Trains, although the station for the latter falls just south of the map.

Uxbridge and Hillingdon are on both the northern branch of the Piccadilly Line, and the Uxbridge branch of the Metropolitan Line, while Northfields, Boston Manor, Osterley and the three Hounslow tube stations (East, Central and West) are all on the Heathrow branch of the Piccadilly Line. Ealing Broadway represents one terminus to the Central Line, and is also on the District Line, as is South Ealing.

Chiltern Railways can be contacted on 08456 005165, while train running times on South West Trains can be accessed on 023 80213600. For times of trains operated by First Great Western Link, call 0845 3303728. National Train Enquiries can be reached on 08457 484950, while the telephone contact for London Travel Information, including tube and bus services, is 020 7222 1234.

BUSES

Getting around by bus is easy in this section, with both the county services covering Buckinghamshire, and the more local London routes, many of which operate out of Uxbridge. The following list sets out the main bus services along this section, although it is advisable to check before using them. This list does not include night buses.

- 58 – *Links Uxbridge with Iver Heath and Iver (First Beeline)*
- 65 – *Ealing to Kingston via Brentford (London United)*
- 83 – *Ealing Broadway, West Ealing, Hanwell and Ealing Hospital (First London)*

181 – *Tattling End, Higher Denham, Denham Green, New Denham and Uxbridge (Arriva the Shires)*

- 182 – *Linking Higher Denham with Denham (Arriva the Shires)*
- 195 – *Hayes, Bulls Bridge Tesco, Southall, Ealing Hospital (Ealing Community Transport)*
- 207 – *Uxbridge, Hayes, Southall, Ealing, Hanwell (First London)*
- 222 – *Uxbridge to Hounslow via Cowley and West Drayton (London United)*
- 235 – *Brentford to Sunbury via Isleworth (Tellings-Golden Miller)*
- 237 – *Brentford and Isleworth (Armchair)*
- 300 – *Uxbridge to High Wycombe via Denham Village (Arriva the Shires)*
- 305 – *Uxbridge to High Wycombe via Denham Village (Arriva the Shires)*
- 331 – *Harefield, Denham, Uxbridge (First London)*
- 459 – *Uxbridge, Cowley, Iver, Uxbridge circular (Jason Tours)*
- 607 – *Uxbridge, Hayes, Southall, Ealing Hospital, Hanwell, Ealing (First London)*
- 635 - *Brentford and Isleworth (Armchair)*
- 698 – *Links West Drayton, Hayes and Harlington and Hayes (First London)*
- A10 – *Uxbridge to Heathrow via Stockley Park (First London)*
- A40 – *Tattling End, Denham, Uxbridge (Carousel)*
- E2 – *Ealing, Northfields and Brentford (Armchair)*
- E3 – *Hanwell, West Ealing and Northfields (First London)*
- E8 – *Ealing, Hanwell, Boston Manor and Brentford (Armchair)*
- H28 – *Osterley Tesco, Isleworth, Bulls Bridge Tesco (Tellings-Golden Miller)*
- H32 – *Links Osterley with North Hyde (London United)*
- H50 – *West Drayton, Stockley Park, Hayes (Tellings-Golden Miller)*
- R21 – *Harefield Hospital, Maple*

Cross, Denham, Uxbridge (First London)
- U3 – *Uxbridge, Yiewsley, West Drayton and Harmondsworth (First London)*
- U4 – *Uxbridge to Hayes (First London)*
- U5 – *Uxbridge, Yiewsley, West Drayton, Stockley Park and Hayes and Harlington (First London)*
- U9 – *Harefield and Uxbridge (Arriva the Shires)*

Contact details for bus operators in this area are listed below, although Traveline, (www.traveline.org.uk) on 0870 6082608, can give details of specific services between 7 a.m. and 10 p.m., and London Travel Information on services operating within their area.

- Armchair (020 8568 8227)
- Arriva the Shires (01923 682262)
- Carousel (01494 533436)
- Ealing Community Transport (020 8813 3210)
- First Beeline (01344 424938)
- First London (01895 236598)
- Jason Tours (0208 8972324)
- London United (0208 4006665)
- Tellings-Golden Miller (0208 755 7050)

TAXIS

The following list gives a selection of the many taxi operators in this section. In addition to mini-cab companies, it may also be possible to hail black cabs for shorter journeys.

- Apex Cars, High St, Uxbridge (01895 233333)
- Boston Manor Cars, Boston Manor (020 8568 7222) – *by the tube station*
- Brentford Cars (020 8560 5999)
- Brentford Express Minicab Co (020 8560 6060)
- Brentford & Isleworth Minicabs (020 8560 6858)
- Carline, High St, Uxbridge (01895 270270)
- Crown Radio Cars, The Common, Southall (020 8571 0008)
- Ealing Local Taxis, Ealing Broadway Railway Station (020 8810 9600)
- Ealing Taxi Service (020 8997 2244)
- Henry's Mini Cabs, Harefield (01895 824422)
- LHR Express Cars, Station Road, West Drayton (01895 444333)
- Parade Car Services, Great West Rd, Brentford (020 8568 4292)
- Peachey Car Services Ltd, Station Rd, West Drayton (01895 444444)
- T W Express, Great West Rd, Isleworth (020 8568 6789)
- South Bucks Executive Cars, Denham (01895 831888)
- South Harefield Taxis (01895 821115)
- Sunshine Minicabs, Southall (020 8571 6060)
- Swan Radio Cars, The Common, Southall (020 8574 4444)
- Village Cars, High Rd, Uxbridge (01895 622222)
- West Ealing Mini Cabs (020 8840 2277)
- Z Cars Minicab, Ealing (020 8840 0004)

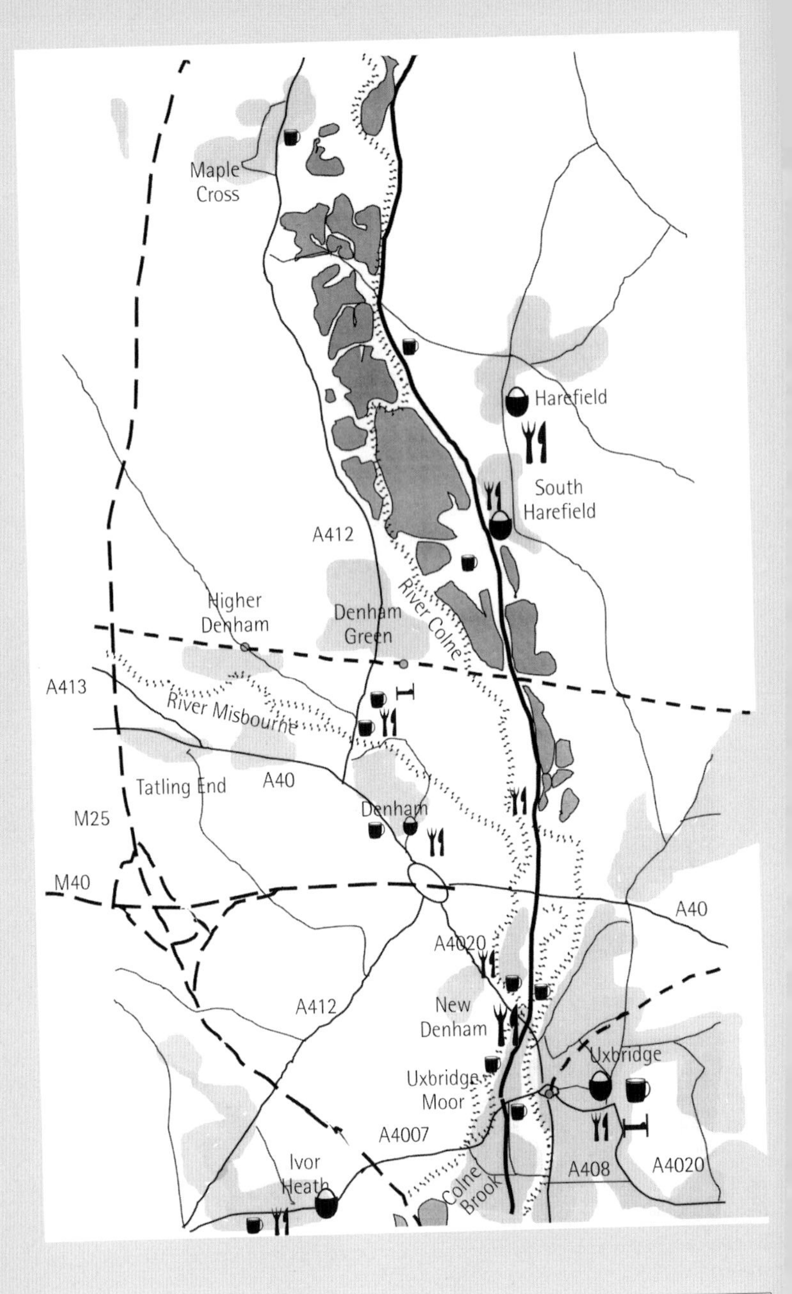
Maple Cross
Harefield
South Harefield
A412
Higher Denham
Denham Green
River Colne
A413
River Misbourne
Tatling End
A40
M25
Denham
M40
A40
A4020
New Denham
A412
Uxbridge
Uxbridge Moor
A4007
Ivor Heath
Colne Brook
A408
A4020

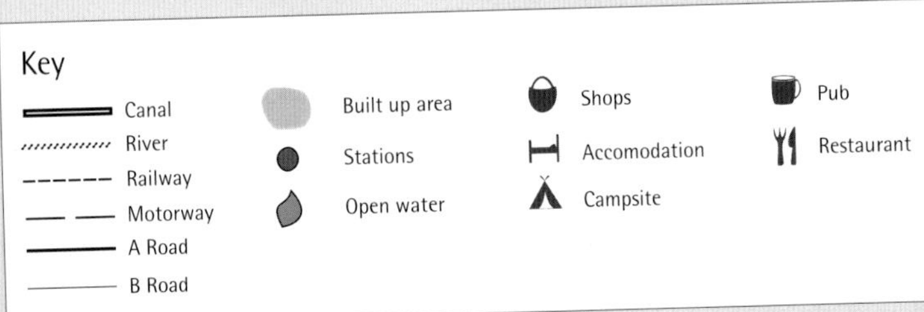
Key
Canal
River
Railway
Motorway
A Road
B Road
Built up area
Stations
Open water
Shops
Accomodation
Campsite
Pub
Restaurant

BASICS

INTRODUCTION

As the canal heads south and then doglegs east towards its final rendezvous with the Thames, the surrounding area becomes more urbanised. Consequently, for its final few miles the towpath is usually never more than a few minutes walk away from some centre of population offering basic services.

The overshadowing presence of Heathrow to the south-east makes its presence known in more ways than one. Never mind Greater London, at times it is possible to feel as if you are travelling through Greater Heathrow. This is reflected in the large industrial and commercial estates that inhabit the area, and in the shape of the communities that have developed to serve the modern transport beast.

Where once the canal would have defined the local area, the airport now does the job. Hotels, large and small, cater for the transient visitor, and shops can be separated into three main categories, described below.

For ease of use, information on basic services in this section has been divided up into the three broad zones described in the 'Shapers' section. Again, these listings do not attempt to be comprehensive but rather to offer a guiding hand through the maze of opportunities available.

Finally, there are three major hospitals in this section:

- Hillingdon (01895 238282), in Pield Heath Road, Uxbridge
- Ealing Hospital (0208 967 5000), between Hanwell and Southall
- West Middlesex University Hospital (0208 560 2121) in Isleworth

Non-emergency health concerns can be addressed by calling NHS Direct on 0845 4647

SHOPPING

In general terms, shopping foci fall into three broad categories: large centres clustered around at least one large covered shopping mall housing all the major High-Street brands; out-of-town, or more accurately out-of-centre, retail parks, which may major on either food (including supermarkets and fast-food outlets) or non-food (such as DIY, shoes, furniture); and local. Under the local banner are what might be regarded as traditional local High Streets, which themselves fall into a number of gradations.

The larger of these may have one or two representatives of national chains, such as WH Smith, Boots or Woolworths, as well as banks. These tend to be surrounded by much smaller outlets, some of which may be recognisable names, for example coffee bars or sandwich shops (or indeed charity shops), but most populous by far will be small independent shops such as grocers. Smaller local opportunities may be clustered into parades of shops, typically including a newsagent, convenience store or post office – often with all three rolled into one outlet.

This section has three main large centres at Uxbridge, Ealing and Hounslow, although the latter is currently in the process of redevelopment. As the landscape

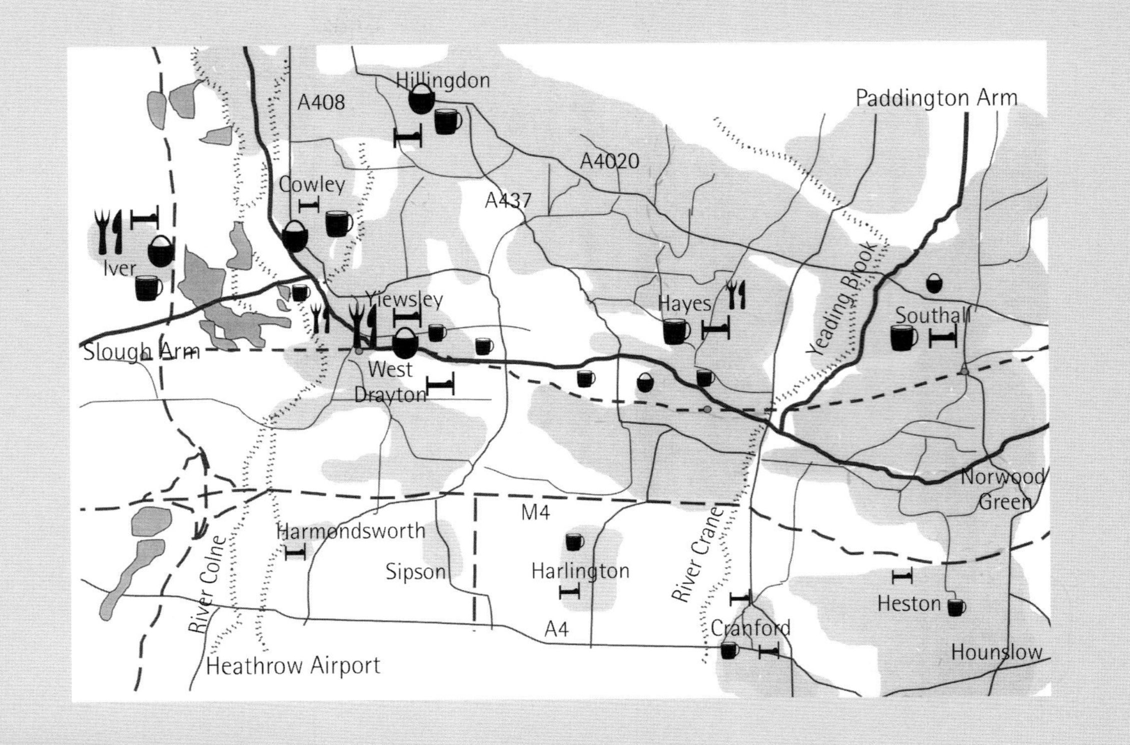

Hillingdon
A408
Paddington Arm
A4020
Cowley
A437
Iver
Yiewsley
Hayes
Yeading Brook
Southall
Slough Arm
West
Drayton
Norwood
Green
M4
Harmondsworth
River Colne
Sipson
Harlington
River Crane
Heston
A4
Cranford
Hounslow
Heathrow Airport

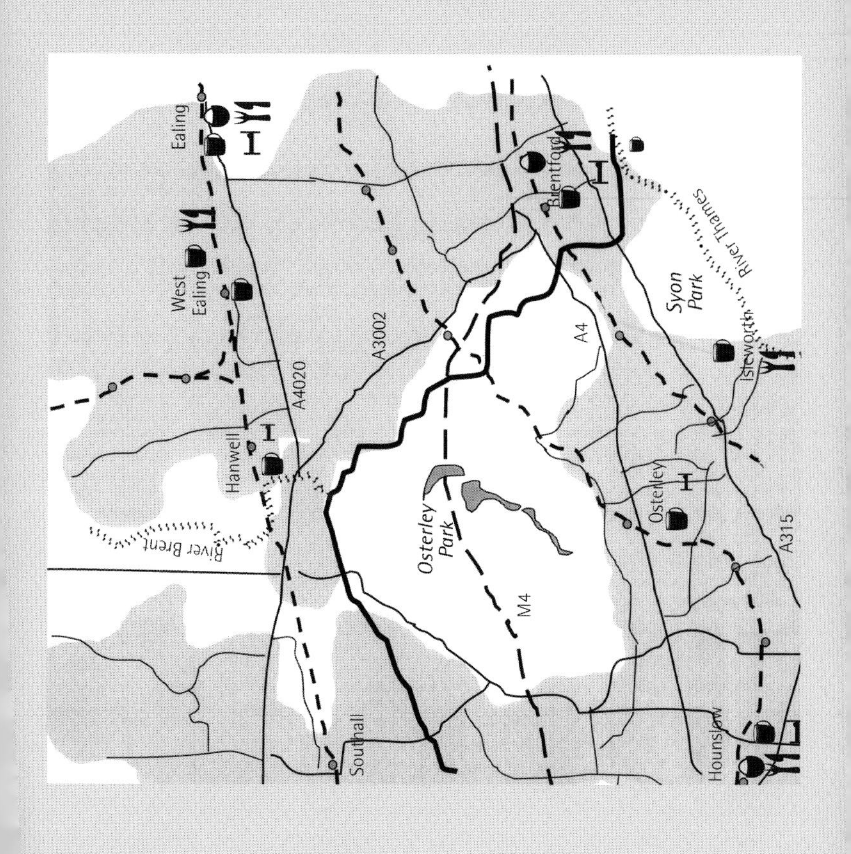
Ealing
West Ealing
Hanwell
River Brent
A4020
A3002
Southall
Osterley Park
M4
Brentford
A4
Syon Park
River Thames
Isleworth
Osterley
A315
Hounslow

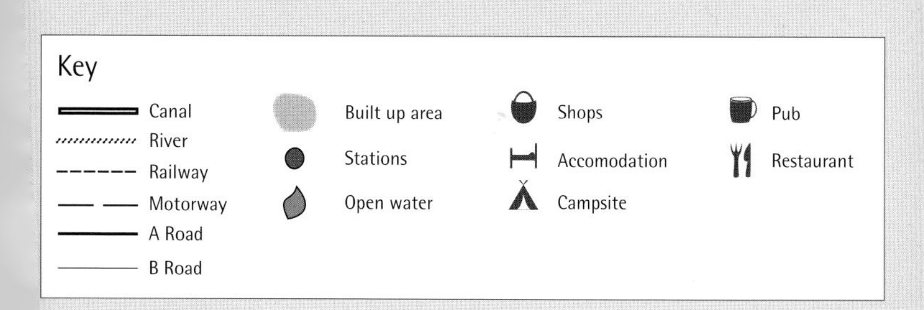
Key
Canal
River
Railway
Motorway
A Road
B Road
Built up area
Stations
Open water
Shops
Accomodation
Campsite
Pub
Restaurant

becomes more built up, most of the shops in the towns and areas within the M25 here fall into the local category, although these vary in extent quite considerably.

Passing through this section, the towpath user therefore has the unaccustomed luxury of knowing that they are never that far from basic supplies, and probably within easy reach of a supermarket, bank or pharmacy. Where a specific centre of population is not mentioned by name, it is generally safe to assume there will be at least one parade of local shops. With some planning, visitors can also arrange a major shopping expedition or, should the fancy take them, wander around a DIY 'shed', in one of the out-of-town centres that often fill any empty land between centres of population.

In the area either side of the M25, to the north of the section, South Harefield has a Londis supermarket as well as a convenience store/post office, while Harefield itself has a much more extensive High Street. As well as a Spar supermarket, a butchers, various hairdressers and a village bakery, there are a number of small specialists where you might be able to pick up those odd nick-nacks you've been searching for for ages. D.H. Mitchell and Sons, White Heath Farm in Mill End Road, Harefield (01895 823303) is a traditional diary producer offering milk, cream and ice cream.

Denham has a small newsagent in the village itself, while the shops by the A40 include a grocer, off-licence, the Denham Bakery, some fast-food outlets and a Thai restaurant, as well as a small HSBC bank.

Iver has a run of shops along its High Street, including an off-licence, a pharmacy, a local bakery, a food and wine shop and a bank, although parking is limited. There is also a convenience store with a sub-post office on the road north, as well as some more local shops.

Also along this road is the Wingrove Farm Shop at Shredding Green Farm (01753 653209), which sells fresh local produce and has a butcher. There is another farm shop, open from June–January, at Bangors Road South, towards Iver Heath, Home Cottage Farm (01753 653064), with a shop and pick-your-own fruit.

Iver Heath has two small, but useful, parades of shops. One of these has a Premier Store and a Martins Convenience Store with a post office, while the other has a Co-Op and pharmacy.

Turning to the area to the east and north of the M4, Uxbridge is one of the section's large centres and has two shopping malls, separated by a more traditional pedestrianised High Street, although most of the larger brand names seem to have migrated to the more comfortable modern surroundings offered by the malls.

The Chimes mall is relatively new, and sits to the side of the tube and rail station on the edge of the older part of town. This has a Debenhams department store as its centrepiece, along with names such as BHS, Boots, Gap and Next. The Chimes is also home to the town's nine-screen cinema. The older Pavillions mall has a Marks and Spencer as well as Tesco and Iceland supermarkets, along with other familiar names.

The High Street in Uxbridge does not seem to have risen to the challenge of coming up with niche alternatives, with the majority of the shops along this thoroughfare fairly mundane. This is the place to go if you need a bank though, and the post office is in the Pavillions. Opposite the Chimes, the town has a comprehensive library which also houses the (less than comprehensive) Tourist Information Point.

Cowley, to the south of Uxbridge, lacks a clear centre, although it has a newsagents, a small grocers, a fast-food outlet and a post office. The shape of shopping here has been influenced by the large industrial estates and business parks, including Cowley's own Office Park, which surrounds the area. Here, cafés, newsagents, bookmakers and local fast-food outlets, including fish and chips, sit alongside basic grocers, all quite close to the towpath. This is a pattern replicated on a number of occasions as the area becomes more built up.

Yiewsley High Street seems to continue straight into West Drayton, the other side of the bridge over the canal, and has an eclectic selection of shops, ranging from Iceland and Aldi, which go some way to set the tone, through to tyre fitters and coffee bars. There are some national names here such as Woolworths, but most shops, including the seemingly ubiquitous fast-food outlets, seem to be of local origin.

Further to the north, Hillingdon has a long parade of shops on one side of the A4020, setting a pattern along this road that continues almost uninterrupted all the way into Ealing, namely long runs of small local shops interspersed with the occasional nationally recognised brand.

Convenience stores and fast-food outlets dominate, but there is also room for all kinds of specialists, ranging from tyre fitters to Indian sweet shops, taking in Cash and Carrys on the way. In fact, a study of the shops in each of the different areas passed through says much about the make-up of the local population.

Southall, for example, has a bustling mixture of jewellers, kitchen-equipment shops, restaurants, sari specialists, grocers and mini-bazaars spread out along its long Broadway. Trading usually spills out onto the pavement, making shopping an experience, but a place to avoid if you're in a hurry.

These High Streets and parades provide a sharp contrast with the neat orderliness of the shopping environment offered in the malls, but do not make the mistake of equating the sometimes run-down and dishevelled look of these streets with a lack of prosperity. These are busy and well-used shops, and the presence of a Rolls Royce dealer in the heart of Hanwell, another local centre, is no accident.

West Ealing acts as a bridge between these local shops and the more sophisticated and antiseptic offerings in Ealing, with outposts of chain stores such as Boots and BHS, as well as a Sainsbury's supermarket. This is not at the cost of its own specialists however, which include an Iranian Caviar shop.

Ealing, the second of the three large centres, has two malls, Arcadia and Ealing Broadway, as well as some more local shopping clustered around Ealing Broadway Station, and a Sainsbury's Local. The Ealing Broadway Centre has a Safeway supermarket. There are some niche outlets here, which include the La Chantal chocolate shop and patisserie, as well as a psychic palmist healer.

Ealing holds a Farmers' Market every Saturday morning, and it is worth checking out Farm W5 (0208 566 1965), which offers organic fresh fruit and vegetables, as well as fresh bread, meat and fifty British cheeses.

Elsewhere in this area, there are occasional retail parks, including one in Hayes, where there is a Sainsbury's and a large Tesco sitting alongside a Toys 'R' Us at Bulls Bridge, right on the canal, as well as out-of-town themed eating places, just outside Southall, for example. There is also a Hayes Health Foods on the Uxbridge Road (0208 561 1624).

The Pavillions Shopping Centre, one of two malls in Uxbridge.

South of the M4, Brentford retains a traditional High Street and has a Somerfield in its centre, as well as the St John's Superstore (a Costcutter) down Ferry Lane, which leads to the river. Near to Brentford there is Syon Park Farm Shop (0208 847 2140), and within Osterley Park, the park's own Farm Shop.

There is a large out-of-town retail park on the edge of Osterley, and the relatively recently built Ivybridge Retail Park on the edge of Isleworth. This has mainly non-food out-of-town superstores, one of which is a Halfords with a Bike Hut. Otherwise, shopping in Isleworth is pretty uninspiring.

Hounslow is the third of the large centres, although it is currently in the process of a major redevelopment called the Blenheim Centre, which is being built in stages. In the meantime, residents have to satisfy themselves with The Treaty Centre. Although this has a Debenhams and a Woolworths, even its biggest fans would probably agree that it has seen better times and that the new centre is overdue.

EATING AND DRINKING

As with shopping, there is no shortage of drinking holes and restaurants along this section, especially towards its end. Once again, for ease of identification, these have been split up into the three broad geographical areas covered in this section in the following lists.

Where practical, the places covered here include those on, or near to, the towpath, as well as a cross-section of those to be found in the towns and villages further afield. These should be regarded as a sample only, with the visitor taking the opportunity to explore the rich variety available.

PUBS:

The following pubs are in the area to the north of the section either side of the M25:

- The Cross, Maple Cross (01923 773266)
- Coy Carp, Harefield (01895 825623) – *pub and restaurant*
- Kings Arms, Harefield (01895 825485) – *on the edge of the green at the end of the High Street*
- Pickle Jar, Harefield (01895 822269) – *claims to offer cold beer and a warm welcome*
- White Horse, Harefield (01895 822144) – *pub and restaurant*
- Horse and Barge, South Harefield (01895 834080) – *next to Bridge 180*
- Green Man, Denham Village (01895 832760)
- The Inn on the Green, Denham (01895 832760)
- Falcon, Denham Village (01895 832125)
- Swan, Denham Village (01895 832085)
- Bull, Iver (01753 651115)
- Chequers, Iver (01753 653869)
- Fox and Pheasant, Iver (01753 653175)
- Swan, Iver (01753 655776)
- Red Lion, between Iver and Iver Heath (01753 654257)
- Black Horse, Iver Heath (01753 653044)
- Prince of Wales, Iver Heath (01753 651378)
- Stag and Hounds, Iver Heath (01753 655144)

The following pubs are in the area of the section to the east of Uxbridge and north of the M4:

- Dolphin, Uxbridge Moor (01895 232656) – *on Bridge 186*
- General Elliott, Uxbridge Moor (01895 237385) – *also on Bridge 186*
- Pipemakers Arms, Uxbridge Moor (01895 252704) – *on the River Colne, also has a Chinese takeaway restaurant*
- The Crown and Sceptre, Uxbridge Town Centre (01895 236308)

The Crown and Treaty in Uxbridge gets its name from unsuccessful talks held there between King Charles and Parliamentary forces during the Civil War.

- Crown and Treaty, Oxford Road, Uxbridge (01895 233891) – *near Bridge 185*
- Good Yarn, Uxbridge Town Centre (01895 239852)
- Ostler, Uxbridge Town Centre (01895 237781)
- Culvert, Cowley Mill Lane, Uxbridge (01895 256699)
- Malt Shovel, Iver Bridge, Cowley (01895 233121) – *canalside pub*
- Cowley Brick, Cowley (01895 234049)
- The Grand Union, Cowley (01895 253248) – *town pub opposite the recreation ground*
- The Lord Hill, Cowley (01895 233029) – *appropriately enough, next door to a post-office sorting centre near to the canal*
- The Paddington Packet Boat, Cowley Peachey (01895 442392)
- The Turning Point, Cowley Peachey (01895 440550)
- George and Dragon, Yiewsley (01895 443286)
- Blues Bar, West Drayton (01895 442020)
- De Burgh Arms, West Drayton (01895 432823)
- Railway Arms, West Drayton (01895 438181)
- Prince of Wales, Hillingdon (01895 254416)
- Vine, Hillingdon (01895 259596)
- Grapes, Hayes (0208 573 7479) – *a 'family-style' restaurant, part of a chain*
- Wagon and Horses, Hayes (0208 573 0233)
- Lamb, Norwood (0208 574 3578) – *by Bridge 203*
- Plough, Norwood Green (0208 574 1945)
- Grand Junction Arms, Acton Lane, Southall (0208 965 5670) – *by Bridge 201*
- Hanborough Tavern, Southall (0208 813 9522) – *by the Paddington Arm*
- Old Oak Tree, Common Road, Southall (0208 574 5851) – *by Bridge 202*
- St George and the Dragon, Southall (0208 813 9429)
- Three Horseshoes, Southall (0208 574 2001)
- Duke of York, Hanwell (0208 567 2319)
- Fox, Green Lane, Hanwell (0208 567 3912) – *50 yards from Hanwell Bottom Lock*
- Ryans (0208 840 4432) – *cocktail bar on the Boston Road out of Hanwell*
- The Viaduct, Hanwell (0208 567 1362) – *opposite Ealing Hospital and adjacent to Brent River Park*

The Paddington Packet Boat ran a daily service that went from here to Paddington. Pulled by a team of horses, it had priority over other craft and was rather notorious in its time.

- The Drayton, West Ealing (0208 997 1019)
- Bell, Ealing (0208 567 0173) – *town-centre pub*
- Grange Tavern, Ealing Common (0208 567 7617) – *pub and dining*
- Haven Arms, Ealing (0208 997 0378)
- North Star, Ealing (0208 567 4848)
- Town House, Ealing (0208 810 0304)
- Wheatsheaf, Ealing (0208 997 5240)

The following pubs are in the area of the section south of the M4:

Charles I is reputed to have rested at the Red Lion in Hayes, while on his way from Oxford to meet the Scottish army at Newark in 1646.

- Red Lion Inn, Harlington (0208 897 7514)
- The Queens Head, Cranford (0208 897 0722)
- Old Queens Head, Heston (020 8570 0486) – *a Hungry Horse pub*
- Beehive, Brentford (020 8560 2421)
- Lord Nelson, Brentford (0208 568 1877)
- Magpie and Crown, Brentford (0208 560 5658)
- Six Bells, High Street, Brentford (0208 560 8804)
- Watermans Arms, Brentford (0208 560 5665)
- Hare and Hounds, Osterley (0208 560 5438)
- Castle, Old Isleworth (0208 560 3615)
- Coach and Horses, Isleworth (0208 560 1447)
- Town Wharf, Old Isleworth (0208 847 2287) – *by the river*
- Triple Crown, Isleworth (0208 892 1929)
- Bell, Hounslow (020 8570 2332)
- Coach and Horses, Hounslow (0208 570 3587)
- Earl Russell, Hounslow (0208 570 1560) – *pub and restaurant*
- Edwards, Hounslow (0208 577 8057) – *wine bar with light meals*
- Moon Under Water, Hounslow (0208 572 7506)
- The Sun and Beamers Carvery, Hounslow (0208 570 4675) – *pub and restaurant*
- Yates Wine Lodge, Hounslow (0208 570 0091) – *converted bank*
- Warren, Hounslow (0208 570 2835)
- Windsor Castle, Hounslow (0208 570 2041)

CAFÉS AND TAKEAWAYS

There are any number of cafés and takeaways along this section, and the following list offers a mere sample of what is available. In addition, each of the main shopping malls in Uxbridge, Ealing and Hounslow, has a number of café and sandwich/coffee bars.

The following cafés and takeaways are in the area to the north of the section either side of the M25:

- The Village Café, Harefield (01895 823994)
- The Busy Bee Café, South Harefield (01895 823015)
- The Café, Iver (01753 650231)
- Simply Snacks, New Denham (01895 461010)

The following cafés and takeaways are in the area of the section to the east of Uxbridge and north of the M4:

- The Toll House Tea Room, by Cowley Lock (no telephone number)
- Packet Boat Marins Café, Cowley Peachey (01895 442290)
- Gordon's Café, Yiewsley (01895 444411)
- Sue's Bakery, West Drayton (01895 422219)
- Coffee Express, West Drayton (01895 444656)
- Corner House Café, Boston Manor (020 8567 2558)

The following cafés and takeaways are in the area of the section south of the M4:

- London Café, Brentford (020 8560 1848) – *on the High Street bridge by the Gauging Locks*
- Bread Lines Café, London Road, Isleworth (0208 560 7679)
- Osterley Cottage, Thornbury Road, Isleworth (0208 560 0455) – *Chinese takeaway*
- Poons Fish Bar, London Road, Isleworth (0208 568 5188) – *fish and chips*
- Sanvishe, London Road, Isleworth (0208 568 5666)
- Swan Chinese Takeaway, Isleworth (0208 560 8779)
- Café Soprano, Staines Road, Hounslow (0208 8572 8191) – *café and snacks*
- Delight Takeaway, Bath Road, Hounslow (0208 570 3170) – *Indian takeaway*
- Rainbows Fish Bar, Hanworth Road, Hounslow (0208 570 5894) – *fish and chips*

RESTAURANTS

There is a rich variety of cuisines available to sample in this section, with Hounslow in particular offering a good mix. The area east of Uxbridge, along the A4020 all the way to Ealing, is notorious for its Asian restaurants, and it would be iniquitous to single out a single establishment. The High Streets and shopping malls in Uxbridge, Ealing and Hounslow also have a number of the national and international-branded food outlets, with eleven in the Chimes in Uxbridge alone.

The performing clock of Ealing's Arcadia Centre.

The following restaurants are in the area to the north of the section either side of the M25:

- Ugly Ducking, Tatling End (01895 832623) – *Harvester family pub and restaurant*
- 128 Chinese Cuisine, Tatling End (07532 883100)
- Black Jacks Mill Restaurant, Harefield (01895 823120) – *Italian restaurant by Bridge 178*
- Harefield Balti and Tandoori Restaurant, Harefield (01895 825844)
- Harry Ramsdens, Harefield (01895 822161) – *fish and chips*
- The Crooked Billet, Uxbridge Road between Iver and Iver Heath (01753 651159) – *an Out and Out pub/restaurant with a large car park*
- Iver Curry and Tandoori Centre (01753 630303)
- Sheeshmahal Indian Restaurant, Iver (01753 655398)
- Da Remo Restaurant, Denham Village (01895 832425) – *upmarket Italian à la carte dining.*
- Sukanya Thai Restaurant, Denham (01895 832048)
- La Rucola Italian Restaurant, New Denham (01895 231568)
- The Shangri-La, Thai and Nepalese Restaurant, New Denham (01895 230430)

> The Weir in Brentford was formerly the White Horse, home to the artist J.M. Turner for a year when he was ten and said to be where he developed his interest in painting.

The following restaurants are in the area of the section to the east of Uxbridge and north of the M4:

- Quackers Riverside Restaurant and Music Bar, Old Mill Lane, Uxbridge (01895 237559)
- Sofra, Rockingham Road, Uxbridge (01895 252248) – *Mediterranean restaurant*
- Webb One, High Street, Uxbridge (01895 252868)
- Golden Curry, Indian Restaurant, Yiewsley (01895 443435)
- Mandarin Chinese Restaurant, Yiewsley (01895 442022)
- Water Palace, Chinese Restaurant, Yiewsley (0800 037 5963)
- The Three Countries, Hayes (020 8845 2624) – *specialises in Italian, Ethiopian and Eritrian cuisine*
- Cypriana, Botwell Lane, Hayes (0208 569 1919) – *Greek restaurant*
- The Olive Restaurant, West Ealing (0208 8507344) – *Mediterranean cuisine and barbeque*
- Charlotte's Place, Ealing Common (0208 5677541)
- Ginos, Ealing (0208 5673681) – *Italian restaurant*
- Mama Amalfi, Ealing (0208 840 5888) – *Italian restaurant*
- The Thai, Ealing (020 8567 5577) – *Thai restaurant*

The following restaurants are in the area of the section south of the M4:

- Fat Boys, Brentford (0208 569 8481) – *Thai restaurant*
- Glistening Waters Bar and Restaurant, Ferry Lane, Brentford (0208 758 1616) – *Caribbean and English restaurant*
- Old Fire Station, High Street, Brentford (0208 568 5599)
- Pappadums, Ferry Lane, Brentford (0208 8471123) – *riverside Indian restaurant*
- The Weir Bar and Dining Room, Brentford (020 8568 3600)
- Beijing Mann, Isleworth (0208 560 2844) – *Chinese restaurant*
- Le Bistro, London Road, Isleworth (0208 568 0504)
- Bridge Inn, London Road, Isleworth (0208 568 8088) – *Thai restaurant*
- Khyber Pass, London Road, Isleworth (0208 560 8284) – *Indian restaurant*
- Cheong Sor House, London Road, Hounslow (0208 572 3102) – *Korean restaurant*
- Crystals, High Street, Hounslow (0208 577 9663) – *Arabic restaurant*
- Gardenia Restaurant, Hanworth Road, Hounslow (0208 577 3260) – *Lebanese restaurant*
- Lahori Karahi, London Road, Hounslow (0208 577 3344) – *Pakistani restaurant*
- Szechuan City, Douglas Road, Hounslow (0208 569 4322) – *Chinese restaurant*
- Sung, Bath Road, Hounslow (0208 570 2161) – *Beijing and Cantonese*
- Hounslow Brasserie, Hounslow (0208 570 5093)

SLEEPING

The proximity of Heathrow means there is no shortage of places to stay along this section. The following list offers a selection of hotels and guest houses:

HOTEL

- The Bull Inn, High Street, Iver (01753 651115)
- The Tower Arms Hotel, Richings Park, Iver (01753 652624)

- The Red Lion Hotel, Royal Lane, Hillingdon (01895 236860)
- Heathrow Lodge, Bath Rd, West Drayton (01753 686970)
- Kings Paget Hotel, Station Rd, West Drayton Middlesex (0208 420 4052) – *modern hotel with own parking*
- Riverside Hotel, Trout Rd, West Drayton (01895 441904)
- Premier Lodge, Hayes (0870 9906612)
- Universal Plaza Hotel, Southall (0208 574 9091) – *new hotel in the centre of Southall*
- The Broadwalk Hotel, West Ealing (0208 840 4134) – *family-run hotel in the heart of West Ealing*
- Abbey Lodge Hotel, Ealing (0208 567 7914) – *seventeen rooms*
- Grange Lodge Hotel, Ealing (0208 567 1049) – *fourteen rooms*
- Boston Manor Hotel, Hanwell (020 8566 1534) – *recently refurbished, forty-eight bed, three-star hotel*
- Kings Arms, Brentford (0208 560 5860) – *bar and hotel*
- Millennium Inn, Cranford (0208 759 9961)
- Travelodge, Heston (0870 191 1600) – *on the M4*
- Master Robert Hotel, Isleworth (020 8570 6261) – *Best Western hotel with ninety-six bedrooms, on the A4*
- Osterley Park Hotel, Osterley (0208 568 9981) – *sixty-one rooms in a Tudor-style hotel*
- Arora International, Bath Rd, Harmondsworth (0208 759 7777)
- Travel Inn Metro, Harlington (0870 6075075)

BED AND BREAKFASTS/GUEST HOUSES

- The Falcon, Denham Village (01895 832125) – *pub and bed and breakfast*
- Lambourn, Iver (01895 232521) – *two bedrooms in a 200-year-old cottage set in an acre of countryside*
- Oaklands Guest House, Iver Heath (01753 653003)
- Brunel Lodge, The Greenway, Uxbridge (01895 460037)
- Debden Guest House, Pield Heath Road, Uxbridge (01895 238507)
- Hayward Guest House, Ivyhouse Road, Uxbridge (01895 638063)
- Hillingdon Heath Guest House, Uxbridge Road, Uxbridge (01895 812499)
- Spackman Guest House, Hillingdon Road, Uxbridge (01895 237994)
- Waterside Bed and Breakfast, Pield Heath Road, Uxbridge (01895 251570)
- Lyttleton Lodge Guest House, Cowley (01895 254970)
- Maygoods Farm, High Street, Cowley (01895 233105)
- The Fox and Pheasant, West Drayton (01895 446033)
- Longford Guest House, Bath Road, West Drayton (01753 682969)
- Ashley Lodge, Yeading Lane, Hayes (0208 569 1586)
- Hayes Bed and Breakfast, Yeading Lane, Hayes (0208 573 9602)
- The Nest Bed and Breakfast, High Street, Hayes (0208 476 7411)
- A Night Inn, Southall (0800 169 3628) – *fourteen rooms*
- Ealing Guest House, South Ealing (0208 840 2807)
- Primrose House, Boston Gardens, Brentford (0208 568 5573)
- The Cottage Guest House, High Street, Cranford (0208 897 1815)
- Lampton Guest House, Hounslow (020 8570 0056) – *twenty rooms*
- Harmondsworth Hall, Harmondsworth (0208 759 1824) – *seventeenth-century Grade II listed building with nine bedrooms*

CAMPING

Unsurprisingly, perhaps, there are no camping sites along this section.

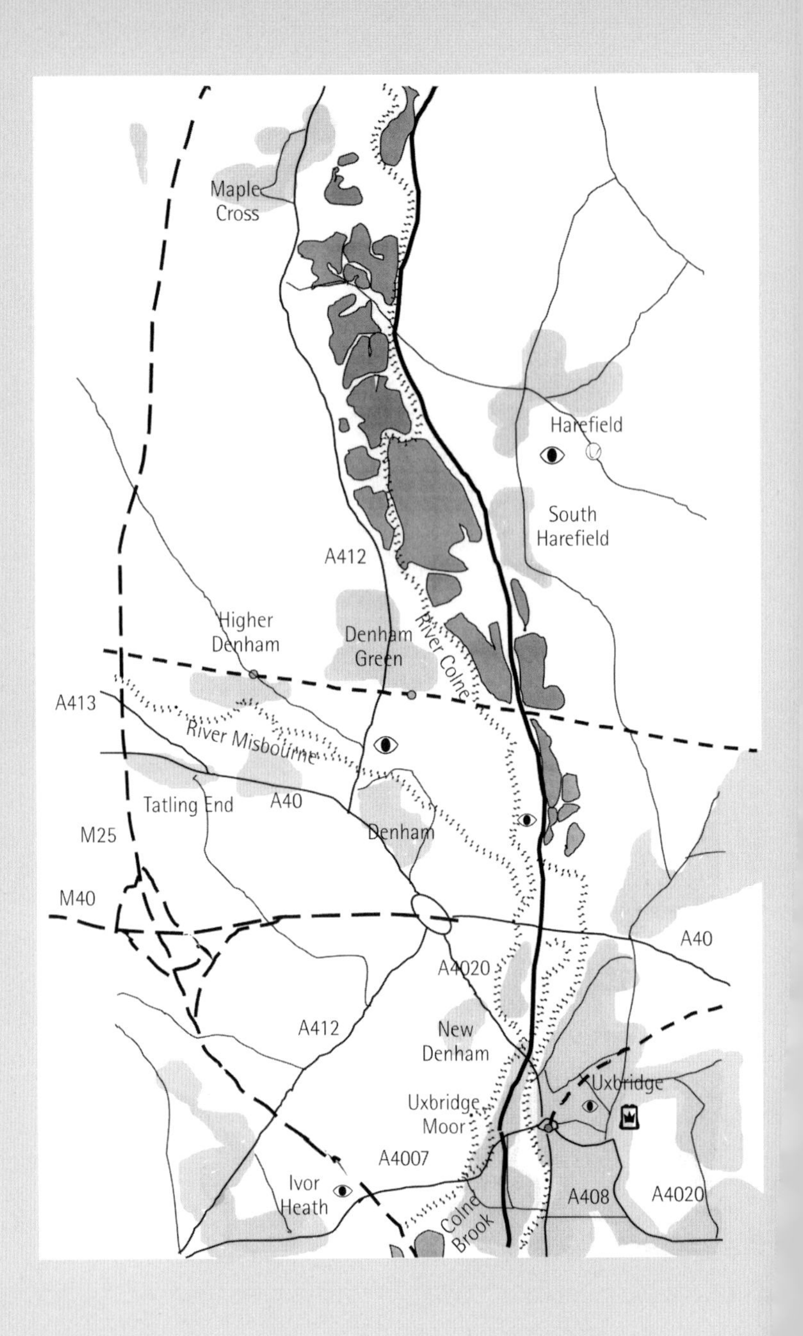
Maple Cross
Harefield
South Harefield
A412
Higher Denham
Denham Green
River Colne
A413
River Misbourne
Tatling End
A40
M25
Denham
M40
A40
A4020
A412
New Denham
Uxbridge
Uxbridge Moor
A4007
Ivor Heath
A408
A4020
Colne Brook

Key
Canal
River
Railway
Motorway
A Road
B Road
Built up area
Stations
Open water
Site/Sight
Leisure
Entertainment
Culture

SEEING AND DOING

INTRODUCTION

This is a section of contrasts, with relatively rural stretches to the north and west giving way to the outskirts of Greater London as soon as the towpath becomes entrenched inside the M25 belt. These contrasts result in a variety of things to see and do in this section, as well as some surprises.

Contrary to what one might reasonably expect, some of the grandest 'country' houses, historical sites and best nature reserves are actually located in the heart of the built-up area to the east of the section. While some of these are well-marketed tourist destinations, others are more oblique and need tracking down – but the hunt is usually worth it, and gives an insight into the history of the local area.

There are two Tourist Information Centres in this section:
- Central Library High Street, Uxbridge (01895 250706)
- The Treaty Centre, High Street, Hounslow (0845 456 2929)

SIGHTS

Dews Farm Sand Pits in Harefield is a small nature reserve based in a sand and gravel quarry. Hollowed grassland provides a breeding ground for butterflies, hoverflies and grasshoppers in the summer. The site can be accessed via Harvill Road opposite New Years Green Lane.

The ANZAC cemetery in Harefield churchyard is dedicated to the graves of 111 AIF personnel, and one nursing sister, who died at the Australian Auxiliary Hospital, Harefield Park, from their wounds or illness. The graves are all the same, being rectangular with a scroll pattern on their base with the dedication 'Erected by his Comrades' and 'ANZAC' on them.

Also in Harefield, it is worth looking out for the distinctive metal sculpture of a hare trapped inside a mesh globe that sits on the green, and on the road down into South Harefield the Countess of Derby's almshouses are also distinctive, with their twisted Tudor chimneys. The hare was erected as a Millennium Memorial, and is a play on the animal in the village's name. The globe features only Britain and Australia, in deference to ANZAC connection. Before leaving Harefield, take in the view over the west of London on the road down towards the turning for the canal.

> The Harefield Hare also makes much play of the village's pioneering heart-hospital, featuring red hearts around its edge.

> The village sign in Denham portrays the chained swan, county emblem of Buckinghamshire, which the village is justly part of.

Denham Village is a hidden gem nestling in the crook of the junction of the A40 and the A412. The village sign proclaims a string of victories in the Best Kept Village competition, although long gaps between them suggest only

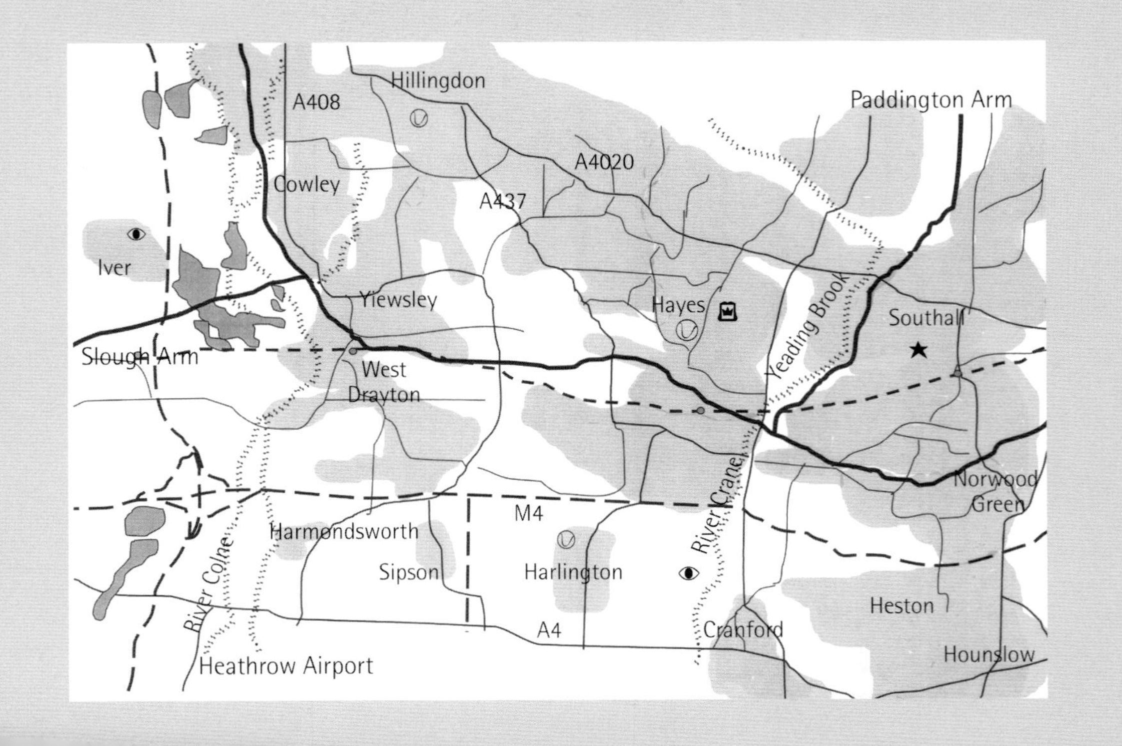

Hillingdon
A408
Paddington Arm
A4020
Cowley
A437
Iver
Yiewsley
Hayes
Southall
Yeading Brook
Slough Arm
West Drayton
River Crane
Norwood Green
M4
Harmondsworth
Sipson
Harlington
River Colne
Heston
A4
Cranford
Hounslow
Heathrow Airport

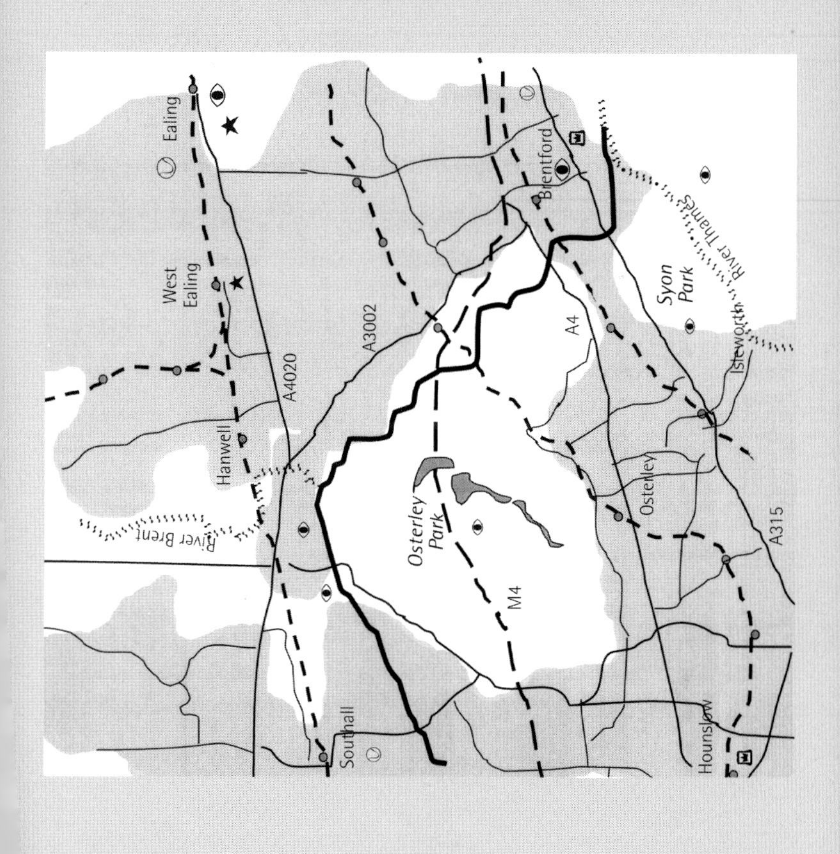
Ealing
West Ealing
Hanwell
A4020
A3002
River Brent
Southall
Osterley Park
M4
A4
Brentford
Syon Park
River Thames
Isleworth
Osterley
A315
Hounslow

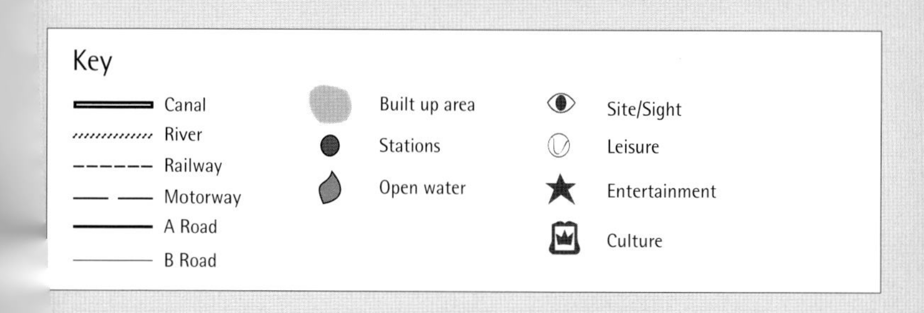
Key
Canal
River
Railway
Motorway
A Road
B Road
Built up area
Stations
Open water
Site/Sight
Leisure
Entertainment
Culture

periodic bursts of enthusiasm for advertising the village's charms to a wider audience, perhaps wisely.

The church has a Norman tower, a thirteenth-century font of Purbeck Marble and a fifteenth-century so-called 'Doom Painting' of the Last Judgement. The village has a number of old properties, such as Southlands Manor, Maltmas Green and Denham Mount, as well as its two main buildings, Denham Court and Denham Place. Denham Place is noted for its friezes, ceilings and chapel, and has a garden landscaped by 'Capability' Brown, while Denham Court sits at the end of an avenue of lime trees.

> Denham's more modern claim to fame is as home to Denham Film Studios, which these days is an industrial estate.

The area around Denham has a particular tradition of supplying flowers to London, and evidence for this can be seen in the long run of nurseries along the A40 leading along the edge of the village.

Denham Lock Wood is an area of Special Scientific Interest, and lies just to the north of Frays Farm Meadows, which shares this status. The former is a wet woodland, and fen and can be accessed via the towpath. Winter wildfowl are a feature, as are the spring flowers. Autumn, however, brings the wood's most notorious inhabitant, the tiny Desmoulin's whorl snail. Frays Farm Meadows boasts kingcups in the spring, followed shortly by ragged-robin. Further information on both of these sights can be obtained from the London Wildlife Trust, on 020 7261 0447.

Iver Nature Study Centre, Slough Road, Iver Heath (01895 270730), is a series of mini-habitats spread out over a 2-acre site. These include woodland, five ponds, a meadow, a mini-rainforest, a sensory area, The Garden of Time and Get Down to Nature. The last of these is a short assault course designed to show how animals move. Open to any member of the community, the centre also hosts educational tours. Iver's church has an Anglo-Saxon window and a tower built with Roman bricks.

> Although not open to the public, and recently converted into flats, the impressive Iver Grove near Shredding Green was originally built by Sir John Vanbrugh in 1724, who was also responsible for the much grander Blenheim Palace.

The Old Mill House on the Uxbridge/New Denham border, near the Swan and Bottle pub, sits on an island bordered by the canal and the River Colne. Dated 1696, this is a reminder of one of the various mills that have existed here over the centuries, and is a rare curiosity in an otherwise very modern landscape. The area around the island is worth visiting, mill or no mill, and these days has a large fountain-cum-sculpture to top it off.

The Grove Nature Reserve in Uxbridge (entrance on Robinwood Grove off Royal Lane) is an area of shaded ponds that act as a habitat for frogs, among grassland and woods. Woodpeckers and tawny owls live in the woods, while herbs and foxtail exist in the grasses.

Uxbridge itself has little to recommend it. Its two shopping centres, clustered around its tube station, dominate the centre, in which commercial properties line the main trunk roads. Although glimpses of the town's historical inheritance can be seen, you have to look hard, with Windsor Street opposite the station a reasonable place to start.

Hanwell Asylum, built by Middlesex County in 1831, in order to meet their statutory obligations to house people with mental-health problems, is visible from both the road and the canal. Over time, the asylum became a self-contained community with a farm, gardens, a laundry, baker and even a brewery – as well as a graveyard.

Many patients worked, as well as lived, here, and six years after it opened there were nearly 1,900 patients. More recently, parts of the asylum have been converted into flats, although the two gatehouses remain, along with surrounding walls.

Near to Boston Manor Station in Hanwell, there is a Gospel Oak. Apparently dead, the tree marks the spot where local parishioners would gather once a year on the Sunday before Ascension Day. Following a beating of the parish bounds, a short service and blessing for the crops would follow.

> There is one other surviving Gospel Oak in London – appropriately enough in Gospel Oak.

Easily missed, Bridge 205 on the canal is known as both Windmill Bridge and Three Bridges, and is the spot where Isambard Kingdom Brunel brought three forms of transport together in Hanwell. One of his last engineering feats, the road (Windmill Lane), goes over the canal, which crosses a railway.

Ealing is dominated by its two shopping centres, The Arcadia, which has a clock that strikes the hour, and the Ealing Broadway Centre, which features a bronze sculpture of a family resting from a hard day's shopping. The borough's Victorian town hall is an impressive edifice on the road out to West Ealing, as is the Anglican High Church of Christ the Saviour.

Pitshanger Manor in Ealing (020 8567 1227) is a restored Regency villa, originally designed by Sir John Sloane, and owned since 1901 by the local authority, who now run it as a museum and a professional contemporary arts venue. There is an extensive display of Martinware Pottery in the museum, and the venue also hosts concerts, workshops and exhibitions.

> Sir John Sloane is perhaps better known as the architect for the Bank of England. Pitshanger House was also the home of the five daughters of the Conservative Prime Minister, Spencer Perceval, who was assassinated in 1812.

Not on the regular tourist trail, Boston Manor House (0845 456 2800) is a Jacobean manor house built in 1623, and set back off the Boston Manor Road. Three-stories high and set in parkland complete with a lake and ancient trees, the house contains the London Borough of Hounslow's art collection – over eighty paintings of historical local scenes.

Another of the great parks dotted around this section, Gunnersbury Park, is a mix of gardens and museum (0208 9921612), with the park being owned by the local councils and open to the public. This includes a boating lake, playgrounds and a pitch-and-putt course. The museum is particularly appreciated by children as it has a rotating exhibition featuring toys, costume and domestic life in the nineteenth century.

Brentford Monument commemorates the supposed crossing point over the Thames by Julius Caesar. This claim is based on the discovery of wooden stakes in Thames at this point, although some archaeological evidence suggests these are more likely to date from medieval times.

> It was from The Butts that the results of Parliamentary elections would be declared - including those which saw the radical John Wilkes elected as the local member in the 1760s.

Also in Brentford, and worth pausing to see, is The Butts, a street and square of red-brick houses from the 1680s. The Butts provides a gateway for imagining how Brentford might have been during the heyday of coaching inns, when the town's location at the end of the road heading west out of London, supported three large coaching inns.

While in Brentford, it is also worth taking in the industrial heritage along the towpath either side of the town, including the large BW warehouse to the west, and Brentford Docks by the Thames.

The grounds of Osterley Park (0208 2325050) dominate the vista south of the towpath along the canal's final loop and turn into Brentford. The house was the handiwork of Robert Adam, who took a crumbling Tudor mansion and made it a neo-classical villa. Today, the house is one of the most complete examples of Adam's work, and the grounds include a Pleasure Gardens and further neo-classical buildings.

South of Osterley lies the Cranford Countryside Park, a 144-acre garden which was originally the grounds of Cranford House. Historical relics are scattered here, such as a walled garden, a restored eighteenth-century stable block, an icehouse and a medieval church. The River Crane also flows through the park.

The remarkable Isleworth Ait can only be accessed by boat, and is only open for special events and on workdays (020 7261 0447 for further details). A small Thames island, this nature reserve is regularly flooded, leading to a tall canopy of mixed woodland, with willows a particular feature. This undisturbed habitat is one favoured by the treecreeper, kingfisher and the inland waterways' friend, the heron.

Henry VIII's coffin stopped overnight at Syon on its way to Windsor for burial, but during the night it burst open and in the morning dogs were found licking at the remains. Many regarded this as divine retribution for Henry's treatment of Syon Abbey.

Syon Park (0208 5600881), between Brentford and Isleworth, remains in the hands of the Earls of Northumberland, as it has been for 400 years. Its name is derived from Mount Zion in the Holy Land, and it was originally the site of a medieval abbey, although it survived only just over a century before it fell victim to Henry VIII's Dissolution. Both the house and the gardens are worth seeing, with the latter housing the Great Conservatory as well as a fine rose garden.

The Aquatic Experience in Syon Park (0208 847 4730) is centred on an exhibition of rescued and endangered species that live in or near water. Highlights include piranhas, the poison-arrow frog and snakes.

Kew Gardens (020 8332 5655) lie south of the river, and are known worldwide for their pioneering conservation work. Now a World Heritage Site, the days when it used to cost a penny to enter have long since gone, although children under sixteen get in free.

Other attractions nearby include Hampton Court Palace (0870 752 7777), Chiswick House (020 8995 0508) and Ham House (020 8940 1950). The first of these is known the world over for its Tudor connections, and is notable for its staterooms and the tour of its kitchens. Chiswick House is one of the country's finest Palladian villas, and is surrounded by extraordinary gardens, while Ham House was built in 1610 and enlarged in the 1670s, at which point it lay at the heart of Restoration court life. Ham also has some very impressive gardens.

CULTURE AND ENTERTAINMENT

Given the area covered by this section, it is not possible within the confines of this guide to offer a comprehensive listing of all culture and entertain-

The Swan and Bottle at Uxbridge, in Edwardian times a favourite stopping place for Sunday cyclists.

ment venues available. It is hoped, however, that the following offers a good introduction as to what might be available.

If its music you're after you could start with the Arts Centre at Brunel University in Uxbridge (01895 273482), which hosts concerts, including a programme of free Friday lunchtime recitals, as well as evening concerts and exhibitions, with the latter held at its Beldam Gallery also in Uxbridge. Arts and music events are also held at St Margaret's church (01895 258766) in Windsor Street, Uxbridge.

The Southlands Arts Centre (01895 442784), meanwhile, hidden away just off the green in West Drayton, stages regular exhibitions and crafts markets.

The Watermans Arts Centre (0208 232 1010) in Brentford is perhaps the main arts venue in this section. Housing a 39-seat theatre and 125-seat cinema, as well as gallery space and a studio, the centre has the added attraction of being on the Thames.

Redlees Studios in Isleworth (0208 583 4457) houses over thirty different artists specialising in areas as diverse as jewellery, glass, ceramics, paint and sculpture. The studios hold regular open events, and it is worth phoning to see when the next one might be.

The main cinemas along this section include:

- The Himalaya Palace Cinema, Southall (0208 813 8844)
- The Gosai Cinema, West Ealing (0208 567 1075) – *for Bollywood movies*
- UGC Cinema, Ealing Broadway (0871 2002000)
- Odeon, the Chimes, Uxbridge (0870 505 0007)

As well as the venues highlighted above, both Hayes and Hounslow have dedicated theatres. The Beck Theatre at Hayes (0208 561 8371) shows films and plays, while the Paul Robeson Theatre in the Treaty Centre in Hounslow (0845 456 2840) is also worth checking out. Finally, the Questors Theatre in Ealing (0208 567 0011) claims to be the largest community theatre in Europe, and has a regular rolling programme with around twenty productions staged every year.

Options for more active entertainment in this section, especially in the sporting arena, are legion. The John Penrose Sports Centre in Harefield (01895 822929) is attached to a school, and is available for public use outside school hours, while the Hillingdon Outdoor Activity Centre (01895 824171), also in Harefield, is a 45-acre watersports lake offering canoeing, windsurfing and sailing.

Yiewsley Swimming Pool (01895 442444) has a gym and 33m-competitive pool. Currently, Uxbridge is short of a good sports complex, although plans to build one are at an advanced stage. In the meantime, there are a number of fitness clubs, including Fitness First (01895 209870) on the High Street.

The Dormers Wells sports and leisure centre in Southall (0208 998 3241) has a sports hall, 20m-indoor swimming pool, dance studio and Boston's Gym. The Elthorne Sports Centre in Hanwell (0208 579 3226) has a sports hall and gym, and the Gurnell Sports Centre (0208 998 3241), to the north of Ealing, has two swimming pools, a sauna and steam room, sunbeds and a fitness suite.

The Hayes Stadium and Sports Centre (0208 573 0093) has a wide range of sporting facilities, while the Hayes Pool (0208 573 2785) in Central Avenue, Hayes, is an indoor swimming pool which also houses a fitness centre. Heston has a David Lloyd Fitness Club on Southall Lane (0208 573 9378).

Brentford Fountain Leisure Centre (0845 4562935), near Chiswick Roundabout, has a gym, a studio, a children's playcentre and three squash courts. In addition, the centre has two swimming pools, one for serious swimming and one for fun.

Finally, on the sporting front, the 1930s-built Isleworth Recreation Centre (0845 456 2980) on Twickenham Road has been recently refurbished, and has three swimming pools, an activities room, a health suite and a gym, as well as a floodlit arena.

We cannot leave sport without mentioning that professional football is played at Griffin Park, home of Brentford FC (0208 847 2511). Known as 'The Bees', Brentford have never achieved a major prize and have enjoyed an honourable history bouncing back and forth among the lower divisions of the football league.

> Brentford FC was formed by members of the local rowing club looking for a winter activity, and their first strip was salmon, claret and light blue, to match the rowing club's colours.

If you like your sport slightly less active, one option may be the Airport Bowl in Harlington (0208 759 1396).

With much of this section dominated by built-up areas, it is no surprise that there are a number of nightlife options. Many of the local pubs offer live music, with Ealing and Brentford getting most of the attention, while there are nightclubs in each of the major centres of population. If you fancy something a little different (and quieter), there is always Stage 5 (020 8758 8510), based at the Ealing Studios, which hosts comedy evenings every Thursday, Friday and Saturday.

By way of a starter, pubs and other venues staging live music in this section include:

- The Ostler, Uxbridge (01895 237781) – *live bands on Thursdays*
- The Viaduct, Hanwell (0208 567 1362)
- Barracuda, Ealing (0208 579 8632) – *a music bar*
- Broadway Boulevard, Ealing (0208 840 0616)
- Finnegan's Wake, Ealing (0208 567 2439)
- The George and Dragon, Ealing (0208 896 9499) – *offering a range of music from rock and punk to jazz, on Thursday and Sunday evenings*
- The Grange Tavern, Ealing (0208

567 7617)
- The Beehive, Brentford (0208 560 2421)
- The Globe, Brentford (0208 560 8932)
- The Six Bells, Brentford (0208 560 8804)
- Stripes Bar and Restaurant, Brentford Football Club (0208 847 2511)
- The Red Lion, Isleworth (0208 560 1457)
- The Shrine, Hounslow (0208 570 1487) – *pub/club playing indie and rock bands or 1970s and 1980s tributes*

Nightclubs in this section include:

- Royale's, High Street, Uxbridge (01895 255513)
- The Priory, The Mall, Ealing (0208 840 0706)
- Club Boulevard, Ealing Broadway (0208 840 0616)
- LA Confidential, Ealing Broadway (0208 567 6733)
- Shannon's, High Street, Hounslow (0208 572 8044)
- Mystique, Cavendish Parade, Bath Road Hounslow (0208 577 8565)

Ealing Town Hall, an impressive Victorian edifice.

SECTION E

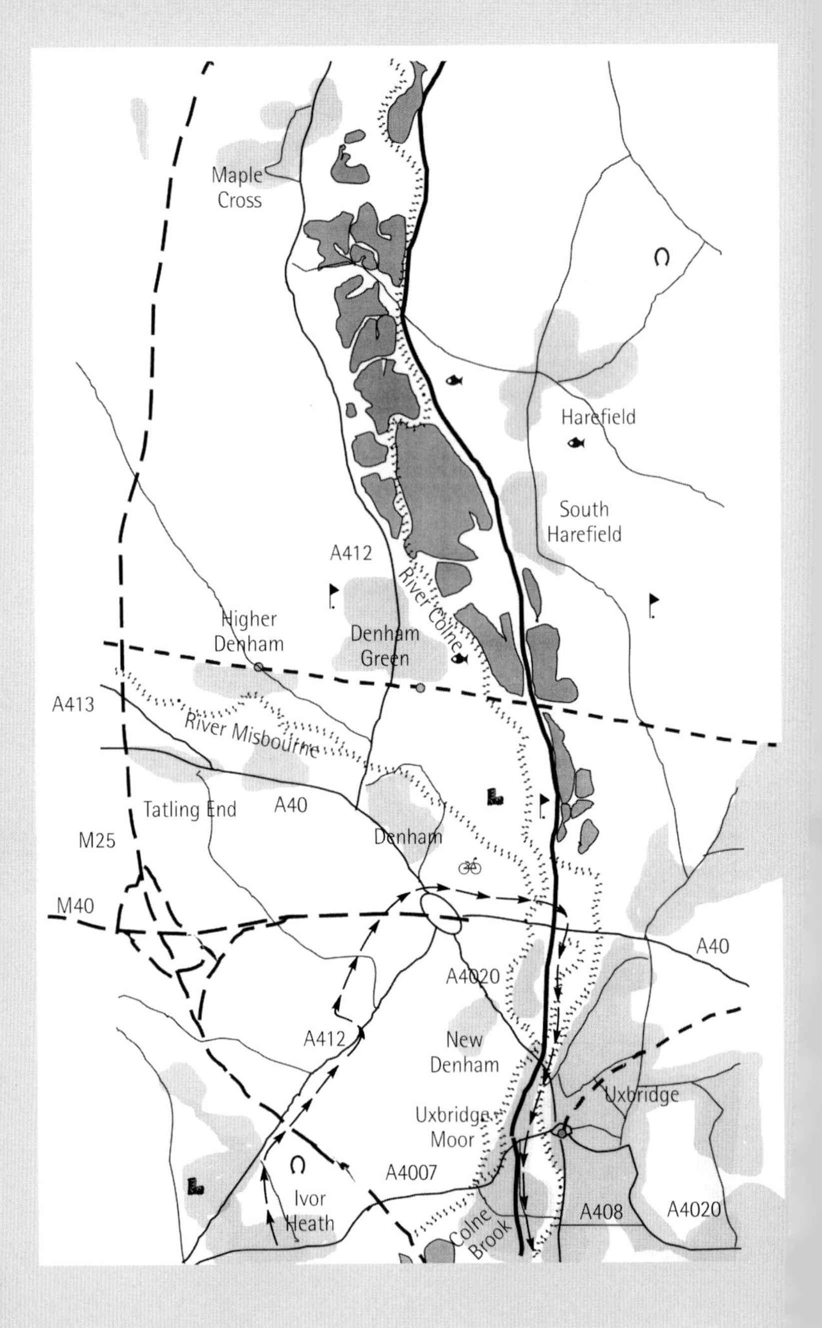
Maple Cross
Harefield
South Harefield
A412
River Colne
Higher Denham
Denham Green
A413
River Misbourne
Tatling End
A40
M25
Denham
M40
A40
A4020
A412
New Denham
Uxbridge
Uxbridge Moor
A4007
Ivor Heath
Colne Brook
A408
A4020

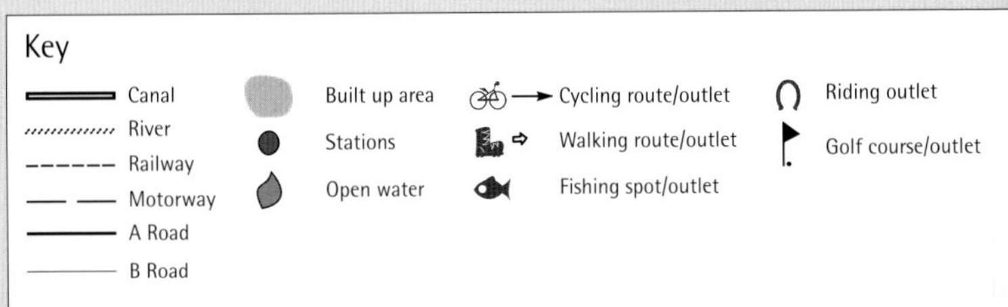
Key
Canal
River
Railway
Motorway
A Road
B Road
Built up area
Stations
Open water
Cycling route/outlet
Walking route/outlet
Fishing spot/outlet
Riding outlet
Golf course/outlet

SAMPLING

INTRODUCTION

This section breaks into two halves. The northern part from Batchworth, as far south as Cowley Peachey, is quite rural, and is dominated by water in the form of lakes and rivers, with the Colne Valley governing the landscape. The eastern section, on the other hand, running from Cowley Peachey through to Brentford, offers a much more urbanised landscape, although it's not all concrete and asphalt. There are a succession of open spaces offering the basis for walks and other ways of sampling the area, not least by using one of the many golf courses to enjoy 'a long walk spoiled'.

WALKING

Walkers are spoiled for choice in both the quantity and variety of walking opportunities in this section, many of which have been consolidated into formal walks by authorities concerned about maintaining the open spaces that have been left following the rapid growth of the western part of London.

The South Bucks Way follows the valley of the River Misbourne and the canal, before linking up with the London Loop at Denham, stretching over a total of 23 miles, and is well marked on Ordnance Survey maps. The London Loop itself is a near circular route around Greater London, covering a total of 150 miles, and the signs for the walk often appear on routes in this section, especially along the canal, in the Colne Valley Park and along the Hillingdon Trail.

The Colne Valley Park stretches from Batchworth down to Denham, and covers 43 square miles. It was created in 1967 by the then Greater London Council for 'recreational and leisure purposes' for the people of London, and is split in two by the M40.

North of the motorway it is the chalk hills that dominate, but these fade out the further south you go, with woodland taking over the area caused by the coming together of the flood plain of the Colne and the Thames, and it is here that the five great reservoirs that command the landscape are formed. The park can be accessed by its visitor centre, just to the north of the roundabout at Junction 1 of the M40, where there is a small charge for parking, but also a tea-room.

Buckinghamshire County Council produce a series of leaflets on walks through the park, and these can be accessed either direct or online (see Learn More and Links). Black Park Country Park, between Slough and the M40, to the immediate west of Iver Heath, is a largely wooded area offering a number of trails, including a cinematic trail in homage to the nearby Pinewood Studios, home to the Bond films, among many others. There is also a large lake and a visitors' centre to the south of the park.

With 69 acres, the Denham Country Park is slightly bigger than the Colne Valley Park. It is bounded by the canal and the Rivers Colne and Misbourne, and links up with a number of local footpaths and bridleways, as well as the South Bucks Long Distance Route. A good place to park in order to access the park is

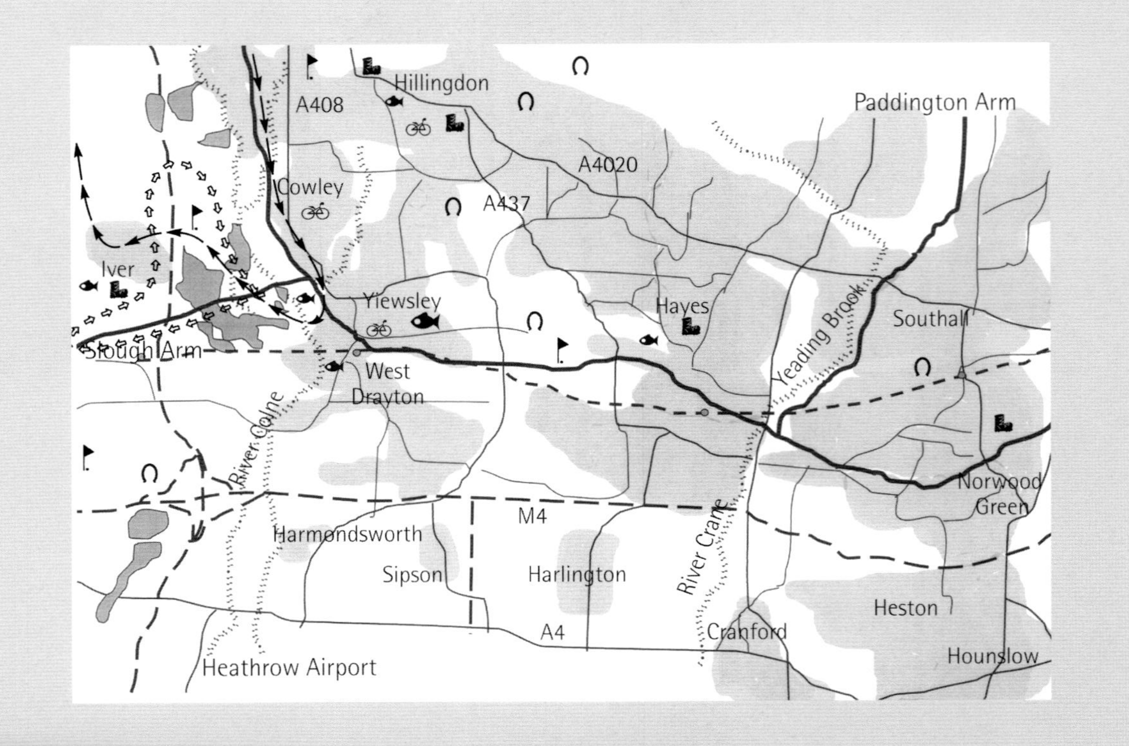

Hillingdon
A408
Paddington Arm
A4020
Cowley
A437
Iver
Yiewsley
Hayes
Yeading Brook
Southall
Slough Arm
West
Drayton
River Colne
Norwood
Green
M4
Harmondsworth
Sipson
Harlington
River Crane
Heston
A4
Cranford
Hounslow
Heathrow Airport

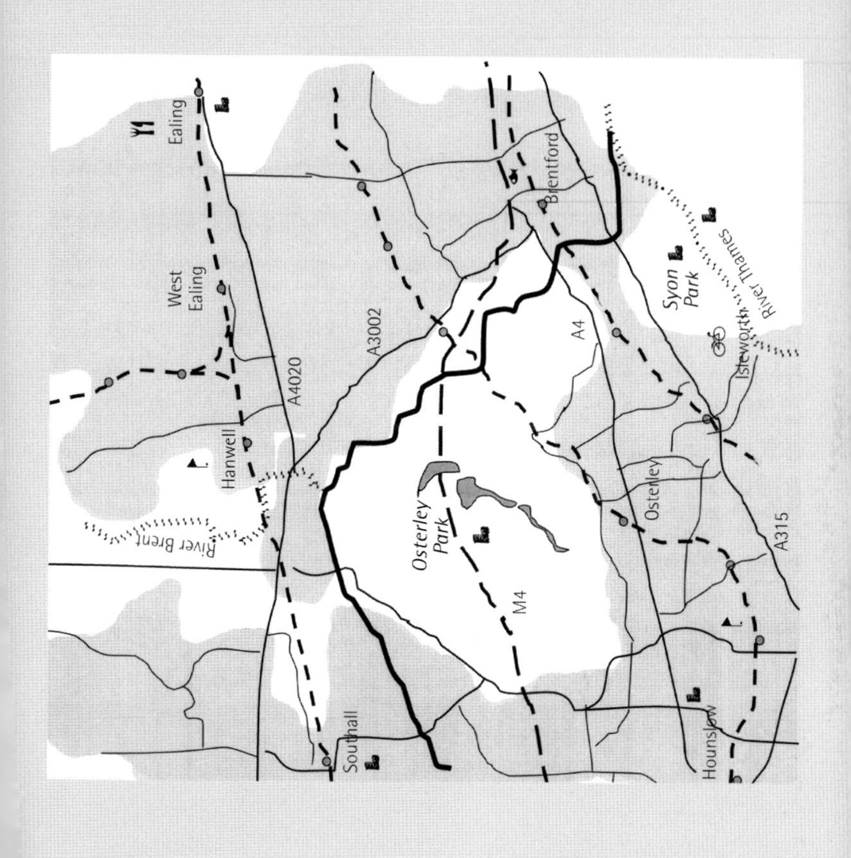
Ealing
West Ealing
Hanwell
River Brent
A4020
A3002
Brentford
A4
Syon Park
River Thames
Isleworth
Osterley Park
M4
Osterley
A315
Southall
Hounslow

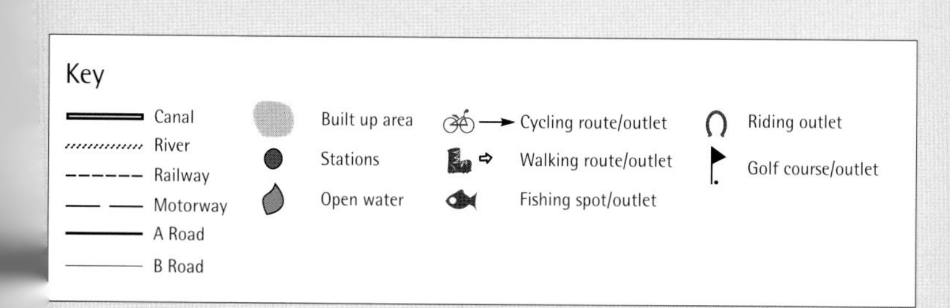
Key
Canal
River
Railway
Motorway
A Road
B Road
Built up area
Stations
Open water
Cycling route/outlet
Walking route/outlet
Fishing spot/outlet
Riding outlet
Golf course/outlet

Denham Quarry on the Moorhall Road between Denham and South Harefield. Denham itself can be explored via a town trail produced by the London Borough of Hillingdon.

Slightly to the south there is also the Kingcup Farm Trail, a 1.5-mile trail round a farm, owned by the County Council, which produces fruit and vegetables for sale on a pick-your-own basis in the summer.

The name Denham means 'village in a valley', although it actually sits in two valleys, those of the Colne and the Misbourne.

The Hillingdon Trail, which often winds through many of the places covered in this section, is a 20-mile trail through the western suburbs of London, starting at Rickmansworth and ending at the River Thames near Isleworth. Its northern section coincides with the Harefield locks on the canal, while its southern part includes stretches of towpath around Hayes. The London Borough of Hillingdon also produces a guide to walking this from the station at Hayes and Harlington, to that at Uxbridge

Beeches Way is a 16-mile route from Cookham to West Drayton, which passes through Burnham Beeches in Buckinghamshire, while the Brent River Park Walk covers a 6-mile route connecting Hanger Lane with Brentford.

The southern portion of this section is also well provisioned with parkland, and includes Osterley Park – a National Trust property, Syon Park and Gunnersbury Park, all covered in more detail in 'Seeing and Doing'. Stockley Park, north of the canal at Bridge 195, covers 450 acres, and although 100 acres of this is business park, there is a large golf course with footpaths and bridleways between the fairways.

Stockley Park was opened in 1993, following what was at the time the largest single civil engineering project involving landfill transfer in Europe. It transformed an area comprising old rubbish, gravel and clay into a beautiful open space.

Other parks include Lake Farm Country Park, which can be accessed by Bridge 198 and Bixley Field, just after Bridge 203 and the meadows surrounding the River Pinn, east of Cowley Peachey.

Finally, there are a number of commons and open parkland among the different towns across this section, including commons and heaths in Hillingdon, Hounslow, Hayes, Southall and Ealing.

Blondin Park outside Boston Manor used to be in the grounds of Blondin House, owned by the tightrope walker Blondin, who once famously crossed Niagara Falls on a wire.

Walk E, however, focuses on the northern part of this section, starting in Iver and part of the Colne Valley Park, before taking in Little Britain Lake and a portion of the Slough Arm.

SECTION E WALK

Iver and the Slough Arm

Description:	*A steady walk sampling the different forms of water in the northern part of the section*
Distance:	*4.75 miles*
Duration:	*2 hours*

Starting point: *Grid Reference 031831, OS Explorer 172*
Nearest Refreshment: *The Swan Inn, Iver (01753 655776)*

Park in the parade of shops on the High Street, or on one of the side roads, and start the walk from the mini-roundabout in the south of the village opposite the church. Go down Swan Lane, past the pub and alongside a private unmade road, persevering along a long straight stretch until the road bends to the left. Just before the bend, pick up the public footpath on the right, going over a stile and along a path constrained by wire fencing. At the next stile, bear right onto a sandy track shaded by horse chestnut trees.

On reaching a gate, cross over a gravel drive and cross the bridge over the Colne Brook. Turn right on the other side and follow a road up and left over the M25. Keep with this as it bends down to the right to Iver Road. Cross the road with care, and go down the path opposite. Two kissing gates sandwich a short avenue of trees, and on going through the second gate you face an attractive section of the River Colne, which acts as the border between Middlesex and Buckinghamshire.

Cross a wooden footbridge and you will come to a weir. Stick with the river, following a sign for the 'London Loop', and soon you will see Little Britain Lake. Go over two more wooden footbridges to a concrete bridge over the river, which takes you to the lake. Bear right at the corner of the lake, and over the top of Packet Boat Lane, following a sign to Stockley Park. The river narrows, and a small incline takes you to an iron bridge over the Slough Arm; cross this and turn right. Further bridges take you over the Colne and Colne Brook. Pass under the M25 and leave the canal at Bridge 4.

Bear left and left again, over the bridge and them immediately right on the other side. Hug the perimeter of an industrial estate until you meet a three-way marker. Take the left turn and strike out over the field towards some houses. On reaching some garages, go up and then right until you reach the village hall. Turn right again, following the main road over the mini-roundabout and back into the High Street.

Walking equipment outlets along this section are thin on the ground, although there is Hi-Gear in Windmill Road, Brentford (020 8847 4422).

CYCLING

Many of the walking routes detailed above are also suitable for cyclists, although users should check first. Towards the southern and eastern part of the section, cyclists should be very road aware, and ideally follow the designated cycle routes.

Specifically, Route 89 of the London Cycle Network runs south down from Uxbridge along Whitehall and Cleveland Roads, through Yiewsley and West Drayton, while Route 43 branches east from West Drayton and follows a path south of Hayes and Southall, to emerge at Brentford. Meanwhile, Route 87 passes north of Brentford and goes through Hanwell, and Route 39 links Uxbridge and Ealing via the A4020.

Brentford Weir at low water – finally tides come into play.

A good way to sample this section by bike is to pick up the South Bucks Way in Denham, and follow it south-east, passing to the north of the Colne Valley Park Visitors' Centre, until you reach the canal towpath. Follow this south, past the outskirts of Uxbridge and beyond Cowley Peachey Junction, until Bridge 191. Here you need to turn right, and pick up the Beeches Way path, heading north-west.

On reaching Ford Lane, turn left and continue along here until you reach Iver Lane, where you again turn left. Follow this through Iver itself, taking the turn right, signed to Iver Heath. Go through Iver Heath and pick up the Denham Road, where you turn right. Follow this over the M25 and over the small stream called Alder Bourne, shortly after which you need to take the road on the left (Southlands Road), turning first left after the farm (Hollybush Lane).

Pass over the M40 and take the first right (Froggy Lane), turning right at the T-junction (Blacksmith's Lane). Where this forks, take the left-hand option. Cross over the A40 and continue along the footpath, picking up the road opposite when you reach the A412. This then leads you back to your starting point – a total of around 14 miles.

Cycling clubs along this section include:

- South Bucks Road Club (01753 869092)
- West London Loiterers, Uxbridge (01895 253288)
- West London Cycle Club, Ickenham (01895 672103)

Cycle outlets along this section include:

- Bike Hut, Halfords, Ivybridge Retail Park, Isleworth (020 8891 4403)
- Bike-Link, Isleworth (020 8568 3999)

- Moore Bros, Isleworth (020 8560 7131)
- Rippingales Cyles, Cowley (01895 232755)
- The Wheely Good Bike Shop, Whiteley's Parade, Hillingdon (01895 811214)
- Wheely Re-Cycled, Yiewsley (01895 445952)

RIDING

Once again, many of the routes described in the walking section are also suitable for riders, notably those through Colne Valley Park, Denham Country Park, Stockley Park and Black Park.

In addition, there are a number of other good riding spots, including Philpots Farm alongside the River Pinn east of Cowley Peachey, Trout Lane west of Yiewsley and Palmers Moor off Iver Lane.

Horse-riding establishments and outlets along this section include:

- Abbeyfields Equestrian Centre, Hayes (020 8841 3362) – *riding school*
- Ealing Riding School, Gunnersbury Lane (0208 9923808)
- Goulds Green Riding School, Hillingdon, Uxbridge (01895 446256) – *riding school*
- Manor Farm, Cowley (01895 442737) – *riding school*
- Norwood Green Stables, Southall (020 8574 5169) – *stables*
- Poplars Riding Centre, Iver (01753 654305) – *livery*
- White Lodge Livery, Wood Lane, Iver (01753 653000)

FISHING

There are plenty of opportunities for fishing along this section, including lakes, rivers and the canal. Waters are controlled by a variety of bodies, and there is a wide range of species available.

The Blenheim Angling Society (01494 764977) has rights over most of the canal between Batchworth and Denham, where carp, roach, bream, perch and pike, as well as some barbel, are the main species.

Boyers Leisure (01753 630302 or 01895 444707) control a number of still waters and stretches of rivers along this expanse. Notable are Mayfields in West Drayton, where pike over 20lb have been caught, along with catfish and good-sized tench; Old Slade Lane Lake and Farlows Lake at Iver, which also has good-sized carp and pike; and part of the River Colne at New Denham, good for pike and barbell as well as bream and tench. Boyers also has Harefield Carp Lake, which has carp up to 40lb.

The London Anglers Association (0208 6207477), featured in the previous two sections, also has some water here, namely a stretch of the canal from Denham Deep Lock through to West Drayton Trout Bridge, split into three sections. This section is well known for large pike, as well as good hauls of roach and chub.

Also featured in previous sections are the Uxbridge Rovers Angling and Conservation Society (020 8428 1739), which controls a number of lengths along this section. These include part of the River Colne by Denham, just north of the M40 (shared with Boyers Leisure), where fishing is allowed only from the canal bank.

There is another stretch of the river through Buckinghamshire Golf Club, running from Denham Viaduct through to Denham Deep Lock. This offers roach and dace, as well as eels and barbell. The society also has the stretch of canal between Osterley and Clitheroe's Locks, where the Brent joins the canal. Roach and perch are the main catch here.

The society also controls the Knightscote Ponds just outside Harefield, a small fishery aimed mainly at young anglers, and stocked with medium-sized carp, tench and perch, as well as numerous small roach and rudd. Finally, the society also has the small Billet Lane fishery in Iver, which has carp up to double figures, as well as bream, tench, chub and roach.

The Gerrards Cross and Uxbridge Angling Society (0208 421 0768) controls sections of the Colne, including a half-mile-long island just south of Uxbridge town centre, within the Uxbridge Moor nature reserve, known for chub, barbell and perch, as well as excellent roach and pike. Other waters controlled by the society include Broadwater Lake in Harefield, a 200-acre lake in the heart of the Colne Valley with bream, tench and pike, and Denham Lake, also in Harefield, which has carp, bream, tench, perch, roach, rudd and pike.

Stretches of canal operated by this society include sections by Denham, accessed via Denham Lake. Carp here are good in the first two months of the season, and there is also some bream. The society controls the Slough Arm, which can be good for fishing due to the low boat traffic. Carp and tench are good towards the Slough end, while bream, tench, rudd, roach, chub and perch dominate the middle section.

Other fishing spots along this section include:

- The Cutting, Packet Boat Lane, Yiewsley (01895 847889) – *carp and pike*
- Gunnersbury Lake, Brentford (0208 7433381)
- Kingfisher Lake, Denham Cross (01895 50111 x 2352)
- Korda Lake, Harefield (01895

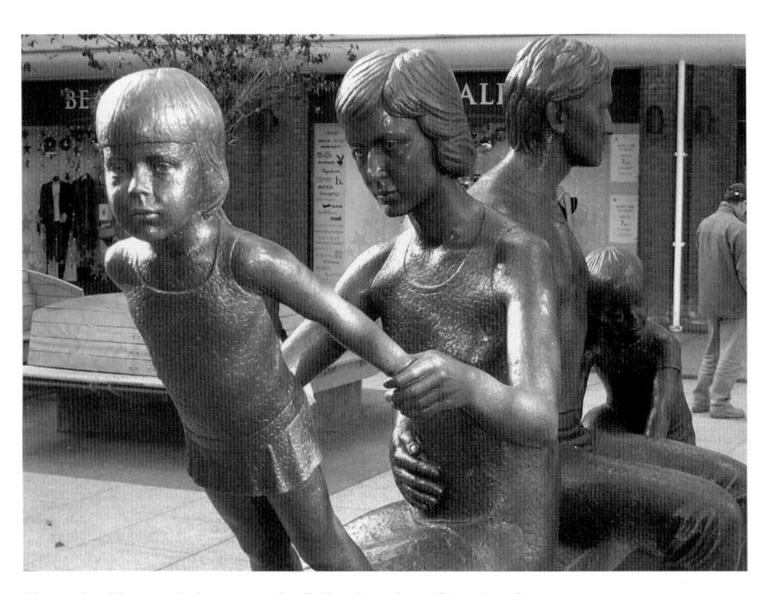

Happy families cast in bronze at the Ealing Broadway Shopping Centre.

824455) – *near Savay Lake*
- Lizard, West Drayton (07931 255897) – *large-sized carp, tench and bream, as well as crucian carp*
- Orlitts Lakes, West Drayton (01895 444707) – *next to the River Colnbrook*
- Potomac Pond, Gunnersbury Park, Brentford (0208 743 3381) – *large carp and pike*
- Savay Lake, Harefield (0207 9696980) – *carp up to 30lb*

Outlets selling fishing supplies along this stretch include:

- William Boyer and Sons, West Drayton (01895 445141)
- Exchange Tackle, West Drayton (01895 442424)
- Harefield Tackle, Harefield (01895 822900)
- Herons Point Fishing Tackle Shop, Iver (01753 630302)
- Judds of Hillingdon Ltd, Westbourne Parade, Hillingdon (020 8573 0196)
- Tacklers, Hayes (020 8573 4767)

OTHER

Many of the open spaces in this section have been occupied by golf courses, allowing plenty of opportunities to sample the surrounding countryside while enjoying a little sport.

The following is a list of the main clubs in the area:

- Brent Valley Golf Club, Hanwell (020 8567 4230) – *18 holes, 5,426 yards*
- Buckinghamshire Golf Club, Denham (01895 835777) – *gently undulating parkland by the Rivers Colne and Misbourne, 18 holes, 6,880 yards with a practice range*
- Denham Golf Club, Denham (01895 832022) – *undulating parkland, 18 holes, 6,462 yards with practice area*
- Harefield Place Golf Club (01895 231169) – *18 holes*
- Hillingdon Golf Club, Uxbridge (01895 467062) – *wooded-parkland course, sloping down to a river, 9 holes, 5,490 yards*
- Hounslow Heath Golf Course, Hounslow (020 8570 5271) – *a 'Pay As You Play' 18 hole-public golf course*
- Iver Golf Club, Iver (01753 655615) – *flat parkland with natural ditches and ponds, 9 holes, 6,288 yards, with an 18-bay driving range and practice area*
- Richings Park Golf and Country Club, Iver (01753 655370) – *flat parkland with an 18-hole 6,209-yard course, and a 5-hole, par 3, course*
- Stockley Park Golf Club (020 8813 5700) – *parkland course, 18 holes, 6,754 yards with practice nets, chipping and putting greens*
- Uxbridge Golf Course (01895 237287) – *undulating parkland, 18 holes, 5,753 yards*
- West Middx Golf Course (0208 5743450) – *18-hole, 5,476-yard course, with public days on Monday and Wednesday*
- Wyke Green Golf Club, Isleworth (020 8560 4874) – *flat parkland, 18 holes, 6,211 yards*

LEARN MORE AND LINKS

For those wishing to delve a little further into the places and events covered in this guide, the following list, while far from comprehensive, should act as a useful starting point:

TOURIST INFORMATION

- Tring, Akeman Street (01442 823347)
- Berkhamsted Civic Centre (01442 228882)
- Hemel Hempstead, Marlowes shopping centre (01442 867827)
- Rickmansworth (01923 776611)
- Batchworth Lock Canal Centre (at Bridge 173 01923 778382)
- Central Library High Street, Uxbridge (01895 250706)
- The Treaty Centre, High Street, Hounslow (0845 456 2929)

WEBSITES OFFERING INFORMATION ON SPECIFIC PLACES OR EVENTS:

- www.mkweb.co.uk – pretty much anything you want to know about Milton Keynes
- www.buckscc.gov.uk/countryside – for details of the various countryside attractions and wildlife scattered around Buckinghamshire
- www.tring.gov.uk – information on Tring
- www.aylesburyvale.net/tring/history – for more on the history of Tring
- www.tring.gov.uk – a mine of information on Tring
- www.rickmansworthherts.freeserve.co.uk – for a history of Rickmansworth
- www.dacorum.gov.uk – covering Hemel Hempstead and Tring
- www.hertfordshire.co.uk – information on businesses and places to go in Hertfordshire
- www.chipperfield.org.uk – information on Chipperfield village
- www.3rivers.gov.uk – portal for the council local to Rickmansworth
- www.watford-history.co.uk – more on the history of Watford
- www.southbucks.gov.uk – website for South Bucks District Council, for details on leisure and sampling opportunities in Denham, Iver and the Colne Valley (call 01895 837200)
- www.buckscc.gov.uk – website for Buckinghamshire County Council, for details on leisure and sampling opportunities in Buckinghamshire, or call (01494) 586600 (Chiltern and South Bucks Area Office). The council sells two Countryside Packs detailing walking routes in the county.
- www.diggerhistory.info/pages-nurses/harefield_pk_hospital.htm – for more on the ANZAC war graves in Harefield
- www.batchworthlock.co.uk – more on the Batchworth Lock Centre
- www.groundwork-tv.org.uk/colne for more on the Colne Valley, including circular walks.
- www.londonanglers.net – website of the London Anglers Association
- www.gxudas.co.uk – website of the Gerrards Cross and Uxbridge Angling Society
- www.uxbridge-rovers.fsnet.co.uk – website of Uxbridge Rovers Angling Society
- www.homepage.ntlworld.com/gordonstorey/blenheim – website of the Blenheim Angling Society
- www.bdas.ukfishinginfo.co.uk
- www.ch.ic.ac.uk/rzepa/hillingdon/ – for more on the Hillingdon Trail
- www.groundwork-tv.org.uk/colne – circular walks through Colne Valley Park
- www.brentfordtw8.com – website for locals by locals, for all things involving Brentford
- www.brentford-dock.net/history-brentford-dock.htm – for more on the history of Brentford

- www.ealing.gov.uk/Services/Tourism – for more on Hanwell and Southall
- www.hounslow.no-ip.com – information on Hounslow
- www.british-history.ac.uk – for more on the local history of specific towns and villages in Section E
- www.hillingdon.gov.uk – website for the London Borough of Hillingdon, covering leisure and providing a general overview of the area. Also includes details of walks and bridleways in the Borough.

LOCALLY PRODUCED FOOD:

- www.bigbarn.co.uk - the UK's main site for locally produced food

BOOKS OFFERING FURTHER DETAIL ON SPECIFIC PLACES OR ASPECTS OF LOCAL HISTORY:

The Anatomy of Canals by Anthony Burton and Derek Pratt, Tempus Publishing 2001

The Grand Union Canal Walk by Anthony Burton and Neil Curtis (Aurum Press 1993)

Waterside Walks in Buckinghamshire by Nick Corble (Countryside Books 2004)

The Grand Union Canal, From Brentford to Braunston by Ian J. Wilson Tempus Publishing 2004)

History and Topography of Buckinghamshire by J.J. Sheahan (Longman, Green, Longman and Roberts 1971)

The Buckinghamshire Village Book (Countryside Books 1987)

TRANSPORT:

www.mkweb.co.uk/transport - for details of bus and other routes in the Milton Keynes area

www.mkweb.co.uk/cycling - for details of cycle routes in Section A, including the Millennium Cycle Ride

www.chilternsaonb.org - for details on walks (including some for the less mobile), cycle and horse riding routes

www.enquire.hertscc.gov.uk/cms - Website for the Countryside Management Service in Hertfordshre, including walk and cycle routes. Can be contacted on 01727 848168

www.watford.gov.uk – public transport and accommodation in Watford

www.londoncyclenetwork.org.uk – for more on cycle routes in London

Sustrans Information Service, PO Box 21, Bristol BS99 2HA (0117 929 0888) www.sustrans.org.uk

Traveline (www.traveline.org.uk) on 0870 6082608 for train routes and times

OTHER:

www.nationaltrust.org.uk – website for the National Trust, useful in particular for more on the properties mentioned in this Guide, and walks around the Ashridge Estate

www.ramblers.org.uk – for more on walking routes covered in this Guide

The British Horse Society, Stoneleigh Deer Park, Kenilworth, Warks CV8 2XZ (08701 202244).

A heron sits patiently on the front of a boat, watching the world go by.

INDEX

Tempus is keen to keep these guides as up to date as possible. If you have any suggestions for inclusion in the next edition of this guide, or would like to point out any changes since it was written, please email us at towpathguides@tempus-publishing.com